A GUIDE FOR

HIKERS • BACKPACKERS • CLIMBERS
CROSS-COUNTRY SKIERS • PADDLERS

Exploring

Colorado's
Wild Areas

D1516252

SECOND EDITION
Scott S. Warren

THE MOUNTAINEERS BOOKS

Published by
The Mountaineers Books
1001 SW Klickitat Way, Suite 201
Seattle, WA 98134

First edition, 1992. Second edition, 2002.

Published simultaneously in Great Britain by Cordee, 3a DeMontfort Street, Leicester, England, LE1 7HD

Manufactured in the United States of America

Project Editor: Christine Ummel Hosler
Copyeditor: Brenda Pittsley
Cover and Book Designer: Ani Rucki
Layout Artist: Mayumi Thompson
Cartographer: Scott S. Warren
Photographer: Scott S. Warren

Cover photograph: *The Maroon Bells*. Photo by Scott S. Warren
Frontispiece: *Along the Continental Divide north of the Needles Range*. Photo by Scott S. Warren

Library of Congress Cataloging-in-Publication Data
Warren, Scott S.
  Exploring Colorado's wild areas : a guide for hikers, backpackers, climbers, cross-country skiers & paddlers / Scott S. Warren.— 2nd ed.
      p. cm.
Includes index.
  ISBN 0-89886-784-3 (pbk.)
  1. Outdoor recreation—Colorado—Guidebooks. 2. Wilderness areas—Colorado—Guidebooks.
I. Title.
  GV191.42.C6 W37 2002
  917.8804'34—dc21
                                                                    2001006486

TABLE OF CONTENTS

Chapter Four. **The Plateau**

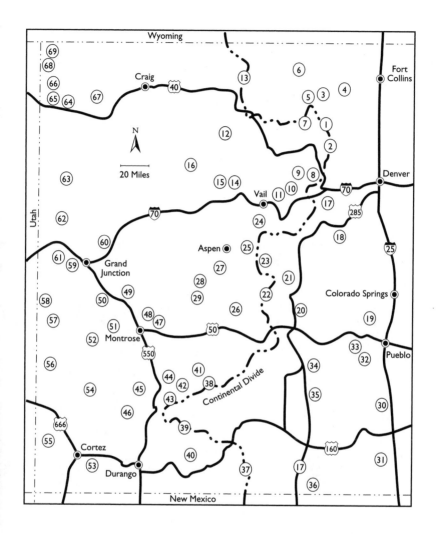

PREFACE

In Colorado, as in other western states, wilderness protection is a hotly contested issue. Mining and timber interests complain that designating wilderness areas on public land ties up resources. Developers view backcountry restrictions as needlessly locking up the land. Off-road vehicle enthusiasts gripe that their chosen recreation is restricted. All of these groups grumble that a wilderness designation stifles growth and, therefore, progress.

But the true worth of wilderness extends far beyond short-term economic gains. As an avid backcountry traveler, I relish the pristine nature of wilderness lands and the opportunities they allow for finding solitude. As a member of society, I am also well aware of the inherent benefits that wilderness lands afford. They are a reliable source of clean water. They reserve pockets of the biological diversity that was once ubiquitous in our country. And they provide an increasingly important escape from the maddening pace of our cities.

Currently, Colorado's national forests, parks, monuments, and Bureau of Land Management (BLM) holdings encompass thirty-nine designated wilderness areas with a total of 3,369,614 acres. Three special management areas add another 99,440 acres to the total. Special management areas are managed as wilderness except for exemptions for water rights. With all three, water development projects have been or could be built upstream from the wilderness. The BLM is studying fifty-four additional parcels of wild land as possible new wilderness areas or as additions to established wilderness areas. These total 346,000 acres. I hope that this comprehensive guide to areas officially established as wilderness and those currently under consideration will raise interest in protecting Colorado's remaining wild lands.

Much has changed in the landscape of wilderness designation since the first edition of this book appeared in 1992. The U.S. Forest Service added acreage to some existing wilderness areas and welcomed several new areas into the fold of permanent protection. Many of its trail systems have been improved or trails have new names. The BLM saw three of its wilderness study areas (WSAs) become designated wilderness areas. Trail systems were expanded in some WSAs, while public access was improved in others. And the National Park Service welcomed a new national monument into its docket of protected lands, plus saw two of its units undergo considerable changes. Black Canyon of the Gunnison National Monument gained park status, and Great Sand Dunes National Monument was greatly increased in size and is in the process of becoming larger still. With the final purchase of adjacent land, the unit will become a national park.

In updating this guidebook, I tried to reflect all the changes relative to Colorado's

Opposite: *Mesa Verde National Park*

wilderness lands. This edition introduces several new wilderness areas. It also incorporates new names if they have changed, new acreage is covered, and some descriptions have been revised. Some of the BLM wilderness study areas that were omitted in the original book are here—their inclusion is possible mostly due to changes in public access and the identification of suitable hiking routes. As with the original book, this second edition omits a few BLM wilderness study areas because they lack suitable access points and trails or other routes.

While writing this guidebook, I struggled long and hard with the notion that such a book would, in effect, advertise Colorado's most spectacular country and bring a flood of people into otherwise uncrowded areas. But after learning that only a handful of the state's wilderness areas receive the lion's share of hikers and backpackers, I realized that this text might help disperse backcountry visitors more evenly.

And if this book also advances support for a wilderness ethic, then so much the better. Legal recognition of wilderness lands may keep the developers at bay, but concern for the land cannot stop there. As each of us takes to the backcountry, we carry with us a responsibility to treat the land with the utmost respect. The adage "leave nothing but footprints, take nothing but photos" proffers the best summation of that responsibility.

INTRODUCTION

When people think of Colorado, they most often think of mountains, and for good reason. With an average elevation of 6,800 feet, Colorado is the highest state in the nation. It possesses three-quarters of all U.S. soil above 10,000 feet and boasts fifty-four summits that top the magical 14,000-foot level. But Colorado is also a land of spectacular canyons and deserts. West of the mountains, the Colorado Plateau sprawls across a third of the state before spilling into Utah. Rugged tablelands and semiarid desert basins, punctuated with slickrock canyons, mesas, buttes, rock formations, and natural arches, typify this landscape. In these vastly differing domains of mountain and desert, Colorado's wilderness lands await discovery.

HOW TO USE THIS BOOK

This text divides Colorado into four regions: the Northern, Central, and Southern Mountains, and the Plateau. To make it simple, the dividing lines follow Interstate 70, U.S. Highway 50, and the eastern edge of the Plateau region.

Wilderness lands discussed in this book are administered by one of three federal agencies: the U.S. Forest Service, the Bureau of Land Management (BLM), and the National Park Service (NPS). The Forest Service holds deed to most of the high mountain areas. The BLM oversees two wilderness areas, portions of two other wilderness areas, portions of two special management areas, and fifty-four wilderness study areas (WSAs). Although these WSAs enjoy some protection, not all have been recommended for wilderness status by the BLM. Congress may still grant protection to any of these WSAs, however, so this book discusses all such areas that offer outstanding recreational opportunities. Unfortunately, given the current national and state political landscape, legislative action on these BLM parcels may be some time off.

The National Park Service holds title to hundreds of thousands of acres of wilderness land in Colorado. This book considers all undeveloped lands within national park and monument boundaries, even though not all the acreage is designated as wilderness. It qualifies for inclusion because the NPS manages backcountry in its parks, preserves, and monuments to enhance its pristine character. However, because management of the newly established Canyons of the Ancients National Monument is still under consideration, and because much of its acreage is already developed in some form or fashion, the only lands within it considered here are those found in the Cross Canyon WSA. The Canyon of the Ancients National Monument is currently managed by the BLM.

Opposite: *Sunset in Chicago Basin of the Weminuche Wilderness*

The Maps

A locator map at the front of the book diagrams the sixty-nine areas covered here. Each chapter begins with its own regional map, and a more detailed map of each wilderness accompanies the individual area descriptions. Designated wilderness areas and wilderness study areas are shaded in gray. Trails are marked by a dashed line. A bold dashed line indicates the Continental Divide. Roads are depicted according to general conditions, and some points of interest are indicated as well. Although these maps are detailed, they should be used for reference only in planning a backcountry trip. They are not a substitute for the appropriate topographic and trail maps produced by the Forest Service, NPS, or BLM.

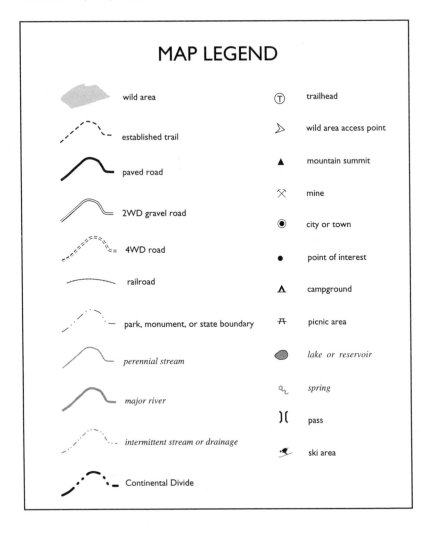

MAP LEGEND

wild area	ⓣ trailhead
established trail	⟫ wild area access point
paved road	▲ mountain summit
2WD gravel road	✕ mine
4WD road	◉ city or town
railroad	● point of interest
park, monument, or state boundary	▲ campground
perennial stream	卅 picnic area
major river	lake or reservoir
intermittent stream or drainage	spring
	)(pass
Continental Divide	ski area

Information Blocks

Each area description opens with a list of quick facts about the area. **Location** information gives the driving distance and direction from the nearest town in which supplies can be purchased. Large wilderness areas may be close to more than just the town that is listed. **Size** reveals the extent of the area in acres. **Status** indicates the area's designation, be it an actual wilderness area, a wilderness study area, a park, or what have you, as well as the date when the designation was enacted.

Terrain describes the prevailing landscape found in the area. It is followed by the highest and lowest **Elevation**. **Management** tells which government agency administers the area. Addresses for these agencies are in the Appendix. A list of the 7.5-minute USGS **Topographic Maps** needed to visit the area finishes the information block.

Text Descriptions

The text portion of each description begins with a brief introduction to the area, followed by a **Seasons** entry, which notes the times of the year the area is generally accessible. These dates should be considered approximate, however, as conditions vary greatly from year to year. Your best bet is to check with the managing agency before starting out. A word of warning: Colorado's high country knows no seasonal boundaries. It can turn cold and snow at any time of the year, so be prepared for inclement weather at all times.

Additional sections cover **Flora and Fauna** and **Geology**. The first looks at species of plants represented in the forests and woodlands, as well as wildflowers and grasses, and larger mammals and birds. The latter reviews the major forces that shaped an area. On occasion, the human **History** of an area also warrants an entry.

Activities

Each description highlights **Activities** suited to the area. Hiking is the most common activity, but cross-country skiing, mountaineering, and river running are also discussed when warranted. This is where you will find the most specific information on places to visit within these wilderness lands. When providing trail lengths, elevations, and conditions, I relied on the Forest Service's Recreational Opportunity Guides (ROGs) as a reference wherever possible. ROGs are one- or two-page write-ups on major trails and seem to be the most consistent source of information available.

WILDERNESS ETIQUETTE

In many respects, pristine wilderness is a privilege, not a right. The regulations governing wilderness use were established with the Wilderness Act of 1964, which defined wilderness as "an area where the earth and its community of life are untrammeled by man, where man himself is a visitor who does not remain."

To perpetuate this ethic, the Wilderness Act sets forth rules that prohibit mechanical transport. This applies to motorized off-road vehicles, obviously, but a debate has come to a head in recent years over the use of all-terrain bicycles or mountain bikes.

Currently, the law does not permit mountain bikes within wilderness areas, nor does it allow hang gliders and other forms of air travel. Simply put, travel on wilderness lands is restricted to foot or pack animal only. Although mountain bikes may be less obtrusive and more environmentally sound than motorcycles or all-terrain vehicles, they do constitute mechanical transport. Fortunately, Colorado still has plenty of open space where mountain bikes are allowed, so the pressure on established wilderness areas in the state is not significant.

Wilderness regulations also ban the use of generators, chain saws, and other motorized equipment. Commercial enterprises such as livestock grazing and outfitting are allowed but only under permit by the managing agency. Fishing and hunting are permitted but are subject to Colorado state regulations. Some areas have restrictions on fires, and camping within 0.25 mile of heavily used lakes may be prohibited. Because dogs can be disruptive to wildlife and other hikers, they should be on a leash at all times, or better yet left at home.

Backcountry travelers should respect these regulations that protect the pristine character of wilderness lands. But because these official rules cannot cover every conceivable threat to the environment, backcountry travelers should also practice no-trace camping during their stay. This means:

- No campfires.
- Dispose properly of human waste by burying it at least 200 feet from water sources and away from where others might camp.
- Don't bury toilet paper; pack it out.
- Stay on the main trail and don't cut switchbacks.
- Avoid camping in sensitive areas.
- Use biodegradable soaps at least 100 feet from water sources.
- Pack out the litter of others as well as your own.
- Never cut standing trees.
- Do not leave behind structures or nails.
- Travel in small groups.
- Do not dig holes or level tent areas.

Animal packers should:
- Picket or hobble livestock at least 200 feet from water and camping areas.
- Not tie animals to trees for long periods.
- Carry sterilized feed for stock and scatter manure.

No-trace camping is important in a wilderness setting; it should be applied to camping at the trailhead as well. Again, all trash should be packed out, and human waste should be properly buried well away from streams, campsites, and traffic areas. Use preexisting campsites that are at least 200 feet from springs, streams, and other water sources. Walk and drive only on existing travel routes to avoid creating new and needless trails. If you do make a fire, use preexisting fire rings or a fire pan, and burn only dead and down wood. The desired result, whether within the wilderness or at the car, is to leave an area without leaving behind any evidence of your passage.

PLAYING IT SAFE

An integral part of the wilderness experience is the inherent danger in traveling away from civilization. No information in this or any other book can substitute for hands-on experience when dealing with wilderness hazards. If you are new to the wilderness, go with someone who has logged many miles of hiking. Actual time spent in the backcountry will help you develop a sense for avoiding danger. Eventually, you too will acquire a knack for safety in the mountains and deserts of Colorado. The possibilities of mishaps are many, but the chances of them actually occurring are quite small if you practice prevention.

Be Prepared

When hiking in Colorado, you should always be ready for a sudden change in weather. Bring extra clothing, a rain parka or poncho, and waterproof matches or other means of starting a fire. Sun block, sunglasses, and a hat will provide protection from the harsh Colorado sun, especially above timberline. Carry plenty of drinking water and pack extra food in case of emergency. Other essentials include a knife, compass, first-aid kit,

Along Grape Creek

flashlight, and the proper maps—either United States Geological Service (USGS) topographic maps or detailed land management maps.

When leaving for a hike, let someone know your exact route, especially if you plan to hike alone. Common sense dictates that you sign in at trailhead registers. This gives search-and-rescue crews more information to go on. If you do get lost, stay in one place and try to keep warm.

Wildlife

Although the threat to hikers posed by wildlife in Colorado is minimal, precautions should be heeded. Practically speaking, there are no grizzly bears in Colorado, but there are black bears, some of which are accustomed to human presence. While maulings by black bears are very rare, it is still prudent to store food out of their reach by hanging it in a tree at least 10 feet off the ground and 4 feet from the tree trunk.

Mountain lions also have become far too confident around people, especially in populated areas along the Front Range. Residents in the foothills regions of Denver and Boulder often spot the animals close to housing, and a young man was stalked and killed by a cougar while running near Idaho Springs. The crux of this problem is that civilization is putting pressure on the mountain lion's range. In wilderness areas far away from urban enclaves, mountain lions, bears, and other creatures still maintain a healthy fear of people.

Lightning

Given Colorado's vast tracts of above-timberline terrain, lightning poses the most deadly threat to backcountry users. Colorado ranks quite high in deaths by lightning strikes per capita—between 1994 and 2000, each year from two to five people were killed by lightning in Colorado. The best way to avoid getting struck by lightning is to avoid places where it is likely to strike. Colorado's prevailing weather patterns form thunderstorms on most summer afternoons. Occurring in both the mountain and plateau provinces, these storms are typically short in duration but often quite intense. They usually do not gather maximum strength until afternoon, but deadly storms can occur at all times of the day. As these storms form, it is best to stay off exposed ridges and peaks.

If you are caught in an electrical storm, flat areas and depressions are the best places to be. Stay away from trees, avoid metal objects, and, if you are riding a horse, get off. Kneeling with hands on the ground and head low is good. Caves and deep overhangs are ideal places to take shelter, but shallow overhangs, stream gullies, and rock ledges are not, because the electrical current tends to move along at ground level near the strike. If you are in a forested area when a storm comes up, avoid taller, isolated trees and instead find a patch of shorter, less obtrusive trees. Cars are very safe during lightning storms; tents are not. You are simply much better off if you get your climbing over with by early afternoon.

Hypothermia

Another killer in the wilds of Colorado is hypothermia. Hypothermia occurs when the heat being lost by the body is greater than the heat being produced. Death can

A stone cabin on Notch Mountain

result if the process is not quickly reversed. Cold and wet weather can crop up suddenly at any time of the year, especially in Colorado's high terrain, so be prepared by packing rain gear, extra clothing, and waterproof matches. Watch for symptoms of hypothermia, including uncontrollable shivering, deteriorating speech, loss of coordination, and impaired judgment. Should these occur, replace wet clothing with dry and then place the victim in a prewarmed sleeping bag. Severe cases may require providing the victim with an external heat source such as huddling with another person. In emergency situations, a fire can provide much-needed heat. Give the victim warm liquids and high-energy food and get her or him to a doctor as soon as possible. Of course, prevention is best. That means avoiding getting cold and wet in the first place, eating plenty of high-energy foods, and keeping active should cold set in.

Giardiasis

While not deadly, another hazard in the wilds is *Giardia*, a microscopic organism that is often present in backcountry streams and lakes. *Giardia* was introduced in the American wilderness only within the last several decades. It is transmitted via beavers, sheep, and other livestock that defecate in mountain streams. Infection with *Giardia* is called *giardiasis*; one of the symptoms is severe diarrhea one to two weeks after it gets into your digestive system. If you should come down with these symptoms, medical treatment is the only cure.

To avoid picking up the parasite, treat water either by boiling it for ten minutes (try boiling the day's drinking water the night before so that it is cool by morning) or by using a suitable filter system. Most chemical treatments do not work on *Giardia*.

HIKING

When hiking in Colorado, keep in mind that both altitude and elevation gain can magnify a hike's level of difficulty. A 5-mile walk in the hills at sea level might not be particularly grueling, but above 10,000 feet it can be. A 2,000-foot elevation gain over 7 miles may not be significant, but the same climb packed into just 2 miles promises to be a real grunt of a march. When choosing a hiking route from this book, consider these factors along with trail distances. Although each person has different hiking abilities, a beginner should allow at least 1 hour for every 1.5 miles over relatively easy grades, and 1 hour for every 1 mile for harder elevation climbs. More advanced hikers may average up to 2.5 miles an hour, depending on their stamina.

Trail miles in this book are one-way distances only. As already mentioned, I relied mostly on information in the Recreational Opportunity Guides (ROGs) for each national forest. However, ROGs, other guidebooks, and signs in the field do not always agree. Keep in mind that the distances presented here are approximate.

Although the Forest Service and the BLM assign trail numbers, this book avoids using them simply because numerical designations sometimes change. Instead, each trail is identified by its official name. In some cases, the beginning and end of a trail—as established by the managing agency—may be obscure, especially when it encounters other trails or crosses into other national forests.

Moonrise over the West Needle Mountains in the Weminuche Wilderness

The text avoids lengthy descriptions concerning road access to the trails. Between the maps presented here and those provided by the Forest Service, the BLM, and the NPS, approach drives should be self-explanatory. Only those that might cause confusion have been detailed here.

Loop hikes are plentiful in Colorado's wilderness areas. When you have the time, loops are a wonderful alternative to backtracking on the same trail. Loop trails are often mentioned in the hiking descriptions, but there may be others to choose from that are not mentioned. Good overnight trips are identified as well, though some hikers can squeeze a 16-mile round-trip hike into one day. Additionally, many routes may be hiked one way if you have a shuttle waiting at trail's end. When shuttles are mentioned in the text, they refer to either a second car parked beforehand at the end of the route or a friend who is willing to pick you up.

Taking Care of the Land

I generally avoid describing cross-country hikes simply because they can be detrimental to fragile environments and because they may lead inexperienced hikers astray. Those who plan to bushwhack should be adept at using both topographic maps and a compass, and also should be aware that their actions pose an additional threat to pristine areas. Footsteps on fragile alpine, subalpine, or desert plants can leave long-lasting scars.

For overnight hikers, common sense and respect for the environment should govern all actions. Campfires can leave burn marks and charcoal that will last hundreds of years. Many areas prohibit fires altogether. Instead, pack a lightweight stove for cooking, extra clothing for warmth, and a candle or portable lamp for light. If you must build a fire, do not make a ring of stones. Instead, clear a spot down to mineral soil. Use small sticks instead of logs. Scatter the ashes after you are sure they are out completely, restoring the area to its natural state.

Bathe and wash dishes at least 100 feet from streams and lakes. Even biodegradable soap can be detrimental to water ecosystems. Carry out all trash. Do not bury or burn it. And, when setting up your tent, try to do so in an area that will not be scarred by your presence.

ANIMAL PACKING

Horses have had an integral role in Colorado's heritage. They were introduced to the region by the Spanish in the 1600s and have been a popular means of wilderness travel ever since. The Ute Indians, who referred to horses as "magic dogs," were quite proficient at equestrian skills.

But horses can inflict considerable damage on fragile alpine and desert environments, and those who travel by horse should take precautions to minimize their impact. Stock should not be tethered or tied within 200 feet of streams, lakes, and other water sources. Feed should be packed in to minimize browsing. Because hay introduces exotic weeds, bring oats or hay pellets instead. Be choosy when tethering your animals so as to disperse the effects of grazing.

Although horses will always be the preferred method of wilderness travel for some, llamas are an increasingly popular beast of burden in the backcountry. Native to South America, llamas are ideal pack animals. Because their hooves are soft and they weigh considerably less, llamas are less damaging than horses are to the soil and plant life. Similarly, their eating habits are not nearly so voracious. In fact, llamas are so environmentally sound that many Forest Service and Park Service trail crews use them for packing gear.

CROSS-COUNTRY SKIING

Because of their relative isolation, Colorado's wilderness areas are not always accessible during the winter months—trailheads are often miles away from the nearest plowed road. On the plus side, however, once you do reach the wilderness boundary the chances of finding solitude are quite good.

In this book, descriptions of cross-country skiing opportunities assume that the trails in the hiking sections can be skied. But be aware that some trails are too dangerous for winter travel because of the threat of avalanches. While a few dangerous routes have been identified, any backcountry slope, especially open areas with more than a 25-percent grade, can be hazardous. It is the responsibility of each backcountry skier to travel in the safest way possible. This means:

- Check on current avalanche conditions before you go. Most mountain areas have an avalanche hotline. Avalanches claim lives in Colorado every year. More often than not, the victims failed to use common sense. Carry avalanche beacons, snow shovels, and probe poles.
- Travel with others who are experienced in winter travel.
- Carry a compass, topographic maps, extra warm clothing, and proper wintertime equipment, such as a tent, sleeping bag, stove, boots, outer clothing, and so on.
- Be considerate and always leave your car in a plowed parking area. These are easy to spot. Parking in other areas along the road may block the snowplows.

MOUNTAINEERING

Mountaineering in Colorado means different things to different people. For some it's the simple pleasure of bagging a peak via the easiest route up. For others, it might entail tackling the most technically difficult route to the top. Where this book is concerned, all mountain ascents fall in the category of Mountaineering. While the simpler routes are described in some detail, the technical climbs are only mentioned to alert those climbers interested in challenges. For further information concerning technical routes, check guidebooks that emphasize climbing or pay a visit to local mountaineering shops. Such stores usually have avid climbers on staff who can provide detailed information on routes and conditions.

Colorado has fifty-four peaks that top 14,000 feet. Any time you are in the vicinity of a "fourteener" you run the possibility of encountering a lot of other people. Strangely, people are infinitely more anxious to climb a 14,001-foot mountain than a 13,999-foot one. In short, if you are interested in finding solitude, go for summits under 14,000 feet.

Columbine Lake in the Weminuche Wilderness

The views are just as rewarding, but you won't have to share them with as many others.

Unfortunately, the degradation of alpine ecosystems has become acute in recent years. To combat the situation, the Forest Service has published guidelines for peak baggers. They include:

- Concentrate travel along standard routes.
- Avoid wet or muddy sections.
- Never cut switchbacks.
- Disperse paths when traveling off-trail.
- Travel on ridges and side hills when traveling off-trail.
- Take extra care when selecting off-trail descent routes.
- Stay aware of changing weather.

Weather conditions are typically most severe on these highest of points. Be prepared for sudden and sometimes violent changes in weather. Watch for lightning, especially on summer afternoons. Watch for signs of fatigue; exertion at high altitudes can lead to disoriented decision making. To help overcome this danger, travel with others. Remember that the consequences of an unwise decision multiply when climbing above timberline. And lastly, be cognizant of your own abilities. Many deaths occur on Colorado's high peaks because inexperienced climbers get in over their heads. Loose rock, severe climbing routes, and dangerous precipices all contribute to mishaps in the mountains.

RIVER RUNNING

Ten of Colorado's wild areas discussed here offer river-running opportunities. They are classified according to their difficulty:

- Class I—moving water with ripples and small waves

- Class II—easy rapids with waves up to 3 feet; clear channels
- Class III—rapids with high, irregular waves capable of swamping an open canoe; narrow channels
- Class IV—long difficult rapids with constricted passages; scouting from shore may be necessary; not runnable by open canoes
- Class V—extremely difficult and long violent rapids; a significant hazard to life in case of mishap
- Class VI—impossible to run

Information concerning permits and the typical length of such trips is also provided. Keep in mind that river beaches and shorelines are fragile environments. Care should be taken to safeguard them. Use toilets when provided, and pack out human waste if they are not. Do not bury trash. Cook with stoves and, if you must have a fire, bring in your own wood for fuel, use a fire pan, and pack out all ashes. Fires may be banned on some stretches of river. As with alpine and desert camping, leave no traces of your stay.

Boaters should consider the hazards associated with river running. Do not attempt waters beyond your ability. Drowning accidents occur with some frequency on Colorado's wild rivers. For those who do not have white-water experience, many of these stretches can be floated on guided trips that are available through local rafting companies.

A NOTE ABOUT SAFETY

Safety is an important concern in all outdoor activities. No guidebook can alert you to every hazard or anticipate the limitations of every reader. Therefore, the descriptions of roads, trails, routes, and natural features in this book are not representations that a particular place or excursion will be safe for your party. When you follow any of the routes described in this book, you assume responsibility for your own safety. Under normal conditions, such excursions require the usual attention to traffic, road and trail conditions, weather, terrain, the capabilities of your party, and other factors. Because many of the lands in this book are subject to development and/or change of ownership, conditions may have changed since this book was written that make your use of some of these routes unwise. Always check for current conditions, obey posted private property signs, and avoid confrontations with property owners or managers. Keeping informed on current conditions and exercising common sense are the keys to a safe, enjoyable outing.

The Mountaineers Books

Opposite: *Alpine scenery in the Ptarmigan Peak Wilderness*

Northern Mountains

chapter 1

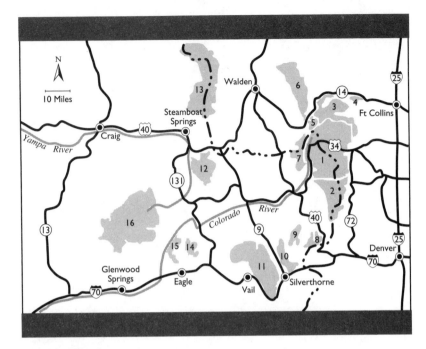

Encompassing a number of ranges, Colorado's northern mountains are home to several designated wildernesses and wilderness study areas. The crown jewel of the region is Rocky Mountain National Park with its extensive holdings of pristine alpine and subalpine terrain. A half-dozen national forest wilderness areas adjoin or nearly adjoin the park on three sides to form a huge tract of unspoiled mountain land. Southwest of Rocky Mountain National Park, along the Interstate 70 corridor, are three tracts of mountain wilderness: Byers Peak, Vasquez Peak, and Ptarmigan Peak. West of them rises the impressive Gore Range, much of which falls in the Eagles Nest Wilderness Area.

Continuing north from the Gores, the Park Range manifests as a gently climbing ridge line covered with timber, some of which falls within the Sarvis Creek Wilderness Area. North of Rabbit Ears Pass, the Park Range rises to the heights of the Mount Zirkel Wilderness Area. Two BLM wilderness study areas are found north of Eagle. Along the region's western boundary is the intriguing Flat Tops Range, home to an expansive wilderness area of the same name.

1 Rocky Mountain National Park

Location: 1 mi W of Estes Park
Size: 265,723 acres
Status: National park (1915)
Terrain: Alpine mountains and deep, forested river canyons
Elevation: 7,800' to 14,255'
Management: Rocky Mountain National Park
Topographic maps: Pingree Park, Comanche Peak, Chambers Lake, Glen Haven, Estes Park, Trail Ridge, Fall River Pass, Mount Richthofen, Longs Peak, McHenrys Peak, Grand Lake, Allenspark, Isolation Peak, Shadow Mountain

Rocky Mountain National Park is dedicated to preserving a vast parcel of the central Rocky Mountain ecosystem. Fully one-third of its more than 250,000 acres are above timberline. Hundreds of summits top the 10,000-foot mark. Its highest point, Longs Peak (14,255 feet), stands as an omnipresent sentinel for the northern portion of the Front Range. Spectacular vistas are found throughout. Alpine wildflowers grace the tundra and several species of big game abound.

Bighorn sheep in Rocky Mountain National Park

For many visitors to Rocky Mountain National Park, the sum of their experience is a drive over Trail Ridge Road. Reaching 12,183 feet in elevation and staying above the tree line for 11 miles, this route is the highest paved through-road in North America. Although most motorists who drive it never stray far from their cars, they are afforded an unusually intimate introduction to the world of alpine tundra.

Of the visitors who do venture into the backcountry, most do so from one of a handful of readily accessible trailheads, such as Bear Lake. On any given summer day, these avenues conduct literally hundreds of hikers to the nearest lake, waterfall, or vista point. Despite such crowds, however, solitude can be found within the park boundaries. The trick is to search out one of the lesser-known trailheads and hike beyond the first point of interest.

Seasons

Like most of Colorado's mountain lands, Rocky Mountain National Park is snowbound from mid-autumn through May and into June or July up high. Trail Ridge Road is usually plowed by Memorial Day and stays open into October, but sudden storms can close the road early.

June, July, and early August are the time for wildflowers, while September witnesses the rutting season for elk. Although an actual contest between two bull elk is a rare sight, their bugling is often heard echoing across the valleys and through the trees.

Flora and Fauna

Rocky Mountain National Park offers a vivid look at the ecosystem of the central Rockies. Dog-hair stands of lodgepole pine and mature forests of ponderosa pine are found at its lower elevation. Above 9,000 feet, Engelmann spruce and subalpine fir dominate. Their ranks are often broken by small parks or meadows, which are favored early-morning haunts for wildlife. Around 11,000 feet, the trees—in response to the harsh wintry conditions—become gnarled and stunted to form what are known as *krummholz* (German for "crooked wood") forests. Above these, the tundra takes over. What may seem like expansive, verdant meadows from afar are actually fragile ecosystems of lichens, sedges, and grasses. Interestingly, many of these specialized plants are the very same species that inhabit other alpine and arctic regions of the world. Because these plants are so delicate, the public is constantly reminded to stay on established trails, especially along Trail Ridge Road.

Among the wildlife species that inhabit Rocky Mountain National Park are mule deer, elk, black bear, coyote, mountain lion, and bobcat. Moose have been moving into the park from the North Park area, and above timberline reside such creatures as bighorn sheep, mountain goats, marmots, pikas, and white-tailed ptarmigan.

Geology

Encompassing the northern reaches of the Front Range, the rugged terrain of Rocky Mountain National Park exhibits classic examples of faulted anticlines—elongated blocks of Precambrian rock that were uplifted after cracks or faults formed in the earth's surface. Geologists believe this process began about 65 million years ago, during a period of worldwide mountain building known as the Laramide Orogeny, and that it lasted for at least 20 million years. More recent uplifts raised the region, and much of the West for that matter, to its present level. Prior to the Laramide Orogeny, considerably older mountains stood in these parts. They eroded away hundreds of millions of years ago, but it is hypothesized that the nearly flat summit of Longs Peak and the gently rolling terrain found along Trail Ridge Road are the remains of their 600-million-year-old surface.

As with much of Colorado's uplands, glaciers played a considerable role in shaping the park's terrain. During the Quaternary period (3 million years ago to present), glaciers formed along the crest of the Front Range. The U-shaped valleys in the park are a telltale characteristic of glacial carving. Most of the lakes resulted from glaciation. Moraines, or accumulations of rock debris that were pushed along by advancing glacial ice, are common at lower elevations. Several small glaciers still exist among the more sheltered cirques above 11,000 feet, but their effect on the terrain is quite localized.

History

Evidence suggests prehistoric people hunted in the park's high country as early as 7,000 years ago, especially in times of drought. Ute and Arapaho Indians also traveled the tundra, leaving trails over Trail Ridge and Flattop Mountain, and along the Fall River.

In 1820, Major Stephen Long spied the peak that now bears his name from out in the plains, but he never crossed into what is now park land. The first white man to enter the area was a trapper by the name of Rufus Sage. He explored the Wild Basin and Moraine Park areas in 1843. Sixteen years later, Joel Estes, along with his son Milton, entered what would become Estes Park and founded the area's first settlement in 1861. Early-day tourists soon followed.

Enos Mills, having arrived in Estes Park in 1884, conceived of turning the area into a park after a solo ascent of Longs Peak. An 1889 meeting with John Muir provided further encouragement, as did a visit to Yellowstone the following year. He began lobbying in 1909, and Rocky Mountain National Park was established by Congress six years later.

ACTIVITIES
Hiking

With 347 miles of backcountry trails, Rocky Mountain National Park is truly a hiker's paradise. Day use of the park's backcountry is unrestricted, but overnight trips require a permit to minimize overuse of popular areas. The most heavily used trails are usually quite crowded and should be avoided during high-use periods—generally June through Labor Day. A great many other routes, though, afford ample solitude.

The most heavily used trails begin along Bear Lake Road in the east-central portion of the park. The parking situation is such that a free bus shuttle operates during peak times to ferry hikers up and down the road. Although most of the hikes in this area are short, the rewards are many.

From the Bierstadt Lake trailhead, it is an easy 1.5-mile jaunt to Bierstadt Lake, where the nineteenth-century painter Albert Bierstadt created one of his many spectacular images of the West. Farther up the road is the Glacier Gorge Junction trailhead. A popular lure here is Alberta Falls. Just 0.5 mile in, this beautiful sight marks the turnaround point for many less adventuresome hikers. Beyond the falls, the North Longs Peak Trail takes off to the left. Eventually this trail connects with the more popular East Longs Peak Trail to provide access to the park's highest point. Shortly after this junction, the main trail divides to follow two spectacular valleys. The left-hand route climbs into Glacier Gorge, an aptly named drainage that dead-ends at the foot of Chiefs Head Peak (13,579 feet), about 5 miles from the trailhead. Up the right-hand fork lies a string of glacial lakes including The Loch, Lake of Glass, and Sky Pond. A spur of this route eventually reaches Andrews Glacier, which is situated at 11,700 feet in the shade of the Continental Divide. Andrews Glacier is a 5-mile, 2,400-vertical-foot walk in.

At the Bear Lake trailhead, a large parking lot complete with restroom facilities awaits the throngs of hikers that arrive daily. Some of these folks are satisfied with walking the 0.5-mile interpretive trail around Bear Lake, but many others head out for points of interest beyond. One of these is Dream Lake, a little over 1 mile in. Billed as the park's most photographed lake, its still waters reflect wonderful views of nearby Hallett Peak and Flattop Mountain. Longs Peak is also visible from here. Emerald Lake, 0.8 mile farther, lies in a rugged gorge headed by Hallett Peak. This trail is said to be the most heavily used in the park.

The Flattop Mountain Trail leads north, then west from Bear Lake, and eventually ascends Flattop Mountain's 12,324-foot summit along the Continental Divide. The 9-mile round trip to the top and back includes a climb of nearly 3,000 feet. The Flattop Mountain Trail connects with other routes as well. About 1 mile from its trailhead is an intersection with the Fern Lake Trail. And, near the summit of Flattop itself, the Tonahutu Creek Trail cuts across Bighorn Flats west of the Divide and drops into the Tonahutu Creek drainage. Crossing nearly the entire width of the park, this route is 18.5 miles in length and requires 2 or more days and a shuttle to complete.

The Fern Lake Trail, also popular with day hikers, begins just west of the Moraine Park Campground, a few miles north of Bear Lake Road. Before encountering Fern Lake, 3.8 miles and 1,375 vertical feet from road's end, this trail visits Pool and Fern Falls. It also passes through open meadows and some beautiful stands of ponderosa pine. It is 8.5 miles from the Fern Lake trailhead to Bear Lake.

Away from the Moraine Park and Bear Lake areas, several other trailheads offer considerably less trampled avenues into the park's backcountry. A number of trails penetrate the North St. Vrain River drainage from the Wild Basin trailhead. Located in the southeastern corner of the park, Wild Basin is reached by driving 12 miles south of Estes Park on Colorado Highway 7. Ouzel Falls, which lies nearly 3 miles up the trail, is one destination; Bluebird and Thunder Lakes, 6 and 7 miles respectively, are other possibilities. The Lion Lakes are 7 miles via a spur trail to the north. Finch and Pear Lakes await hikers who follow the southern arm of this trail system. All of these hikes involve elevation gains of 1,400–3,000 feet and can be completed in a long

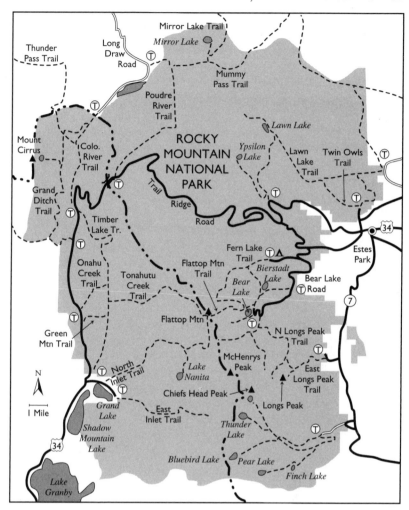

day. Defined by Longs Peak to the north and the Continental Divide to the west and southwest, Wild Basin lives up to its colorful name.

Entering the remote northeastern corner of the park is the Lawn Lake Trail. Following the Roaring River, this route climbs more than 2,000 feet in 6.2 miles before finding Lawn Lake. Constructed during the first decade of the last century, the Lawn Lake dam burst in 1982, flooding Estes Park and claiming three lives. A southern spur climbs to Ypsilon Lake, and another branch drops down Black Canyon to the Twin Owls trailhead.

Hiking trails that enter the park from the Roosevelt National Forest to the north include the Mummy Pass, Mirror Lake, and Poudre River Trails. The Mummy Pass Trail, 13 miles in length, can be picked up from either the Corral Creek trailhead near the end of Long Draw Road or at Pingree Park to the east. Although both trailheads are outside of the park boundary, backpackers must obtain a permit from the backcountry office adjacent to park headquarters. The Mirror Lake Trail is reached from the Peterson Lake trailhead, also on Long Draw Road outside the park, and it ends at Mirror Lake, which sits in a classic, glacier-carved cirque. A route that offers an uncharacteristically easy grade is the Poudre River Trail, which follows the Cache la Poudre River into the park to its source near Milner Pass on Trail Ridge Road. All of these hikes are considered overnight treks.

In addition to rivers that flow eastward, Rocky Mountain National Park is also home to the headwaters for the Colorado River. From the Colorado River trailhead in the northwest corner of the park, two trails explore the uppermost reaches of this renowned waterway. The Colorado River Trail travels an easy 7.3 miles north to La Poudre Pass on the northern boundary of the park. Near the remains of Lulu City, an 1880 mining camp 4 miles in, the Thunder Pass Trail branches left to eventually cross the Continental Divide and connect with State Highway 14 near Cameron Pass.

Contouring along the eastern slope of the Never Summer Range is the Grand Ditch, a canal built in the early 1900s that diverts water across the Divide. The Grand Ditch Trail provides access to the Lake of the Clouds, situated below Mount Cirrus. Because it too intersects the Thunder Pass Trail, this route can be combined with the Colorado River Trail for a loop trip.

Within the park, the young Colorado River meanders south through the Kawuneeche Valley, from which three trails access high country to the east. The Timber Lake and Onahu Creek Trails both approach Long Meadows from different directions. Timber Lake is almost 5 miles and a 2,060-foot climb in. The Green Mountain Trail connects with the Onahu Creek Trail but not before crossing Big Meadows on the way.

From the Grand Lake area—the only vehicle entry point for the park on the west side—hikers can follow the North Inlet Trail 11 miles to Lake Nanita, situated below Andrews Peak. The Tonahutu Creek Trail begins at the same trailhead. Big Meadows is where the Tonahutu Creek Trail breaks off to connect with the Flattop Mountain Trail in Bighorn Flats. Before making the climb to Flattop Mountain, the Tonahutu Creek Trail connects with the North Inlet Trail, allowing a 27-mile loop trip. The East Inlet Trail, which begins at the east end of Grand Lake, covers 7.8 miles to reach Spirit Lake—a climb of 2,000 feet.

Cross-country Skiing

Covered with a thick blanket of snow, Rocky Mountain National Park is a winter wonderland for backcountry skiers and snowshoers alike. Although Trail Ridge Road closes with the first heavy snows, most of the lower roads are plowed regularly, especially those on the eastern side of the park. This means that many of the trails described in the hiking section are accessible to cross-country skiers.

One of the more popular trails is the one that climbs up Glacier Gorge. Rated as moderately difficult, the route passes Alberta Falls and a handful of lakes along the way and affords dramatic views of Longs Peak and other summits in the area. Another popular ski trip follows the Fern Lake Trail for as far as your energy will take you. For a considerably shorter tour, try the mile-long route from Glacier Basin Campground to Sprague Lake. With easy conditions the entire way, this route is good for beginners.

On the west side of the park, the road is usually plowed part way up the Kawuneeche Valley. A notable ski tour here follows the Green Mountain Trail to Big Meadows before heading south on the Tonahutu Creek Trail. From Big Meadows the trail slowly descends alongside Tonahutu Creek for 4 miles to the Tonahutu/North Inlet trailhead. The entire route is 6 miles in length and requires a shuttle.

You are not limited to these suggestions as the entire Rocky Mountain National Park trail system is open to cross-country skiers. Overnight trips require a permit from the Park Service. Any trip should take into account the ever-present danger of avalanches and exposure to wind and cold.

Mountaineering

Rocky Mountain National Park has a century-long tradition of mountaineering, much of it centered around Longs Peak (14,255 feet). Major John Wesley Powell and a party of six made the first ascent of Longs on August 23, 1868. Enos Mills climbed the peak 297 times while serving as a guide in what would become Rocky Mountain National Park. Today, upwards of 7,000 people make the summit each year.

Although several routes access Longs Peak, the most popular is the Longs Peak Trail, which begins at Longs Peak Campground in the southeast portion of the park. From the trailhead it is 8 miles and 4,855 feet to the top. After passing through subalpine forests, the route eventually tops the tree line and then crosses a boulder field. The trail passes through the Keyhole and up the Homestretch—an angled face of granite—before reaching the top. Cables used to exist to assist climbers but were removed as part of an effort to enhance wilderness characteristics in the park. Although there are pitches where toe and handholds greatly assist in the climb, most folks make it to the top without ropes and technical equipment.

Other routes up Longs Peak are more challenging to experienced climbers, and the most renowned of these ascend the east face of the mountain. An impressive 1,700-foot wall of granite, the east face has proved to be the nemesis of many a climber. The first successful attempts came in the 1920s, and other first ascents followed at sporadic intervals. The last route to be climbed was the Diamond, considered one of the sheerest faces in the West. First conquered by a pair of climbers in 1960, the Diamond has been climbed many times since.

Like Longs Peak, most of the other summits in the park are approachable by both easy scrambles and technically challenging routes. Typically, the west and south faces of these peaks are considered walk-ups, while the east and north faces offer more vertical facades. Within the vicinity of Longs Peak, Mount Meeker (13,911 feet), McHenrys Peak (13,327 feet), Mount Alice (13,310 feet), Chiefs Head Peak (13,579 feet), and Hallett Peak (12,713 feet) tempt many climbers. The Mummy Range, although somewhat gentler in profile, contains a number of 13,000-foot summits, and the Never Summer Range in the western portion of the park boasts some lofty mountains as well.

While casual peak baggers can have a field day in Rocky Mountain National Park, technical climbers also will find many rock walls and ice faces worth attempting.

2 Indian Peaks Wilderness Area

Location: 25 mi W of Boulder
Size: 73,391 acres
Status: Wilderness area (1978)
Terrain: Alpine summits and timbered lower slopes
Elevation: 8,400' to 13,502'
Management: Arapaho–Roosevelt NF, Rocky Mountain National Park
Topographic maps: Monarch Lake, Isolation Peak, Ward, Shadow Mountain, Allenspark, East Portal, Nederland

The Indian Peaks are a grand selection of lofty summits, sculpted by glaciers and named after several important Native American tribes of the West. A few small glaciers still dot the highest of these summits and sparkling lakes abound. The Continental Divide runs the length of this area—from the Rocky Mountain National Park border to Rollins Pass.

Because the Indian Peaks Wilderness is so readily accessible to the Denver–Boulder area, it is heavily used. Annual visitation numbers top the 100,000 mark, with some 90 percent of use occurring on the east side. This popularity has led to the institution of a wilderness permit system that regulates the number of people camping in each of the eighteen travel zones. One zone is off-limits to overnight use entirely, while four others have designated camping areas. The permit system is in effect between June 1 and September 30, and there is a reservation fee. Campfires are banned in all areas east of the Divide and in some areas west as well.

Seasons

Because much of the Indian Peaks Wilderness is above 10,000 feet, the hiking season may not arrive until July. Thunderstorms can be a daily hazard in the summer. Wildflowers reach their peak in late July or early August. The first heavy snows usually arrive in October, and it does not take many blizzards to lay down an adequate base for cross-country skiing.

Flora and Fauna

A majority of this wilderness area lies above timberline and is therefore typified by stretches of alpine tundra. White-tailed ptarmigan, marmots, and pikas are common in this life zone. Below timberline, stands of spruce and fir form krummholz forests.

Interestingly, because the winds are so terrific in the Indian Peaks, a false timberline is found in some areas. One such area lies at 10,300 feet on the east end of Brainard

Arapaho Glacier in the Indian Peaks Wilderness

Lake. Although timberline is normally around 11,000 feet, the trees here have taken on many characteristics of a krummholz forest.

Aside from a mix of spruce and fir, lodgepole pine is also prevalent in many forested areas in the Indian Peaks Wilderness. Within these forests, deer, elk, black bears, coyotes, cougars, and bobcats reside.

Geology

As part of the Front Range, the Indian Peaks were uplifted during the Laramide Orogeny, beginning about 65 million years ago. During this period of worldwide mountain building, the underlying basement rock was broken into long, narrow blocks. These blocks then tilted along their lengths and began rising. Known as a faulted anticline, the Indian Peaks feature the characteristic single spine of high peaks that is the apex of the uplift. Although most of Colorado's mountain ranges were formed in this manner, the Front Range is far and away the state's longest. Geologists theorize that during the 20 million years it took to rise, the Front Range was displaced as much as 25,000 feet. The range never reached such grand heights, however, because erosion was continually grinding away at the mountains. In the Indian Peaks, erosion's most visible effect resulted from glaciation. These glaciers, occurring about 2 million years ago, were responsible for many of the dramatic stone faces found here. Cirques and U-shaped valleys are widely evident, and several lakes—nearly fifty of them—are the result of glacial scouring. Today, remnant glaciers still cling to the highest peaks.

ACTIVITIES
Hiking

The most easily accessible trails in the Indian Peaks Wilderness are on the east side, but they are also the most heavily traveled. Several trails start from Brainard Lake—reached via the paved Brainard Lake Road (FS Road 112)—and offer quick access into the heart of the area's most scenic terrain. Because these trailheads are above 10,000 feet, the climb into the high country is not too difficult.

Following the South St. Vrain drainage to its head, the Isabelle Glacier Trail climbs 1,500 feet to an active glacier. Along the way it passes two beautiful lakes—Long Lake and Lake Isabelle—and the spectacular profiles of Navajo, Apache, and Shoshoni Peaks are seldom out of sight. The trail ends at Isabelle Glacier, about 3 miles in. Camping in this drainage is prohibited due to widespread overuse. Branching off from this trail is the Pawnee Pass Trail. The 12,541-foot pass, 4.5 miles from the trailhead, is along the Continental Divide and allows overnight hikers to cross over to the west slope of the wilderness and out to Monarch Lake in the Lake Granby area.

From the Mitchell Lake trailhead—also near Brainard Lake—two hikes access areas to the west and north. Like the South St. Vrain drainage, the Mitchell Lake area is off-limits to camping, but it does make for a nice day hike. Mitchell Lake itself is about 1 mile in, while slightly higher Blue Lake is about 1.5 miles farther. Traversing a ridge to the north, the Beaver Creek Trail climbs to 11,300 feet before dropping to meet the Buchanan Pass Trail in the Middle St. Vrain drainage. A spur route branches off to the left to climb up Mount Audubon (13,233 feet). Only 2 miles in, Mount Audubon is one of the easiest summits to climb in Colorado.

Like Pawnee Pass, Buchanan Pass allows enough of a break in the mountains for a trail to cross the Continental Divide. Access to this route from the east is attained by driving a rugged 4WD road past Beaver Reservoir to Coney Flats. In 3.5 miles the trail climbs from 9,800 feet to the 11,837-foot pass, from which it drops nearly 6 miles down Buchanan Creek to the Cascade Creek Trail, which then descends to Monarch Lake. A 22-mile extended loop is possible by following the Buchanan Pass and Pawnee Pass Trails. Other trails that take off from Coney Flats include spurs to Coney Lake and the St. Vrain Glaciers. Additionally, the St. Vrain Mountain Trail passes by St. Vrain Mountain (12,162 feet) near the park border before dropping into Allenspark 9 miles from its start.

South of Brainard Lake, parcels of private land push the wilderness boundary westward to the Continental Divide. An extension of designated wilderness land does eventually bow eastward again to include the Rainbow Lakes. Only 1 mile in, all eight Rainbow Lakes are quite popular for fishing. The trailhead is found at the Rainbow Lakes Campground, which is also the start of the lengthier Arapaho Glacier Trail (about 6 miles long), which leads to the Arapaho Glacier overlook.

Quicker access to Arapaho Glacier can be had from the Fourth of July Campground at the end of a rough 2WD road that passes the Eldora Mountain Ski Resort. Follow the Arapaho Pass Trail for about 1 mile; then turn right to pick up the Glacier Rim Trail for another 2.5 miles. Although it is only 3.5 miles to the glacier from the Fourth of July trailhead, the route climbs from 10,121 feet to 12,700 feet, making it moderately strenuous. Arapaho Pass (11,900 feet) provides access to areas west of the Divide. For part of the 3-mile walk to the top of the pass, the trail follows an old stage-coach road. It also passes the remains of the Fourth of July Mine near timberline. Once on top, the Arapaho Pass Trail drops 9.3 miles down Arapaho Creek to Monarch Lake.

In the southern end of the Indian Peaks Wilderness, the Continental Divide can be traversed via Devils Thumb Pass. Beginning at the Hessie trailhead west of Eldora, the Devils Thumb Lake Trail climbs 2,000 feet in 5.5 miles to Devils Thumb Lake. The trail traces an old road for part of the way, intersecting with the Woodland Lake Trail after 2.5 miles. Woodland Lake is 2 miles farther. After reaching Devils Thumb Lake, the trail climbs steeply for another mile to the 12,100-foot pass. At the pass, the route intersects the midway point of the 6-mile-long High Lonesome

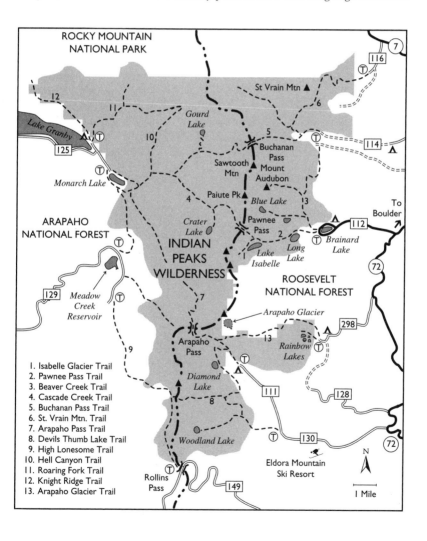

ROCKY MOUNTAIN
NATIONAL PARK

7

116

St Vrain Mtn ▲

12

11

6

114

Gourd
Lake

5

Lake Granby

125

10

Buchanan
Pass

Sawtooth
Mtn

Mount
Audubon

Monarch Lake

4

Paiute Pk ▲

Blue Lake

13

To
Boulder

ARAPAHO
NATIONAL FOREST

Crater
Lake

Pawnee
Pass

112

INDIAN
PEAKS
WILDERNESS

Lake
Isabelle

2

Long
Lake

Brainard
Lake

72

129

Meadow
Creek
Reservoir

ROOSEVELT
NATIONAL FOREST

7

Arapaho Glacier

298

9

Arapaho
Pass

13

Rainbow
Lakes

111

Diamond
Lake

128

8

1. Isabelle Glacier Trail
2. Pawnee Pass Trail
3. Beaver Creek Trail
4. Cascade Creek Trail
5. Buchanan Pass Trail
6. St. Vrain Mtn. Trail
7. Arapaho Pass Trail
8. Devils Thumb Lake Trail
9. High Lonesome Trail
10. Hell Canyon Trail
11. Roaring Fork Trail
12. Knight Ridge Trail
13. Arapaho Glacier Trail

Woodland Lake

130

72

Rollins
Pass

149

Eldora Mountain
Ski Resort

N

1 Mile

Trail. A right-hand turn will take you out of the wilderness and down into Devils Thumb Park. Turn left and you can follow a surprisingly level grade south along the Continental Divide to Rollins Pass. This route is quite scenic as it is above timberline the entire way. Topped by a jeep road, 11,670-foot Rollins Pass marks the southernmost tip of the wilderness area.

Not surprisingly, visitor numbers on the west side of the Indian Peaks Wilderness are considerably lower than those on the east. Most trails that penetrate the western slope originate from the Lake Granby–Monarch Lake area. The Roaring Fork Trail, which begins at the east end of Lake Granby, climbs steeply for the first mile along its aptly titled namesake. Eventually, it tops an 11,200-foot saddle before dropping down. The view from the saddle is spectacular. Alternate routes include a side excursion to Watanga Lake and a return trip down the appropriately named Hell Canyon Trail to the Cascade Creek Trail. The Forest Service describes the Hell Canyon Trail as the most difficult in the wilderness but points out that it receives only light use.

By comparison, the Cascade Creek Trail, which begins near the west end of Monarch Lake, is heavily used, especially on weekends. Climbing over 4,000 feet in 10.5 miles, this route eventually tops Pawnee Pass. Along the way are pristine forests of lodgepole pine and beautiful waterfalls. Pawnee Lake lies not far off the trail, 8 miles in. Beyond it, the trail climbs through more than two dozen switchbacks before reaching the 12,541-foot pass. An interesting and popular side trip from the Cascade Creek Trail begins 6.7 miles in and climbs 1 mile to Crater Lake. Crowned by Lone Eagle Peak (11,920 feet), a grand spire of stone, the scenery here is stunning.

Also branching off from the Cascade Creek Trail and providing access to the east side of the wilderness is the previously mentioned Buchanan Pass Trail. Starting a little more than 3 miles up Cascade Creek, this route climbs nearly 6 miles to 11,837-foot Buchanan Pass. Along the way, a side trail climbs for 2.7 miles to Gourd Lake. Nestled below the pass in a glacial valley is Fox Park—home to many wildflowers in late July and August.

The Arapaho Pass Trail, like other trans-Divide routes, runs considerably longer on the west side. Although the pass is 3.5 miles from the nearest trailhead on the east side of the Divide, it is nearly 11 miles from the Monarch Lake trailhead via the Arapaho Pass Trail. The route cuts through timbered canyons for much of the way, but Coyote Park does offer one reprieve about 6 miles in. Timberline is reached at Caribou Lake, and the pass lies above a series of steep switchbacks.

Cross-country Skiing

Wintertime access to the east side of the Indian Peaks Wilderness is easy thanks to the fact that the road is plowed to within 2 miles of Brainard Lake. Wind can be a problem along the road, so most cross-country skiers follow the Waldrop North Trail (instead of the Brainard Lake Road) 2.7 miles to the various trailheads. From there, skiers can follow any of the trails discussed in the previous section. The Isabelle Glacier Trail, for instance, offers easy skiing terrain for 2 miles to Lake Isabelle before encountering steeper slopes. The threat of avalanches may exist beyond this point; check on conditions before venturing farther. On the Mitchell Lake Trail, the possibility of avalanches exists beyond Blue Lake. Experienced skiers may want to tackle a trip up Mount Audubon. Although the mountain is not particularly steep, avalanche conditions may exist and the wind can be tremendous. But under ideal conditions, it is a superb ski up one of the higher summits in the range.

The Middle St. Vrain drainage also conducts skiers into the wilderness, although it is a considerably longer trip—nearly 5 miles—from the road to the wilderness boundary. Beyond this point, it is another mile to Red Deer Lake and 3.5 miles to the base of the St. Vrain glaciers. This route is considered difficult.

You may also enter the wilderness to the south at Coney Flats (the plowed road ends at Beaver Reservoir). From here, the Buchanan Pass Trail travels 3 miles to Buchanan Pass, while the Beaver Creek Trail heads south over a divide to the Brainard Lake area. All of these extended trips are long and avalanches are a real possibility, especially at Buchanan Pass. A general rule of thumb is to consider the possibility of avalanches whenever leaving the safety of the timber.

The St. Vrain Mountain Trail in the northeastern corner of Indian Peaks begins on Rock Creek Road about 1.5 miles south of Allenspark. The route climbs steadily once inside the wilderness. The first half of the trail is set in a narrow valley where trees cut down the exposure to wind; as it nears St. Vrain Mountain, however, the trees thin out and wind exposure coupled with avalanche danger can pose a problem.

South of Brainard Lake, cross-country skiers will find wilderness access at road's end just beyond the Eldora Mountain Ski Resort. Several destinations are possible, including King Lake, 5.5 miles in; Woodland Lake, a little more than 5 miles from the wintertime trailhead; and Devils Thumb Lake, a 14-mile round trip. All of these routes climb more than 2,000 feet and pass through places where avalanches are possible.

Mountaineering

Peak bagging in the Indian Peaks Wilderness can be as easy or as challenging as you want to make it. Barely 2 miles in is Mount Audubon (13,223 feet). Another easy climb is Sawtooth Mountain (12,304 feet), which lies just south of Buchanan Pass. From Pawnee Pass, Pawnee Peak (12,943 feet) and Shoshoni Peak (12,967 feet) are reachable summits, and both are walk-ups. Paiute Peak (13,088 feet) stands about 1 mile west of Audubon's summit and is connected by a rugged ridge. This traverse involves exposure and loose rock.

More technical climbs include those up Apache Peak (13,441 feet) and Navajo Peak (13,409 feet). Routes up the north face of Navajo are especially difficult. Both Apache and Navajo peaks can be approached via the South St. Vrain drainage. The most alluring precipice in Indian Peaks Wilderness may be Lone Eagle Peak. A thin spire of granite towering above Crater Lake, this mountain has been ranked as one of the best technical climbs in the state.

Farther south on the Continental Divide, North Arapaho and South Arapaho Peaks, 13,502 feet and 13,397 feet respectively, are approached via the Arapaho Pass Trail out of the Lake Eldora area. Both are rugged scrambles to the top.

3 Comanche Peak Wilderness Area

Location: 40 mi w of Fort Collins
Size: 66,791 acres
Status: Wilderness area (1980)
Terrain: Alpine peaks and heavily timbered canyons
Elevation: 8,000' to 12,702'
Management: Roosevelt NF
Topographic maps: Boston Peak, Kinikinik, Rustic, Chambers Lake, Comanche Peak, Pingree Park, Crystal Mountain, Estes Park, Glen Haven

Picking up where Rocky Mountain National Park ends, the Comanche Peak Wilderness Area includes a large parcel of backcountry directly adjacent to the park's northern border. Some trails here offer hikers relatively easy access into the park's northern frontier, while others crisscross the wilderness area itself. Thick forests cover much of the Comanche Peak Wilderness, and several beautiful streams run through the area. Most of the summits, including the area's namesake, are along its southern border.

Seasons
Winter holds fast to the Comanche Peak area from October through May and into July at higher elevations. Many permanent ice fields and snowbanks exist in protected spots. During the summer months and often into fall, afternoon cloudbursts accompanied by lightning are common. Wildflowers typically bloom soon after the snow melts in July and August. The bugling of elk may be heard in September.

Flora and Fauna
With elevations between 8,000 and 11,000 feet, much of the terrain is characterized by thick stands of either lodgepole pine or Engelmann spruce and subalpine fir. Patches of aspen are also plentiful, along with open meadows. At timberline, krummholz forests are common; beyond the last trees, alpine tundra takes over with its array of lichen, sedges, and grasses.

Wildlife found in the Comanche Peak Wilderness Area include mule deer, elk, black bears, coyotes, cougars, marmots, pikas, and an occasional band of bighorn sheep that has wandered over from the park.

Geology
The Comanche Peak Wilderness Area encompasses the northern end of the Mummy Range, so named because some peaks resemble reclining mummies. Part of the Front Range, the Mummies formed as a result of faulted anticlines some 65 million years ago. The Mummies, however, are quite gentle by comparison to neighboring ranges.

Typically, the western slopes of the Mummies are rounded and smooth, but, thanks in part to the carving action of glaciers, their northern and eastern faces often erupt as precipitous cliffs of granite. Several permanent ice fields still exist.

ACTIVITIES
Hiking

With more than a dozen trails penetrating the Comanche Peak Wilderness, an inviting array of hikes awaits backcountry visitors. Gravel roads skirt the western, northern, and eastern fronts of the wilderness, providing access to a number of trailheads.

A popular hike for fishermen is the Big South Trail, which follows the Cache la Poudre River for 12 miles before becoming the Poudre River Trail in Rocky Mountain National Park. Access to the Big South Trail is found along Colorado Highway 14 and at Peterson Lake off Long Draw Road. Because this route closely follows a river bottom, its grades tend to be gentle and trees limit the vistas. A bill signed by President Clinton in October 2000 dedicated the Big South Trail to Jaryd Atadero, a 3-year-old boy who disappeared while hiking on the trail with others in 1999. The Fish Creek and Little Beaver Trails, which also follow streams, are close by and reachable from the Pingree Park Road.

The Zimmerman Trail starts on Colorado Highway 14, about 2 miles east of Big Bend Campground. It follows a drainage bottom for the first few miles, crosses into the Sheep Creek drainage, and climbs again. At about 9 miles in the trail meets with the end of the Crown Point Road, and 12 miles from the start, it ends at a junction with the Flowers Trail. Elevation on the Zimmerman Trail ranges from 7,600 to 10,400 feet.

The Flowers Trail, a wagon road in the 1800s, crosses the wilderness from Peterson Lake to Beaver Park. The Beaver Park access is at the end of the 6-mile, 4WD Flowers Road (FR 152). Climbing to within 0.5 mile of Crown Mountain (11,637 feet), the Flowers Trail tops out above timberline, opening up to some spectacular views in the

Along the hike to Emmaline Lake

process. The Beaver Creek Trail connects with the Flowers Trail near its midpoint. Seven miles long, the Beaver Creek route begins about 4 miles west of the Tom Bennett Campground near Pingree Park. It also passes Comanche Reservoir—a popular fishing spot—just outside the wilderness area. The Hourglass Trail, which cuts south from Comanche Reservoir, climbs from 8,400 to 12,000 feet in 4 miles to meet with the Mirror Lake Trail just north of the park boundary.

The Flowers Trail also intersects with the Browns Lake and Mirror Lake Trails. Browns Lake and nearby Timberline Lake, both favorite spots for anglers, are 4 miles south of the Browns Lake trailhead on the Crown Point Road. The 9-mile Mirror Lake Trail takes off from a point on the Flowers Trail and heads south toward Mirror Lake, a few miles outside the park. A high-altitude route, it reveals many spectacular vistas along the way.

From the Pingree Park area, several routes traverse the wilderness before entering the park to the south. The Stormy Peaks Trail, for instance, crosses into the park after 2 miles and tops Stormy Peaks Pass once inside. The route eventually joins the North Fork Trail, which follows the Big Thompson River across the northeast corner

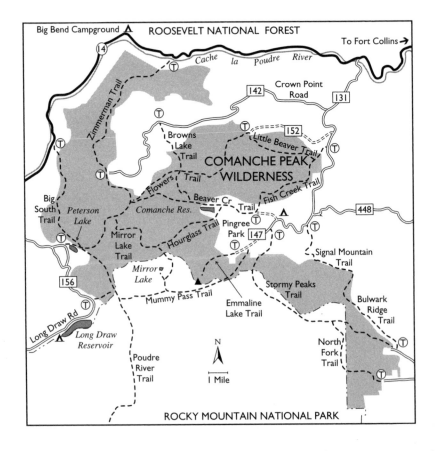

of Rocky Mountain National Park and back out to the Comanche Peak Wilderness. A return route to the Pingree Park area follows the Bulwark Ridge and Signal Mountain Trails, which cross over Signal Mountain (11,262 feet).

Also starting at Pingree Park are the Emmaline Lake and Mummy Pass Trails. These routes divide after following a 4WD road for 2 miles. The Mummy Pass Trail enters the park before reaching the pass 5 miles from the trailhead. The Emmaline Lake Trail continues up the Fall Creek drainage until it reaches the lake, 4 miles in. Situated at timberline in a beautiful cirque of granite walls and ice fields, Emmaline Lake is overshadowed by Fall Mountain and Comanche Peak. The Fish Creek and Little Beaver Trails follow streams and are reachable from Pingree Park Road.

Cross-country Skiing

Although access to the Comanche Peak Wilderness is not always assured due to an uncertain plowing schedule, many of the routes discussed under Hiking double as fine cross-country skiing routes. Trails that take off from Pingree Park Road include the Emmaline Lake, Mummy Pass, Stormy Peaks, Signal Mountain, and Little Beaver routes. Long Draw Road is not plowed but can be easily skied to reach the Peterson Lake area. The Big South Trail begins on Highway 14 but follows a canyon bottom, which makes for some difficult skiing terrain.

Mountaineering

Because of their gentle stature, summits in the Comanche Peak Wilderness can be reached via relatively easy walk-ups, but technical climbers can find several challenging routes up cirque walls. One such climb is up Comanche Peak from Emmaline Lake. The easy route follows a ridge line to the northwest, but more difficult routes are found among the walls directly above the lake. From Comanche Peak, the summit of Fall Mountain is an easy traverse.

4 Cache la Poudre Wilderness Area

Location: 30 mi W of Fort Collins
Size: 9,380 acres
Status: Wilderness area (1980)
Terrain: Steep canyons and semiarid forests
Elevation: 6,200' to 8,600'
Management: Roosevelt NF
Topographic maps: Big Narrows, Rustic, Pingree Park

Small and often overlooked, the Cache la Poudre Wilderness Area safeguards some of the steep canyon terrain found along the Cache la Poudre River. The wilderness is bounded by Colorado Highway 14 and features only one established trail.

Seasons

Unlike other wilderness areas in this region, the Cache la Poudre is situated at a relatively low elevation, making the hiking season as long as ten months.

Flora and Fauna

Because deep snow cover is infrequent here, Cache la Poudre is an important big game winter habitat. Mule deer and elk rely on areas like this to sustain them through the winter months as they browse on bitterbrush and mountain mahogany, two major food sources. Other species you might see here include black bears, coyotes, cougars, and bighorn sheep. With many rock outcrops and cliff faces, this wilderness is also home to the rare peregrine falcon. Forest types include lodgepole and ponderosa pine.

Geology

Absent here are the effects of glacial activity. Rather, the topography has been shaped by the cutting action of the Cache la Poudre River and some of its tributaries. Through this process of stream erosion, outcrops of Precambrian basement rock have been exposed.

History

The Cache la Poudre or "Hide the Powder" River was named by employees of the Hudson Bay Company who were en route from St. Louis to Green River in November 1836. Slowed by deep snow, the men buried gunpowder and other provisions in order to lighten their load. The next spring, they returned to the site along the river to collect their belongings.

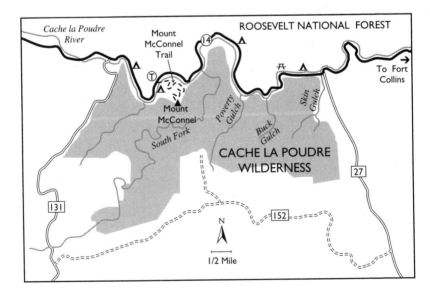

Pine forests typify most of the Cache la Poudre Wilderness.

ACTIVITIES
Hiking

Because there is only one established trail within the Cache la Poudre Wilderness Area, backcountry use is comparatively low. The busiest time is during deer hunting season.

The Mount McConnel National Recreation Trail is a 4-mile loop that climbs Mount McConnel (8,010 feet). Part of this route is also designated as the Kreutzer Nature Trail. Dedicated to William Kreutzer, the first official forest ranger in the United States (he was assigned to the Colorado Timber Land Reserve in 1898), this self-guided walk is a little more than 2 miles. Along both routes, spectacular views of the Cache la Poudre River Canyon open up frequently. From the summit of Mount McConnel you can also spy the distant peaks of the Mummy Range.

According to the Forest Service, to maintain the area's wilderness character, no new trails are planned. They suggest that visitors try bushwhacking along stream bottoms in the area or follow game trails and ridge tops. While such travel is rewarding, it is also prudent to bring along topographic maps, a compass, and the skill to use both.

5 Neota Wilderness Area

Location: 60 mi W of Fort Collins
Size: 9,924 acres
Status: Wilderness area (1980)
Terrain: Flat-topped alpine ridges and thick forests
Elevation: 10,000' to 11,800'
Management: Roosevelt NF, Routt NF
Topographic maps: Chambers Lake, Fall River Pass, Clark Peak

A small wilderness area, the Neota is separated from the neighboring Rawah and Comanche Peak wilderness areas by established roads. Few people visit the Neota, mostly because it is comparatively small and only two trails access it. Nevertheless, the opportunities for finding solitude and spotting wildlife make the Neota Wilderness a gem.

Alpine terrain in the Neota Wilderness

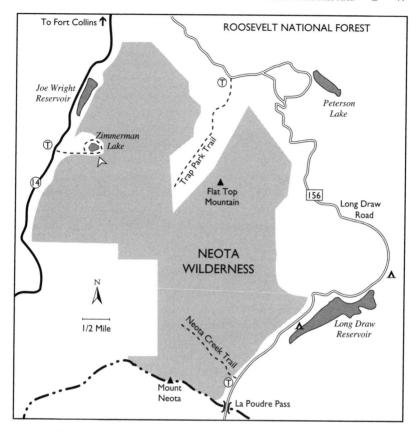

Seasons

Because of its high elevations, heavy snow cover can be expected in the Neota Wilderness from October through June or July. Alpine flowers bloom mostly in July, and September brings on the bugling season for elk.

Flora and Fauna

One-third of the Neota Wilderness is alpine tundra, so the inhabitants in that portion are the species that frequent higher elevations, including bighorn sheep, marmots, and pikas. Mule deer, elk, and the shy pine marten live among the thick Engelmann spruce and subalpine fir forests that cover the lower elevations. Beaver dams are a common sight along stream bottoms and in marshy areas.

Geology

At the northern end of the Never Summer Range, the Neota area is primarily volcanic in origin, having been formed during the Tertiary period. Glaciers subsequently etched shallow cirques into the higher reaches and gave drainages a U-shaped profile.

ACTIVITIES
Hiking
One official trail accesses the upper ridges of the Neota. The Neota Creek Trail begins close to the end of Long Draw Road and climbs 1.5 miles before the view opens to the expansive tundra. From there, the high country is easily accessible. Low-impact travel and camping techniques should be used, as the tundra is quite fragile. A closed-off jeep road is now a hiking trail into Trap Park. It also starts from Long Draw Road at a point about 3 miles from Colorado Highway 14. The gentle alpine ridges above are easily gained from the park.

Cross-country Skiing
Long Draw Road is frequented by both skiers and snowmobilers in the winter, but skiers can leave the noisy machines behind by turning up one of the previously mentioned trails.

A marked ski trail that is very close to but not actually in the wilderness area circumnavigates Zimmerman Lake, which sits 1.5 miles from Highway 14. Experienced skiers can pick their way through the timber from Zimmerman Lake to the open tundra above—another mile and several hundred feet up.

 6   Rawah Wilderness Area

Location: 60 mi W of Fort Collins
Size: 76,424 acres
Status: Wilderness area (1964)
Terrain: Alpine summits and forested lower slopes
Elevation: 8,400' to 12,951'
Management: Roosevelt NF, Routt NF
Topographic maps: Rawah Lakes, Glendevey, Shipman Mountain, Clark Peak, Boston Peak, Chambers Lake

Covering the eastern slope of the rugged southern end of the Medicine Bow Range, the Rawah Wilderness Area features some spectacular hikes and vistas. The main spine of the range is topped by 11,000- and 12,000-foot peaks and is dotted with alpine lakes. From the highest peaks, the view to the west stretches across North Park to the distant Mount Zirkel Wilderness Area. To the north you can peer into Wyoming and the Snowy Range, timbered drainages drop off to the east, and, to the south, the many summits of Rocky Mountain National Park rise in unison.

Seasons
The hiking season begins in May or June in the lower elevations, while the high country may not open up until well into July. Summers bring thunderstorms and vivid dis-

Twin Crater Lakes at sunset

plays of wildflowers, while the first hints of autumn signal the start of the elk rutting season. Mid- or late October typically brings the first heavy snows.

Flora and Fauna

Among the lower elevations of the Rawah, thick stands of lodgepole pine predominate, but aspens fill in some areas. Higher up, Engelmann spruce and subalpine fir comprise most of the wooded areas. Near timberline, krummholz forests of severely stunted trees are common; one such forest is found in the vicinity of Twin Crater Lakes. Winter winds sweeping off the high peaks blast the area and strip branches off the taller trees. Beyond the krummholz growth, alpine tundra is interspersed with boulder fields and rocky ridges.

Among the creatures that inhabit the Rawah are elk, mule deer, black bears, and snowshoe hares. Coyotes roam all regions of the mountains, including those above timberline. A herd of bighorn sheep has made a home in the higher reaches. White-tailed ptarmigan also live in alpine areas. Among the pine forests of the lower elevations, moose have been doing well since being introduced to the North Park region in 1978 and 1979. Another northern species whose range extends this far south is the pine marten.

Geology

Like the Front Range to the south, the Medicine Bow Range was formed after faults formed in the earth's surface and great, elongated blocks of Precambrian substrata tilted upward. Known as a faulted anticline mountain chain, such a formation resulted in the exposure of very old basement rocks, such as granite and schist. If you look down the spine of the Medicine Bow, it is easy to imagine them as a single block that has tilted to one end. Geologists theorize that, like most of Colorado's mountains, the Medicine Bow began rising during the Laramide Orogeny, 65 million years ago.

In more recent millennia, glaciation played a major role in shaping the Rawah Wilderness. Many of the highest valleys are U-shaped, and a string of glacially carved lakes constitutes the "Lake District" along the higher southern end of the wilderness. The erosive action of streams and creeks has affected the lower topography.

History

The names Rawah and Medicine Bow indicate that this wilderness area was a one-time haunt of Native Americans. Rawah is Ute for "wilderness," while Medicine Bow refers to an Indian legend that wood collected in these mountains for bows is bestowed with "good medicine" by the gods.

Fur trappers no doubt crossed the area in the early nineteenth century. Although mining never really got started in the Rawah, cattle grazing was prominent after 1900. Some old cabins date back to early settlers. The range was recognized for its wilderness qualities early on, and a 16,000-acre tract of protected land was established in 1927. In 1953 it was expanded to 26,797 acres and classified as a wild area. The Wilderness Act of 1964 brought congressional recognition, and subsequent legislation expanded the Rawah Wilderness to its current size.

ACTIVITIES
Hiking

Situated relatively close to population centers along the Front Range, the Rawah Wilderness Area is heavily used. A permanent fire ban covering most of the range's tundra region has gone a long way toward remedying the impact backpackers have made on this fragile land, but it will be many decades before the scars are fully erased. Given the growing popularity of this wilderness, a permit system is probably just around the corner.

The heart of the Rawah Wilderness is the Lake District, where some two dozen lakes dot a high alpine and subalpine landscape. Several summits top 12,000 feet, including the highest in the range, Clark Peak (12,951 feet). Access to any part of this area requires a hike of at least 4 miles and usually an elevation gain of 2,000 feet or more.

The easiest hike into the Lake District, and consequently the most heavily used trail in the wilderness, is the Blue Lake Trail. Beginning on Highway 14 not far from Cameron Pass, this route climbs a little more than 1,000 feet in 6.5 miles before reaching Blue Lake at 10,800 feet. From the lake, a sweeping vista to the south takes in the Mummy Range and parts of Rocky Mountain National Park. So popular is the Blue Lake area, however, that camping is restricted to a handful of designated sites and horses are prohibited along the entire trail.

North of Blue Lake, the trail continues over Blue Lake Pass to connect with the West Branch Trail. The West Branch trailhead is near Tunnel Campground on graveled

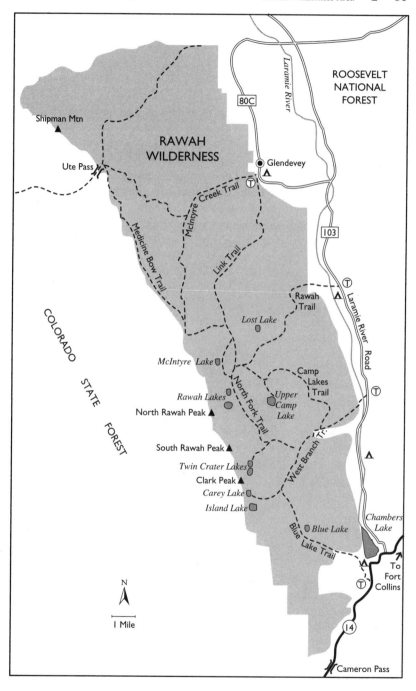

Laramie River Road. The West Branch Trail leads to Island and Carey Lakes, 7 miles and 2,440 vertical feet from its trailhead. Two other trails branch off to the north creating an inviting network of optional routes. Three miles in from the West Branch trailhead, the Camp Lakes Trail begins a 6-mile traverse to the Camp Lakes area, then continues on to the spectacular Rawah Lakes. The second branch follows the North Fork drainage for a more direct route to the Rawah Lakes. As this trail climbs toward Grassy Pass, a 1.5-mile side trail climbs steeply to Twin Crater Lakes. Set in a rugged cirque of peaks, Twin Crater Lakes are a picturesque reward for those who make the 6-mile, 2,500-foot hike in from the trailhead.

Just as the Rawah Lakes can be reached from the West Branch Trail via the Camp Lakes and North Fork Trails, they are also accessible by way of the Rawah Trail, which starts across from the Rawah Guest Ranch on Laramie River Road. Climbing from 8,400 feet to 10,700 feet in a little over 9 miles, this route is not necessarily more direct than those previously mentioned, but it does offer a less-used alternative when the West Branch trailhead parking lot is full. Whichever route you choose, expect to meet a lot of other hikers and horsepackers from Blue Lake north to the Rawah Lakes.

North of the Rawah Lakes, one last cluster of alpine lakes attracts hikers following the Link Trail. Eight miles and 2,200 vertical feet in is McIntyre Lake. About 1 mile beyond, the trail connects with the Rawah Trail, making possible an extended journey into the Lakes District of the Rawah.

North of the McIntyre Lake area, the Medicine Bow Range drops below timberline to become a forested ridge line rather than a chain of rugged summits. Because this area lacks alpine lakes and rocky crags, it is considerably less crowded than the southern end of the wilderness. Beginning near the Browns Park Campground, near Glendevey on County Road 80C, the McIntyre Creek Trail ascends to two points along the top of the range. To the north it reaches 9,869-foot Ute Pass after 10 moderately easy miles. A southern spur tops out to the south, about 2 miles from McIntyre Lake. Running between the Link Trail and Ute Pass is the Medicine Bow Trail. Because it follows the Medicine Bow Divide for nearly 10 miles, it opens up to some beautiful views of North Park to the west. Other notable highlights along this trail system are Honsmer and Shipman Parks, two natural meadows often frequented by deer and elk.

Cross-country Skiing

Because Laramie River Road is not plowed in the winter, access to many trailheads is restricted. To reach the West Branch, Rawah, and Link–McIntyre trailheads, snowmobiling up the Laramie River Road might be your best bet.

One trail easily reached along Highway 14 is the Blue Lake Trail. Although considered difficult, this route is quite popular among skiers for it allows access to the Rawah high country. Avalanche dangers exist on the steeper slopes. Another route that lies just south of the wilderness boundary off Highway 14 and just up the road from the Blue Lake trailhead climbs for 1.1 miles to Montgomery Pass. Topping out on the Medicine Bow Divide, this ascent is quick and difficult, but the views from the pass make it well worth the effort.

Mountaineering

Climbers will find numerous technical routes with exposed granite faces and even a few permanent ice fields, especially in the vicinity of Clark, Ashley, and Rawah Peaks. Access to these summits is also possible via walk-ups. To reach Clark Peak (12,951 feet), follow the ridge southwest from Blue Lake Pass for 2 miles. The second-highest point in the Rawah Wilderness, South Rawah Peak (12,644 feet), can be reached from either Twin Crater Lakes or the Rawah Lakes area. North Rawah Peak (12,473 feet) is a 2-mile ridge walk from South Rawah.

Never Summer Wilderness Area

Location: 30 mi SE of Walden
Size: 20,692 acres
Status: Wilderness area (1980)
Terrain: Alpine peaks and forested lower slopes
Elevation: 8,900' to 12,810'
Management: Routt NF, Arapaho NF
Topographic maps: Mount Richthofen, Bowen Mountain, Grand Lake

Small by Colorado standards, the Never Summer Wilderness Area nestles up to the western boundary of Rocky Mountain National Park. The Continental Divide forms part of the shared border before cutting west across the wilderness area. Never Summer is a derivative of the Arapaho name for these mountains, *Ni-chebe-chii* or "No Never Summer." Given the lofty stature of the area, it is a fitting name indeed. The Colorado Wilderness Act of 1993 added 6,990 more acres, mostly in the Bowen Gulch and Cascade Mountain areas. Further, an 11,600-acre Protection Area also has been established. It bars future development but permits snowmobiles and mountain bicycles.

Seasons

The high country does not open up in most years until early July, while the first heavy snows fall in October. Severe thunderstorms with plenty of lightning are the rule of thumb during the summer months, and surprise snow showers can occur anytime. The wildflower season runs from late July through early August.

Flora and Fauna

Sixty percent of the Never Summer Wilderness is either alpine meadow or barren, rocky terrain. Forests of either Engelmann spruce and subalpine fir or lodgepole pine occur along the lower slopes. Open meadows, often thick with willows, are found along the valley floors.

Elk and mule deer are found in most reaches of the Never Summer Range. Bighorn sheep inhabit the uppermost elevations, as do marmots, pikas, and ptarmigan.

Black bears and coyotes are relatively common here, and pine martens can be sighted in the timbered regions. As a result of a privately funded transplant project, moose now frequent the lower elevations.

Geology

Unlike the nearby Mummy and Medicine Bow Ranges, the Never Summers resulted more from volcanic activity than from faulting or folding action. In addition to being darker than neighboring mountain ranges, peaks in the Never Summers display colorations typical of heavy mineralization. Harder than some other mountains, the Never Summers proved more resistant to the sculpting power of glaciers.

ACTIVITIES
Hiking

Because of its remote location and its comparatively small acreage, the Never Summer Wilderness does not receive the high numbers of visitors that other wilderness areas do. Because of this, the area provides plenty of solitude for those willing to travel that extra mile.

From the Rocky Mountain National Park side, two trails follow drainages west into the southern half of the wilderness. The Bowen Gulch Trail begins 6 miles north of the park entrance in the Kawuneeche Valley. For much of the way, this route follows an old jeep road built in the 1880s to access the Wolverine Mine, now long abandoned. Eight

Wilderness sign near Baker Pass

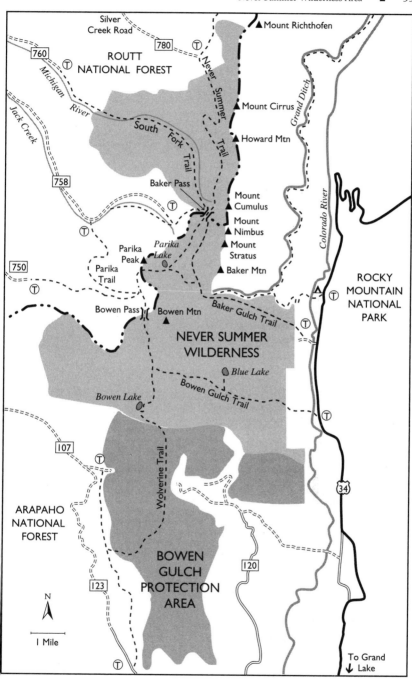

miles and a 2,500-foot ascent in, the Continental Divide is reached at 11,476-foot Bowen Pass. Along the way, side trails lead to two lakes—Blue Lake is 1 mile north of the Bowen Gulch Trail, and Bowen Lake is 2 miles south. From atop the pass, the Parika Trail drops down to a 4WD road that approaches from the west. Stream crossings can be difficult along the Bowen Gulch Trail, especially in spring and early summer.

Heading south from Bowen Lake is the Wolverine Trail. After passing Bowen Lake near the current southern boundary of the wilderness, this route runs along Blue Ridge, cutting through the Bowen Gulch Protection Area. Access to the southern portion of the trail is found on the Supply Creek Road, approximately 5 miles south from Bowen Pass.

From a trailhead 2 miles north of the Bowen Gulch trailhead, the Baker Gulch Trail follows Baker Gulch Creek to its headwaters at 11,253-foot Baker Pass, also on the Continental Divide. It is a moderate climb the entire way, gaining 2,300 feet in 6 miles. Along the way, the route encounters the Grand Ditch, an 1890s water-diversion project that transports water across the Continental Divide and into the Cache la Poudre drainage for consumption in the Fort Collins area. The fishing is good in much of Baker Gulch Creek. A side route 4 miles in leads to Parika Lake. Spectacular summits encircle the headwaters of this drainage.

Although it lies at the very heart of the Never Summer Wilderness, Baker Pass is easily accessible from the western slope of the range. From the end of a steep 4WD road that climbs to the head of the Jack Creek drainage, it is only 1 mile to Baker Pass. Following an old road now closed to vehicles, this route climbs quickly out of the trees to the Continental Divide. From there, the views of the surrounding peaks and valleys are spectacular. Also reaching Baker Pass from the west is the 6-mile South Fork Trail. Following a branch of the Michigan River almost the entire way, this route is easy. Highlights include virgin forests and open parks.

Once on top of Baker Pass you can pick up the Never Summer Trail. Spanning much of the length of its namesake wilderness, virtually the entire 9-mile route runs above tree line. Parts of it are rugged and not recommended for horses, but the nonstop scenery makes this trail a real treasure. North from the pass, the Never Summer Trail covers 5 miles before intersecting with the 4WD Silver Creek Road just outside of the wilderness. It passes below a line of rocky peaks named after cloud formations—Mounts Cirrus, Cumulus, Nimbus, and Stratus—as well as Howard Mountain, the highest point in the wilderness at 12,810 feet. Heading south from Baker Pass, the Never Summer Trail continues on to Parika Lake, then crosses back to the western flank of the Continental Divide via a 12,000-foot saddle between Fairview Mountain and Parika Peak. Exiting the wilderness at this point, it drops 2.5 miles to a trailhead on a forest road along the upper Illinois River.

Mountaineering

Although quite steep and often cloaked with talus slopes, the greater peaks of the Never Summer Range can be scrambled with no technical assistance. Mounts Cirrus (12,797 feet), Nimbus (12,706 feet), and Stratus (12,520 feet), as well as Howard Mountain (12,810 feet), are climbable from either the Never Summer Trail or the Big Ditch Trail in the park. Baker Mountain (12,397 feet) can be reached from the Baker Gulch Trail. Rising just north of the wilderness is Mount Richthofen (12,940 feet), which is reachable from the Cameron Pass area.

8 Vasquez Peak Wilderness Area

Location: 3 mi S of Winter Park
Size: 12,300 acres
Status: Wilderness area (1993)
Terrain: Alpine peaks with timbered lower slopes
Elevation: 8,600' to 12,521'
Management: Arapaho NF
Topographic maps: Berthoud Pass, Byers Peak

A small parcel of mountain land tucked between Berthoud Pass and the Fraser Experimental Forest, the Vasquez Peak Wilderness offers a beautiful taste of Colorado's high country. The Continental Divide runs through part of the area, creating a wonderful alpine ridge with spectacular views along the way. Vasquez Peak Wilderness was established by the Colorado Wilderness Act of 1993.

Seasons

Winter's grip lasts long in this high land, usually from October through June or July. Wildflowers begin blooming in late July, and summer afternoons often witness the formation of thunderstorms, which can be quite dangerous on exposed ridges and summits.

Flora and Fauna

The lower elevations of this area are heavily forested with Engelmann spruce and subalpine fir. Smaller stands of lodgepole pine are also present. Krummholz forests are found at timberline, and stretches of alpine tundra constitute the primary plant community above timberline.

Mountain goats reportedly inhabit the Vasquez Peak Wilderness, as do mule deer, elk, black bears, and coyotes. Above timberline, high-pitched chirps are a reminder of the area's pika population.

Geology

Constituting the western end of the Front Range, the Vasquez Mountains were uplifted during the Laramide Orogeny as faulted blocks. Glaciers wielded a considerable influence on the area, as evidenced by the many glacial bowls and cirques.

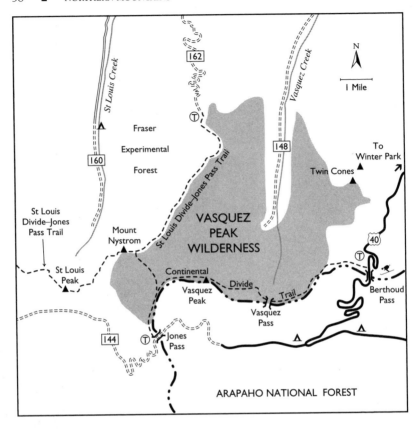

ACTIVITIES
Hiking

A good point of access for the Vasquez Peak Wilderness is by way of the Continental Divide Trail—a consortium of trails that follow the Continental Divide from Mexico to Canada. The Divide crosses 11,315-foot Berthoud Pass, and you may park for an excursion into the Vasquez Peak area at this convenient stretch of paved road. Follow the ski-hill service road on foot for 1 mile to the top of the chair lift west of the pass. The trail then continues west and south up an obvious ridge. Follow the Continental Divide Trail, which is marked by blue signs, for several miles to Jones Pass, just beyond the western end of the wilderness area.

The St. Louis Divide–Jones Pass Trail begins its 16-mile journey at Jones Pass before crossing the western end of the Vasquez Peak Wilderness to Mount Nystrom. Mount Nystrom can also be reached from the north via a 5-mile trail that follows the divide between the Vasquez Creek and St. Louis Creek drainages.

Additionally, an old road climbs to 11,700-foot Vasquez Pass from the end of Forest

Opposite: *A memorial along the Continental Divide in the Vasquez Peak Wilderness*

Road 148. This walk is 3 miles each way. It intersects the Continental Divide Trail at the pass.

Cross-country Skiing

With a chair lift servicing the slope west of Berthoud Pass, winter access to the Vasquez Peak Wilderness Area is easy. From the top of the lift, it is possible to continue along the Continental Divide toward Jones Pass. This being a steep, wind-blown area, the avalanche danger can be very high and exposure to cold is a constant threat. Skiing is best from November to May.

9 Byers Peak Wilderness Area

Location: 10 mi SW of Winter Park
Size: 8,095 acres
Status: Wilderness area (1993)
Terrain: Alpine ridges with forested lower slopes
Elevation: 9,000' to 12,804'
Management: Arapaho NF
Topographic maps: Byers Peak, Bottle Pass, Ute Peak

Like the Vasquez Peak Wilderness, the Byers Peak Wilderness Area borders on the Fraser Experimental Forest. With much of its acreage above timberline, the Byers Peak Wilderness features a wealth of high-altitude vistas. Formerly known as the St. Louis Peak Further Planning Area, Byers Peak was not recommended for wilderness designation by the Forest Service, but Colorado's congressional delegation included it anyway.

Seasons

The short hiking season usually begins in late June or July and lasts until October. Lower elevations may be accessible a few weeks earlier. Thunderstorms are an almost daily hazard in the summer, and freezing temperatures can occur almost anytime.

Flora and Fauna

The forests in this area consist mostly of Engelmann spruce and subalpine fir, with some stands of lodgepole pine mixed in. Among these timbered lands you might spot deer, elk, black bears, and several species of nongame animals. Pikas, marmots, and white-tailed ptarmigan are common in alpine reaches. Mountain goats are also known to visit the area.

Geology

Part of the Front Range, the Byers Peak region was uplifted during the Laramide Orogeny, although it does not exhibit the same north–south trend as the eastern part of the range. Glaciers have formed broad cirques and a few small alpine lakes.

ACTIVITIES
Hiking

The 16-mile St. Louis Divide–Jones Pass Trail follows the eastern boundary of the Byers Peak Wilderness. For the most part, this route stays high on a ridge crest, opening up to some glorious views. It is accessible south of the wilderness thanks to a rough but passable 2WD road to the top of 12,453-foot Jones Pass. Situated on the Continental Divide, 5 miles west of U.S. 40 near Berthoud Pass, Jones Pass offers spectacular views in all directions. From Jones Pass, follow the Continental Divide Trail north 1.5 miles to the turnoff for the St. Louis Divide. In 1 mile the route tops Mount Nystrom and then continues west and north along the rim of mountains (see Vasquez Peak Wilderness Area map).

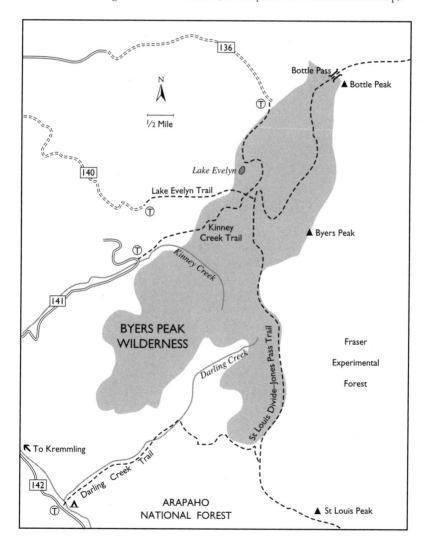

A stream in the Byers Peak Wilderness

Three trails drop into the Williams Fork drainage to the west from the St. Louis Divide–Jones Pass Trail: the Lake Evelyn, Kinney Creek, and Darling Creek Trails. Each of these routes eventually accesses the diminutive Lake Evelyn located at 11,700 feet and terminates at trailheads along Forest Service roads below. The most direct approach follows the lake's namesake trail east from a trailhead along Forest Service Road 140.

A shorter hike accesses the top of 12,804-foot Byers Peak. From the Byers Peak trailhead located in the Fraser Experimental Forest east of the wilderness, it is a 1.5-mile hike to the highly scenic summit.

10 Ptarmigan Peak Wilderness Area

Location: 5 mi NE of Silverthorne
Size: 13,175 acres
Status: Wilderness area (1993)
Terrain: Alpine ridges and forested slopes
Elevation: 8,800' to 12,757'
Management: Arapaho NF
Topographic maps: Loveland Pass, Byers Peak, Dillon, Ute Peak

The Ptarmigan Peak Wilderness Area includes the mountainous country just north of Interstate 70 from the Eisenhower Tunnel to Silverthorne, and from the Williams Fork Mountains up to Ute Pass. This proximity to a major thoroughfare—a detraction for some and an attribute for others—makes this wilderness unique. A far cry from the 54,000 acres originally considered for protection, the Ptarmigan Peak Wilderness (previously known as the Williams Fork Further Planning Area) once extended east of the present boundary to include a broad and beautiful drainage. Conflicts with the city of Denver's plans to develop its rights to Williams Fork water led to this pristine drainage being dropped from consideration as part of the wilderness area.

Seasons
Expect winter snows to last from late October through May in the lower elevations and possibly into July up high. Lightning storms are a definite hazard on exposed ridges in the summer. September is a good time to hear the elk bugle in the woodlands of this area.

Flora and Fauna
Forests within the Ptarmigan Peak Wilderness consist of lodgepole pine, Engelmann spruce, and subalpine fir. Mule deer and elk are common, as are black bears and many smaller nongame mammals. Along the highest ridges, the forests give way to alpine tundra where wildflowers grow in abundance.

Geology

The Ptarmigan Peak Wilderness encompasses the west- and south-facing slopes of the Williams Fork Mountains, offshoots of the Front Range. Uplifted during the Laramide Orogeny, this block of Precambrian basement rock is more a high ridge than an actual range of peaks. The Eisenhower Tunnel just beyond the eastern end of the wilderness penetrates Precambrian granite. Dropping east from the crest of the range, the Williams Fork drainage provides a vivid example of stream erosion at its best.

ACTIVITIES
Hiking

The Ute Pass Trail begins at a low pass on County Road 3 and climbs 5 miles along the crest of the Williams Fork Mountains to the top of Ute Peak (12,298 feet) on the north-

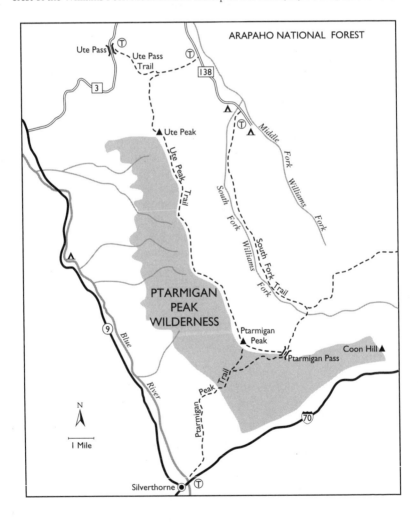

ern boundary of the Ptarmigan Peak Wilderness. South from Ute Peak it is 10 miles along the crest of the Williams Fork Mountains to Ptarmigan Pass. At Ptarmigan Pass you can either descend 3 miles to the South Fork Trail, which runs through the Williams Fork drainage to the east, or you can drop into Silverthorne via the 7-mile Ptarmigan Peak Trail. Faded in places, this route descends significantly to an obscure trailhead on County Road 2021.

Eagles Nest Wilderness Area

Location: 2 mi W of Silverthorne
Size: 133,325 acres
Status: Wilderness area (1976)
Terrain: Rugged alpine peaks with forested lower slopes
Elevation: 8,600' to 13,534'
Management: Arapaho NF, White River NF
Topographic maps: Dillon, Frisco, Vail Pass, Willow Lakes, Red Cliff, Vail East, Vail West, Squaw Creek, Mount Powell, Piney Peak

One of the most rugged mountain chains in the state, the Gore Range is a sight not easily forgotten. Rising from the Blue River Valley to more than 13,000 feet, its summits rake the sky in grand fashion. Their distinctive profile is readily visible from as far away as Trail Ridge Road in Rocky Mountain National Park.

Up close, the Eagles Nest Wilderness indeed lives up to all expectations. Heavily glaciated, much of its precipitous highlands remain trailless and inaccessible to the casual backcountry traveler. Typically, the trails that do penetrate the wilderness dead-end before reaching the crest of the range. The fact that these mountains pretty much escaped the push of nineteenth-century miners adds to their wild character. Whereas other ranges are pockmarked with old tailing piles and roadways, the southern Gore Range is quite pristine. Unfortunately, some of its trails and lakes are being loved to death by hikers.

Seasons
Winter keeps a snowy grip on the upper reaches of the Eagles Nest Wilderness from mid-October through June and sometimes into July. Almost daily afternoon showers in the summer bring with them the threat of lightning. Freezing temperatures and sudden snow squalls can occur any time of the year. The wildflower season begins shortly after the last snowbanks melt away.

Flora and Fauna
The ecological countenance of this wilderness begins with lodgepole pine and aspen forests at the foot of the mountains. Engelmann spruce and subalpine fir grow across its middle section, and alpine tundra interspersed with rocky ridges and outcrops typify

the highest reaches. Open meadows—which are often boggy in the early summer—characterize many subalpine valleys. Such parklands are good places to spot wildlife. Dozens of lakes dot the higher terrain, and the fishing is good in many of them.

Thanks in part to its incredibly rugged stature, the Eagles Nest Wilderness is home to both bighorn sheep and mountain goats. Mule deer and elk are common as well. Black bears, coyotes, and mountain lions can be spotted in the area. Nongame residents include snowshoe hares, marmots, and pikas.

Geology

Like the nearby Front Range, the Gore Range is a faulted anticline. Beginning 65 million years ago, an elongated block was pushed up after faults formed in the basement rock. As a result, the heart of the Gore Range consists of hard Precambrian rock, including granite. Unlike much of the Front Range, however, remnant deposits of sedimentary rock are still found on parts of the crest and red rock formations are found on the west flank of the Gores near Vail Pass. Glaciers played an important role in shaping the upper reaches of the range. Not only are U-shaped valleys, glacial lakes, and cirques common in the Eagles Nest Wilderness but the very ruggedness of its summits is partially attributable to the impressive power of glacial carving.

History

The Gore Range was named after Sir St. George Gore, a wealthy Irish nobleman who mounted a hunting expedition through the Colorado Rockies in 1883. The famous mountain man Jim Bridger served as his guide. John Wesley Powell climbed Mount Powell, the range's highest point, in 1868, a year prior to his epic journey down the Colorado River.

ACTIVITIES
Hiking

Because of the Gore Range's ruggedness, many of the trails in the Eagles Nest are in-and-out routes that begin at the foot of the mountains and ascend into the higher reaches of the range. One exception is the 54.5-mile Gore Range Trail, a long-distance backcountry avenue that runs the length of the wilderness. The Gore Range Trail can be picked up at nine access points along the way. The trail begins (or terminates, depending on your point of view) across from the Copper Mountain Ski Resort on Interstate 70. Climbing from 9,600 feet, the trail reaches 11,900-foot Uneva Pass 5 miles from the trailhead. From there, it traverses more high country to Eccles Pass and then begins dropping down the South Willow Creek drainage to a point just inside the wilderness. From there the route roughly parallels the eastern border of the wilderness to its end. Although the trail stays low among the trees for most of the way, the forest cover occasionally opens up to reveal spectacular views to the west. Near its northern end, the Gore Range Trail passes close to a handful of lakes before concluding at the Mahan Lake trailhead on FS Road 1831, a branch off Spring Creek Road.

Spring Creek Road 23

ARAPAHO NATIONAL FOREST

Green Mountain Reservoir

404

1832

1831

449

Mahan Lake

Lower Cataract Lake

30

1725

1700

Surprise Lake

Eaglesmere Lakes

Mirror Lake

Eagles Nest Mtn

N

1 Mile

9

Soda Lakes

18

17

Meridian Peak

Mount Powell

7

16

Upper Slate Lake

Slate Lake

6

Rock Cr Road

701

Piney Lake

786

EAGLES NEST WILDERNESS

WHITE RIVER NATIONAL FOREST

700

Vail

15

14

13

12

Salmon Lake

8

Willow Lakes

Zodiac Spires

Red Peak

9

Silverthorne

Red Buffalo Pass

Buffalo Mtn

Eccles Pass

10

Frisco

70

Uneva Pass

Copper Mtn Ski Resort

1. Gore Range Trail
2. Eaglesmere Trail
3. Surprise Trail
4. Mirror Trail
5. Elliot Ridge–East Meadow Creek Trail
6. Boulder Creek Trail
7. Slate Creek Trail
8. Willow Lakes Trail
9. Mesa Cortina Trail
10. East Meadow Creek Trail
11. Gore Creek Trail
12. Deluge Lake Trail
13. Bighorn Creek Trail
14. Pitkin Creek Trail
15. Booth Creek Trail
16. Piney Lake–Soda Lakes Trail
17. West Meadow Creek Trail
18. Piney River Trail
19. North Piney River Trail

Along the way, the Gore Range Trail intersects with shorter trails that access the eastern half of the wilderness. Lower Cataract Lake marks the start of two very popular trails. Heading north and west from the road, the Eaglesmere Trail climbs nearly 3 miles before reaching the Gore Range Trail. A right-hand turn takes you 0.5 mile to the Eaglesmere Lakes, which are situated at 10,500 feet. Surprise Trail heads south from Lower Cataract Lake and also picks up the Gore Range Trail partway in. Turn right off Surprise Trail onto Gore Range Trail and follow it about 0.3 mile to reach Surprise Lake nestled in the trees. Follow the Gore Range Trail farther still and you will reach the turnoff for Upper Cataract and Mirror Lakes, both of which are situated at the 10,800-foot level just below Eagles Nest Mountain. Upper Cataract Lake is 5.5 miles in, while Mirror Lake lies 1 mile beyond. Known as the Mirror Trail, this route continues past Mirror Lake and over Elliot Ridge, eventually connecting with the Elliot Ridge–East Meadow Creek Trail on the western slope of the range. All trails in the Cataract Lake area are heavily used.

Two other corridors that approach the heart of the range are the Boulder and Slate Creek Trails. Hiking access is from Rock Creek Road and both drainages cross private land before entering the national forest. The trailhead is 7 miles north of Silverthorne beyond a locked gate off of Rock Creek Road. The Gore Range Trail is 0.3 mile from the gate. Follow it north 1.8 miles to the Boulder Creek Trail. Boulder Lake is less than 0.5 mile in. The trail continues for nearly 3 miles beyond Boulder Lake to a nest of smaller lakes near the crest of the Gore Range. This section of trail is not recommended for horses, as it can be boggy in early summer.

The Slate Creek Trail spurs off the Gore Range Trail 4.4 miles north of the intersection with the Boulder Creek Trail. The trail follows an easy grade for 2 miles, but steepens and becomes rocky as it nears Slate Lake. Upper Slate Lake is reached after another mile of steep trail. It is 9 miles one way from the trailhead on Rock Creek Road to Upper Slate Lake.

The Willow Lakes Trail branches off from the Gore Range Trail and climbs to Salmon and Willow Lakes. Access to the Willow Lakes Trail is from a Rock Creek Road trailhead and then following the Gore Range Trail about 5 miles south, or from the Mesa Cortina trailhead on Aspen Drive just outside of Silverthorne. The Mesa Cortina Trail intersects the Gore Range Trail approximately 4 miles south of the Willow Lakes turnoff. The lakes are perched above 11,000 feet and the scenery is memorable. The Willow Lakes, which are the farthest in, are 7.5 miles from the Rock Creek Road trailhead and 8.5 miles from the Mesa Cortina trailhead.

A relatively easy route to the high country is one of two Meadow Creek Trails in the wilderness. Beginning from a trailhead just north of the Frisco exit on Interstate 70, the East Meadow Creek Trail climbs steadily for 4 miles to a juncture with the Gore Range Trail. From there it is nearly 1 mile to the top of 11,900-foot Eccles Pass. From this natural vantage point there is an incredible, up-close view of the Gore Range. North of the pass sits Buffalo Mountain, Red Peak, and Red Buffalo Pass. Red Buffalo Pass was considered as a possible site for Interstate 70, which was fortunately routed through a canyon farther south.

From Eccles Pass it is a little more than a 1-mile traverse to Red Buffalo Pass via the Gore Range Trail. From this saddle you can drop down into the west side of the mountains via the 5-mile Gore Creek Trail. This trail is quite popular thanks to its easy access from Interstate 70.

North of Gore Creek, other drainages bisect the western side of the Gore Range, each accompanied by a hiking trail. The Deluge, Bighorn, Pitkin, and Booth Creek Trails each offer popular in-and-out wilderness routes. The scenery along each is outstanding and all but Bighorn terminate at a high alpine lake. The longest of these options, the Booth Creek Trail, climbs a little more than 3,000 feet in 6 miles.

In the northwest corner of the Eagles Nest Wilderness, a network of trails offers round-trip possibilities. Pick up the lengthy Piney Lake–Soda Lakes Trail at the end of FS Road 449 (off Sheephorn Creek Road) on the northern boundary of the wilderness. Follow the trail south toward Meridian Peak, then return via the West Meadow Creek, Piney River, or North Piney River Trails. Under 20 miles in length, this trip can be completed in 2 days, or more if time to explore more of the high country is added in.

For those in search of high, rugged terrain, the Elliot Ridge–East Meadow Creek Trail is the answer. It begins at Blue Lake off FS Road 1831. With its trailhead situated at 11,154 feet, this route follows the Gore Range divide south for 7 miles before dropping down to Soda Lakes. Beyond the lakes, the trail picks up West Meadow Creek and follows the Piney River. This route boasts 360-degree, panoramic scenery and passes through the Meridian Peak–Eagles Nest Peak area. It also allows access to the Mirror Trail in the eastern portion of the range.

Cross-country Skiing

Since many of the trails previously discussed run mostly below timberline, they are relatively safe from avalanche danger. Where they do encounter open slopes, however, the possibility of snowslides always exists.

Winter access to these trails can be something of a chore, as most approach roads are not plowed regularly. One trail that begins near an all-season road is the West Meadow Creek Trail, which climbs from the Frisco exit on Interstate 70 to Eccles Pass. The route follows an old wagon trail under the cover of trees for the 3 miles before breaking out into a broad and open valley floor. It is only in the last mile of the trail, near Eccles Pass, that avalanches pose a threat. Enjoy the relative safety of the meadows area rather than attempting the pass itself.

Mountaineering

Eagles Nest offers mountaineers an impressive array of challenges. Its 13,397-foot namesake, located in a cluster of high peaks in the northern end of the wilderness, can be approached from Upper Cataract Lake via the ridge to the west. Also in this group are Mount Powell (13,534 feet), the range's highest point, and Meridian Peak (12,390 feet). All of these summits offer both walk-up and more technical routes. Other peaks in the vicinity somehow escaped being named and are known only by a letter designation. Most of these top out very near the 13,000-foot mark and offer uncrowded alternatives to the more popular summits in the range.

In the southern end of the wilderness, the Willow Lakes area up the Willow Lakes Trail is a popular destination for climbers. Nearby Red Peak (13,183 feet) and East Thorn (13,330 feet) are two possible climbs, while a number of lesser crags and spires, including the Zodiac Spires a little to the west, offer good technical routes. Climbers also frequent the extensive snowfields in the cirque above Willow Lakes.

In the Eccles Pass–Red Buffalo Pass area, Red Peak is approachable from the south, as is Buffalo Mountain (12,764 feet), an off-crest summit that looms impressively over Silverthorne. A number of lesser high points just west of Eccles Pass provide short but rewarding ascents as well.

Sarvis Creek Wilderness Area

Location: 17 mi SE of Steamboat Springs
Size: 47,140 acres
Status: Wilderness area (1993)
Terrain: Heavily timbered drainages and ridges
Elevation: 7,000' to 10,687'
Management: Routt NF, Arapaho NF
Topographic maps: Gore Mountain, Green Ridge, Walton Peak, Blacktail Mountain

The Sarvis Creek Wilderness Area includes drainages that drop west off the southern end of the Park Range. Unlike most other mountain wilderness areas in Colorado, the Sarvis Creek area encompasses tree-covered ridges rather than high, glaciated peaks. This tract was formerly known as the Service Creek Further Planning Area. Sarvis was the original name given to Service Creek; it refers to the old Sarvis Timber Company, which once operated in the area. Although they had their eye on the area's remaining old-growth timber, modern-day logging companies lost out in this wilderness battle.

Seasons
Winter sets in here by late October or November and usually stretches until April or May. During the autumn months, isolated patches of aspen turn bright gold and elk fill the woods with their bugling.

Flora and Fauna
More than 80 percent of this wilderness is forested, much of it with lodgepole pine. Stands of Engelmann spruce and subalpine fir are found at higher elevations; some of the spruce was killed by an infestation of bark beetles 50 years ago. Small patches of aspen occur, especially on the western end. Big-game residents of the Sarvis Creek Wilderness include mule deer, elk, and plenty of black bears. Squirrels, snowshoe hares, and pine martens also reside here.

Geology
As the southern terminus of the Park Range, this area is made up mostly of Precambrian granite that began uplifting during the Laramide Orogeny. This gentle upland was once covered with glaciers though it lacks many of the telltale signs that typify such activity.

Opposite: *Along the Sarvis Creek Trail*

ACTIVITIES
Hiking

Two main trails constitute most of the routes found within the Sarvis Creek Wilderness. The Sarvis Creek Trail begins at the Sarvis Creek State Wildlife Area on the western border of the national forest and runs 12.2 miles to Buffalo Park on the crest of the range. Although the trail climbs more than 2,000 feet, the grades are mostly easy. The route follows a stream bottom for part of the way and encounters small stretches of parkland and an old homestead. Branching north from the upper end of the Sarvis Creek Trail is the Routt Divide Trail, which travels 7 miles along the wilderness boundary before ending at Harrison Creek Road.

The Silver Creek Trail similarly follows a drainage from west to east. Eleven miles in length, this route encounters a bit more rugged terrain near the bottom. For backpackers interested in an extended loop trip, it is possible to connect the Sarvis Creek and Silver Creek routes by walking 4 miles along Buffalo Park Road. Ten miles of road separate the two western trailheads.

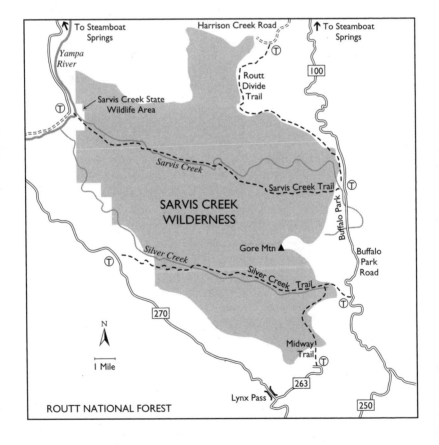

13 Mount Zirkel Wilderness Area

Location: 12 mi NE of Steamboat Springs
Size: 160,568 acres
Status: Wilderness area (1964)
Terrain: Alpine ridges and summits with forested valleys
Elevation: 8,500' to 12,180'
Management: Routt NF
Topographic maps: Teal Lake, Buffalo Pass, Rocky Peak, Pitchpine Mountain, Mount Ethel, Floyd Peak, Boettcher Lake, Mount Zirkel, Farwell Mountain, Pearl, Davis Peak, West Fork Lake

The Mount Zirkel Wilderness has long been a popular destination for backpackers. Although it embraces the highest reaches of the Park Range, this wilderness is laced with hiking routes, making it relatively accessible. Its highest point and namesake, Mount Zirkel, barely tops the 12,000-foot mark. The heart of the wilderness is characterized by glaciated terrain and striking alpine scenery. There are some sixty-five lakes here, as well as several streams that feed the North Platte and Yampa Rivers.

Seasons
The hiking season usually begins in late June and runs until mid-October. Some snowbanks may last year round. In the spring, runoff is heavy, making for difficult stream crossings. Summertime means daily afternoon showers and the threat of lightning in the high country. Wildflowers are abundant in Mount Zirkel Wilderness, especially in July and August. The aspen begin changing color in September.

Flora and Fauna
Across the highest regions of the Mount Zirkel Wilderness lie beautiful stretches of alpine tundra. Wildflowers found in these areas include the magnificent blue columbine and the Indian paintbrush. Bighorn sheep are rare but may be spotted in this high terrain, while marmots and pikas are abundant. Below timberline, the predominant forest type is a mixture of Engelmann spruce and subalpine fir, although stands of lodgepole pine and aspen are also present. An unusual natural phenomenon occurred on October 25, 1997, and changed the complexion of the Mount Zirkel Wilderness for hundreds of years to come. On that day, a ferocious windstorm with speeds topping 120 mph blew over more than 4 million trees. The results of this storm are best observed in a 5-by-30-mile swath running south to north along the western slope of the mountain range. Certainly such a massive blowdown poses both an inconvenience and a hazard to hikers.

Open parks and meadows are plentiful, and it is in these settings that you may be able to spot mule deer and elk grazing in the early morning hours. Other wildlife species represented in the Mount Zirkel Wilderness include mountain lion, black bear, coyote, fox, and pine marten.

Geology

Like other mountain ranges in the area, the Park Range is a faulted anticline. These lengthy blocks of uplifted Precambrian rock are bounded by faults, and most of the west slopes have steep faces. The Park Range carries the Continental Divide for several miles along its crest, separating the Yampa and North Platte River drainages. Evidence of glaciation is plentiful throughout—glacially carved valleys, lakebeds, and cirques characterize the high country here. Some permanent snowfields here are believed to have started forming within the last few thousand years.

History

Mount Zirkel was named after Ferdinand Zirkel, a geologist who traveled through the Park Range with the King Survey of the 40th Parallel in 1871. Theodore Roosevelt hunted in the range before the turn of the twentieth century; as president he established the Park Range Forest Reserve in 1905. The Mount Zirkel–Dome Peak Primitive Area was established in 1931. The Mount Zirkel Wilderness Area became a reality with the Wilderness Act of 1964. It has been expanded twice since then, first in 1980 and again in 1993.

ACTIVITIES
Hiking

With several trails to choose from, the route possibilities in the Mount Zirkel Wilderness are many, as are the opportunities for finding solitude. The most heavily used entry point is Slavonia, about 30 miles north of Steamboat Springs. Two trails head east into the wilderness from here and eventually join. The Gilpin Trail covers 4 miles before reaching Gilpin Lake, following an easy grade most of the way. Similarly, you can hike 4 miles to Gold Creek Lake via the Gold Creek Lake Trail. Camping and fires within 0.25 mile of either lake are prohibited. The trails intersect about 1 mile beyond both lakes to make a 10-mile loop.

The Gold Creek Lake Trail continues to climb up the drainage east to Ute Pass. After crossing the Continental Divide at the 11,200-foot pass, the Gold Creek Lake Trail then drops 6 miles into the eastern side of the wilderness. About 1 mile beyond the Gold Creek Lake/Gilpin intersection, the Red Dirt Pass Trail branches left to continue north toward its 11,560-foot namesake. Along the way it passes the abandoned Slavonia Mine, which is about 7 miles from the trailhead. The top of Red Dirt Pass, and the Continental Divide, is 8.5 miles in. A seldom-traveled trail continues from the pass into Frying Pan Basin east of the Divide. And 12,180-foot Mount Zirkel is an easy traverse from the pass. Heading north from the Gilpin Trail, the Mica Basin Trail leads to Mica Lake, which sits squarely beneath Big Agnes Mountain (12,059 feet), one of the most prominent summits in the range.

A small lake along the Wyoming Trail

Another popular wilderness trail located a few miles south of Slavonia is the Three Island Lake Trail, which begins on Forest Road 443, approximately 3 miles from Seedhouse Road. About 3 miles in from the trailhead, Three Island Lake is beautifully situated among the trees. Because of overuse, camping and fires are prohibited within 0.25 mile of the lake. The trail continues beyond the lake to eventually join with the Wyoming Trail on the Continental Divide.

Beginning 1.5 miles beyond the Three Island Lake trailhead is another trail system that accesses other wilderness lakes. The North Lake Trail climbs about 5 miles to North Lake before connecting with the Wyoming Trail 1 mile beyond. The Swamp Park Trail runs from the South Fork Road near Slavonia to the Mad Creek trailhead about 5 miles north of Steamboat Springs. For 17.5 miles this route dips in and out of the drainages that bisect the western slope of the wilderness. It has five side trails along the way; one offshoot, the Luna Lake Trail, climbs east from this low-elevation route to the Divide.

The Wyoming Trail, a long-distance route, begins at Buffalo Pass, which is 12 miles east of Steamboat Springs via a good gravel road. From this point just below timberline on the Continental Divide, the Wyoming Trail heads north through scattered forests and open parks. The grade is negligible—the route starts at 10,600 feet—and the trail's condition is excellent, making it popular with hikers and horsepackers. Following the Continental

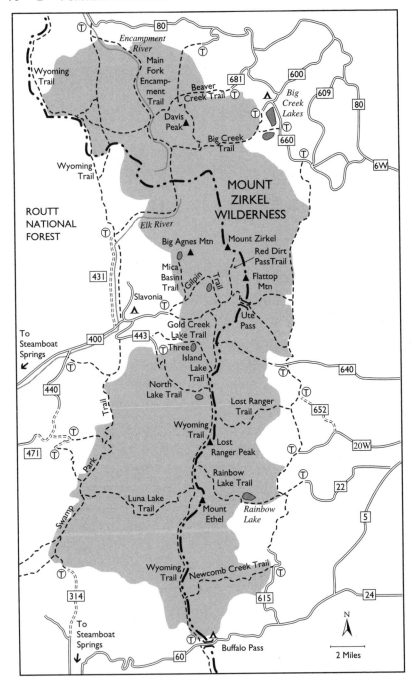

Divide for much of the way, the Wyoming Trail passes among clusters of alpine lakes, high summits, and sublime mountain scenery. Several side trails branch off the main route. After extending for nearly 20 miles inside the wilderness area, the Wyoming Trail combines with the Gold Creek Lake Trail. It begins again north of the Seedhouse Campground outside the wilderness, terminating just inside the Wyoming state line.

Many of the shorter routes that hook up with the Wyoming Trail follow drainages from the eastern side of the wilderness. The Newcomb Creek Trail climbs nearly 2,000 feet in 5 miles before finding the Wyoming Trail a little north of Buffalo Pass. The 7.5-mile Rainbow Lake Trail encounters several lakes, including the Rainbow and Slide Lakes, before arriving at the Wyoming Trail. And the Lost Ranger Trail covers 7 miles before it intersects with the Wyoming Trail 1 mile north of Lost Ranger Peak (11,932 feet). It features spectacular views of Red Canyon.

On the northern end of the wilderness, a network of trails laces what is known as the Encampment River area. The Main Fork Encampment Trail follows its namesake into the Encampment Meadows from the northern tip of the wilderness. In the 1890s this area was logged for railroad ties that were floated down the Encampment River to Wyoming. A few old cabins remain. A ford across the river marks the actual wilderness boundary and from there the route crosses the Continental Divide before dropping into Diamond Park on the western side. The Beaver Creek Trail connects with the Main Fork Encampment Trail at the river crossing. A more popular route leading into this area is the 9-mile Big Creek Trail. Beginning at the Big Creek Lakes campground, this route passes Big Creek Falls and the Seven Lakes before it joins up with the Main Fork Encampment Trail. This route is not recommended for horses.

Cross-country Skiing

Because the entry points to the Mount Zirkel Wilderness Area are found mostly at the end of dirt or gravel Forest Service roads, wintertime access is limited. This makes ski touring in the wilderness mostly an overnight endeavor. Nevertheless, for those cross-country enthusiasts with time on their hands, this is an ideal trip.

Buffalo Pass Road (FS Road 60) is plowed for only a few miles, leaving 8 miles of skiing to reach the pass. And it is 7 miles from road's end at Hinman Park to the Slavonia trailhead. Other entry points may become accessible in spring as the snows begin to melt at lower elevations. Once you reach the wilderness boundary, the tour possibilities are as numerous as the hikes previously mentioned. A few things to keep in mind, though, are the possibility of avalanches while crossing steeper slopes, the constant threat of exposure to cold that exists above timberline, and, because trails are not marked for skiers, topographic maps and a compass are needed to find your way.

Mountaineering

Most of the Mount Zirkel Wilderness is gentle by comparison to other Colorado wilderness areas. Nevertheless, a few mountaineering opportunities do exist. The climb up Mount Zirkel (12,180 feet) is via the ridge line running northwest from Red Dirt

Pass. Big Agnes and Flattop Mountains are other possibilities in the Mount Zirkel area. To the south, Mount Ethel and Lost Ranger Peak are both easy high points along the crest of the range.

Castle Peak Wilderness Study Area

Location: 10 mi N of Wolcott
Size: 12,237 acres
Status: Wilderness study area (1978)
Terrain: Mountains and forested drainages
Elevation: 8,400' to 11,275'
Management: BLM (Glenwood Springs Field Office)
Topographic maps: Castle Peak, Eagle

Crowned by its scenic namesake, the Castle Peak Wilderness Study Area (WSA) offers some interesting mountain terrain located between the Interstate 70 corridor to the south and the Colorado River to the north. This wilderness study area is a bit unusual for the BLM in that it is somewhat high in elevation. Small lakes, scenic terrain, and pristine forests await those who venture within.

Seasons
Winter snows and the resulting muddy roads typically preclude access to the Castle Peak WSA from October to May. Summers often mean afternoon showers with occasional lightning activity. Flowers bloom from June to August, and aspen trees put on a show of color in September.

Flora and Fauna
The Castle Peak WSA features a variety of ecosystems—sagebrush and grasslands; aspen stands; timberlands of mixed pines, spruce, and firs; and scenic meadows, to name four. Wildlife in the region include mule deer, elk, black bears, mountain lions, and the like.

Geology
Castle Peak itself is capped by a remnant of an old lava flow, the same formation that tops the Flat Tops Wilderness to the north. Underlying strata dates from the Mesozoic Era.

ACTIVITIES
Hiking
Although somewhat isolated from major roadways, the Castle Peak WSA is accessible in two places. Reaching the eastern edge of the WSA is possible by driving 3 miles

An old fenceline along the edge of the Castle Peak WSA

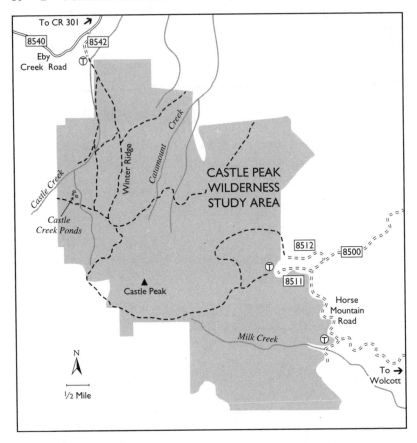

north from Wolcott on State Highway 131 to the Milk Creek Road (County Road 54). Turn west, drive 1.5 miles, bear right on the Horse Mountain Road (BLM Road 8500) and continue another 4 miles or so to the WSA boundary. The road continues north along the boundary for another 1.5 miles. From this section of the road it is possible to bushwhack up drainages that continue west toward Castle Peak. A few old jeep roads, now closed and overgrown in places, provide possible routes as well.

A second access point for the Castle Peak WSA is located at the area's northwest corner. From here an old pack trail continues south up the Castle Creek drainage. At about 1 mile in, a second trail branches left to head up Winter Ridge. Beyond this a network of old routes reaches Castle Creek Ponds and drops into the Catamount Creek drainage to the east. These trails are not regularly maintained, and many sections may be faded and hard to find. Hikers should come armed with a topographic map and wayfinding skills. To reach the northwest corner of the WSA, drive downstream from McCoy on County Road 301 (the Colorado River Road) to the top of Blue Hill. It is 3.3 miles to the turn-off for BLM Road 8542. The trailhead is a short way beyond on this road. Bear left and continue a bit farther to a parking area.

Drawing close to the west side of the Castle Peak WSA, the Eby Creek Road looks like a good access route on the map. It is closed to public traffic on both ends, however.

Bull Gulch Wilderness Study Area

Location: 13 mi NE of Dotsero
Size: 15,201 acres
Status: Wilderness study area (1978)
Terrain: Deep canyons and forested ridges
Elevation: 6,400' to 10,020'
Management: BLM (Glenwood Springs Field Office)
Topographic maps: Burns South, Gypsum

The Bull Gulch Wilderness Study Area (WSA) borders the south bank of the Colorado River north of Eagle. Its namesake, along with Posey and Alamo Creeks, drains off the slopes of Greenhorn Mountain and flows directly into the Colorado River. In so doing, these drainages dissect the WSA along a southeast-to-northwest axis. Colorful geologic formations are exposed, and an interesting ecological countenance results.

Seasons
During the winter months access is difficult if not impossible due to snow accumulations and impassable roads. Muddy roads can make access difficult in late fall and spring. Watch for lightning during frequent afternoon showers during the summer months. Wildflowers are plentiful during June and July, and late September ushers in the autumn foliage season.   .

Flora and Fauna
Pinyon pines and junipers are typical across the lower elevations, while ponderosa pine, Douglas fir, Colorado blue spruce, and aspen glades are commonplace higher up. The WSA's mid-level elevations provide important winter range for deer and elk. Other residents include mountain lions, bobcats, coyotes, and bald eagles.

Geology
Like the Maroon Bells near Aspen, colorful formations within the canyons and gulches of the Bull Gulch WSA are made up of metamorphosed sandstones. Stream erosion is readily evident throughout, and volcanic intrusions are found in places.

ACTIVITIES
Hiking
Given the fact that the Colorado River runs along the northern border of the Bull Gulch WSA, hiking access is problematic in places. To reach the upper end of Bull Gulch

you must turn south from County Road 301 (the Colorado River Road) at Blue Hill, 2 miles east of Burns, and follow the Eby Creek Road (BLM Road 8540) south for 3.5 miles to where a rugged 4WD route (BLM Road 8544) turns right. Follow this route for about a mile to its end then continue on foot west into the head of Bull Gulch.

The mouth of Bull Gulch, while offering fine hiking in the canyon bottom, is accessible only by boat from the Colorado River. This hiking route begins as a narrow, winding canyon but soon opens up into a broader basin.

The headwaters of Posey Creek are similarly accessible by an overland route. This route requires driving several miles of 4WD road, however. It begins at Gypsum along Interstate 70 and continues north on County Road 51 (the Trail Gulch Road) to the turn-off for BLM Road 8487. Bear right and continue for several more miles to the WSA boundary. The last few miles of Road 8487 are not recommended for vehicles other than ATVs. Given the fact that there are several side roads along the way and private land must be skirted, it is best to consult the BLM in Glenwood Springs for more complete directions. Once reaching the start of the hike, expect to find no trails or obvious routes.

Hikers can access the mouth of Alamo Creek from the Colorado River Road. Drive 13 miles north of Dotsero to where the creek drains into the Colorado River. A BLM sign marks the access point just west of the creek. The canyon bottom offers a suitable route for a mile or more. There is private property nearby so be mindful of fences and signs.

Because BLM Road 8479 runs along the WSA's southwest boundary for several miles, this region is accessible as well. There are no established trails in this area, however, and any hiking is strictly cross-country. BLM Road 8479 can be reached by driving about 1 mile downstream from Alamo Creek along the Colorado River Road.

River Running

Although the Colorado River does not actually enter the Bull Gulch WSA, the 7 miles of floatable water that parallels the northern border does offer some fine river running

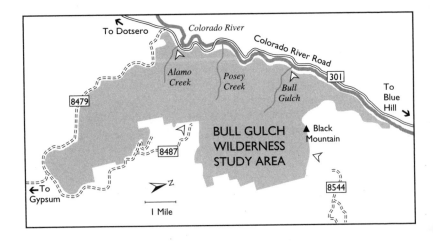

A sign at the mouth of Alamo Creek

possibilities. The put-in for this stretch of the Colorado is at the BLM-administered Pinball Recreation Site. The first developed take-out below the WSA is 12 miles downstream at Lyons Gulch. Rapids along this stretch are mostly Class II but some particular hazards such as bridge pilings do exist. The BLM can supply more complete river running information, including a map.

16 Flat Tops Wilderness Area

Location: 15 mi SW of Yampa
Size: 235,035 acres
Status: Wilderness area (1975)
Terrain: Flat-topped alpine mountains with forested drainages
Elevation: 7,600' to 12,354'
Management: Routt NF, White River NF
Topographic maps: Trappers Lake, Dome Peak, Orino Peak, Devils Causeway, Ripple Creek, Big Marvine Peak, Oyster Lake, Blair Mountain, Deep Lake, Sweetwater Lake, Sugarloaf Mountain, Meadow Creek Lake, Buford, Lost Park, Dunkley Pass, Sand Point

The Flat Tops are somewhat unusual in the state of Colorado. Instead of rising to jagged summits, these mountains have lofty escarpments with broad, level tops. The area is dominated by the White River Plateau, which tops 12,000 feet in elevation. Special features include the Chinese Wall along the precipitous eastern face of this tableland.

Because the Flat Tops are so high, they capture a lot of moisture and therefore contain some eighty alpine lakes and several miles of streams. Two major rivers, the Yampa and the White, have headwaters in the Flat Tops. As Colorado's third-largest designated wilderness area, the Flat Tops offer solitude in a grandly beautiful setting.

Seasons

The higher elevations of the Flat Tops are accessible on foot from early July through mid-October, and sometimes into November. During the summer months you can expect almost daily thundershowers by afternoon. Sudden snow squalls can occur any time of the year. Runoff is heavy in the spring, making stream crossings difficult. July and August bring on floral displays that are quite spectacular, and September is the rutting season for elk. Listen for their bugling among timbered drainages and in the high meadows.

Flora and Fauna

Because it is a high tableland, twenty percent of the Flat Tops Wilderness is above timberline, with vast expanses of alpine tundra dotted by clusters of trees. In this rolling tundra, pikas and marmots are plentiful, and elk and mule deer find suitable grazing in the early morning and evening hours. Other wildlife residents include coyotes, black bears, porcupines, red foxes, beavers, and bobcats.

Engelmann spruce and subalpine fir dominate the forested regions of the Flat Tops. In the 1940s a spruce bark beetle epidemic left some 68,000 acres of timber devastated. Although now on the comeback, a forest of sun-bleached snags is still readily visible and travel through it can be difficult because of deadfall.

Geology

Encompassing much of the 50-mile-long White River Plateau, the Flat Tops rose as a broad, flattened dome of sedimentary rock during the Cenozoic era. Beginning about 24 million years ago, during a period of widespread volcanic activity, lava flows covered much of the plateau with a hard layer of rock. As the region was pushed upward, erosion ate away at the exposed layers of softer bedrock. Where lava flows had capped the terrain, the area's characteristic flat-topped mountains resulted. Streams have continued to etch out portions of the plateau, leaving beautiful canyons in the process.

History

The Flat Tops were recognized early on for their wild and scenic value. Colorado's first national forest reserve included this area in 1891. In 1918 Arthur Carhart was sent to Trappers Lake by the U.S. Forest Service to survey the possibility of allowing summer homes in the area. Impressed by its natural beauty, he returned to Denver to report that it instead should be set aside as wild lands, thus giving the idea of a Flat Tops Wilderness early impetus.

ACTIVITIES

Hiking

Because hundreds of miles of hiking trails interlace this vast chunk of pristine land, backpacking opportunities abound. Loop routes, both short and long, can be devised, while countless lakes, geological features, and such make attractive destinations. Because the terrain is generally level, many sections of trail follow comparatively easy grades.

A popular entry point on the Routt National Forest side of the wilderness is at Stillwater Reservoir, 15 miles southwest of Yampa. From there, the Bear River Trail

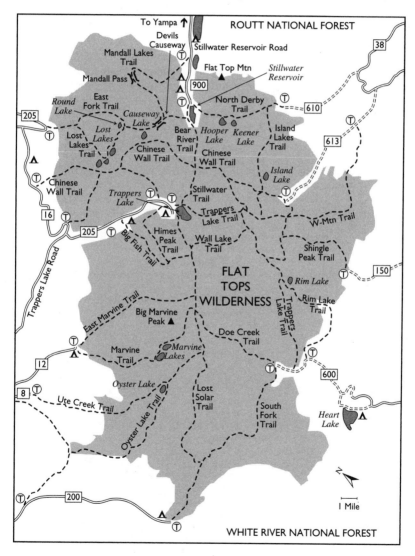

provides the quickest conduit into the heart of the wilderness. Climbing from 10,280 feet to 11,400 feet in three miles, this trail tops out on the divide between the Routt and White River National Forests. West from the divide, it is 4.5 miles to Trappers Lake. On the White River side, the route is known as the Stillwater Trail. The Chinese Wall Trail intersects near the divide. Running north, the Chinese Wall Trail follows the national forest border quite closely and eventually leads to the Lost Lakes area. It then continues on to end at Forest Road 16 on Ripple Creek Pass 12 miles from the Stillwater Trail. The trail's namesake, a grand escarpment of layered rock, parallels the trail to the west. In places where no tread exists, following the Chinese Wall Trail is a matter of following the highest ridge line. South from the Stillwater Trail, the Chinese Wall Trail continues for nearly 5 miles to an intersection with the Island Lakes Trail, which, in turn, runs east to a trailhead on 4WD FS Road 610. The Island Lakes Trail connects with the lengthy W-Mountain Trail, which heads south and east to exit the wilderness in the southeast corner.

The East Fork Trail begins nearly 1 mile up the Bear River Trail from the trailhead at Stillwater Reservoir. The East Fork route climbs to 11,600 feet on the ridge that divides the Bear River and Williams Fork drainages.

Travel 0.3 mile southwest on this ridge and you will be afforded a view of the Devils Causeway, a narrow ridge some 1,500 feet above the valley floor. The East Fork Trail continues north into the Williams Fork Valley with its beautiful, forested topography. Five miles from the trailhead the route finds Causeway Lake, and about 1 mile farther it encounters Round Lake and the end of the Lost Lakes Trail. The East Fork Trail leaves the wilderness 14 miles from the Stillwater Reservoir trailhead near the Pyramid Forest Service Station.

Heading south across the Stillwater Reservoir dam is the North Derby Trail. It is a 2-mile, 1,000-foot climb from the trailhead to the Routt–White River National Forest border. You can leave the trail and follow this dividing ridge east for 2 miles to the top of Flat Top Mountain (12,354 feet), the highest point in the wilderness. A mile beyond the forest boundary, the trail passes Hooper and Keener Lakes, then continues down the North Fork of Derby Creek for another 3 miles before reaching a 4WD road at Stump Park.

The 5-mile-long Mandall Lakes Trail begins at Bear Lake Campground and ends at Mandall Pass. Heading north before eventually looping south again toward the Devils Causeway, this route passes several high lakes along the way. Five miles in is 11,960-foot Mandall Pass. Remaining high until reaching its terminus at the causeway, the route passes through miles of spectacular alpine country.

On the White River National Forest side, the handiest trailheads are found along Trappers Lake Road, which is bounded by wilderness land on both sides. In addition to the Stillwater Trail, Trappers Lake ushers three other routes—the Trappers Lake, Wall Lake, and the Himes Peak Trails—into the wilderness. The Himes Peak Trail is 5 miles long. It climbs from Trappers Lake Road to the Big Fish Trail. Sixteen miles in length, the Trappers Lake Trail crosses the entire wilderness, from the lake itself south

Opposite: *Alpine scenery above Stillwater Reservoir*

to Indian Camp Pass near Heart Lake. Several wilderness lakes and lengthy stretches of alpine terrain along the way provide the scenery.

Several routes hook up with the Trappers Lake Trail to give hikers a variety of loop excursions. Five miles in, the Island Lakes Trail cuts off toward the eastern portion of the wilderness where it connects with the W-Mountain and other trails. The Wall Lake Trail heads northwest and eventually loops back to Trappers Lake 7 miles away. Near its midpoint, the Trappers Lake Trail finds the Shingle Peak Trail, and the Rim Lake Trail takes off some 12 miles from the trailhead. Both the Rim Lake and Shingle Peak Trails continue south toward the wilderness boundary.

As previously mentioned, the Wall Lake Trail branches off from Trappers Lake and eventually terminates at Trappers Lake Trail. But first it intersects with the Oyster Lake Trail, a 25-mile route that beelines across the western reaches of the wilderness. The terrain along this route changes from forests and open parkland to alpine tundra near its northern end. The scenery takes in several peaks. And as with the Trappers Lake Trail, the Oyster Lake Trail connects with several other side trails. Heading north to Trappers Lake Road is the Big Fish Trail. The East Marvine Trail covers 9 miles before finding the Marvine Creek Campground on the northwest boundary of the wilderness. A spur trail climbs Big Marvine Peak (11,879 feet) for a stunning view of the surrounding landscape. The Marvine Trail also leads to the Marvine Creek Campground but encounters the Marvine Lakes near its midway point. The Doe Creek Trail heads south from an intersection with the Oyster Lake and Marvine Creek Trails. Six and a half miles from the Wall Lake–Oyster Lake junction, the Lost Solar Trail continues southwest as the Oyster Lake Trail turns west. Eight miles long, the Lost Solar Trail joins the South Fork Trail and then exits the wilderness in the southwest corner. Finally, near Oyster Lake itself, the Ute Creek Trail begins its 10-mile run down Ute Creek to a trailhead just off County Road 8, the road from Meeker to Trappers Lake.

Cross-country Skiing
Because the higher terrain is mostly gentle, many backcountry ski tours are relatively safe in the Flat Tops. Winter access is extremely limited, however, as avalanches are possible along the slopes leading up to it. All forest roads in the area go unplowed in the winter and are frequented by snowmobiles. The best plan is to follow the Stillwater Reservoir Road in. Plowed to the forest boundary, this route leaves another 8.5 miles of road to ski before reaching the wilderness. Once there, however, you can choose from a number of long-distance tours. Be extra wary of avalanche danger on steeper slopes.

Opposite: *Aspen are plentiful in the Raggeds Wilderness.*

chapter 2 **Central Mountains**

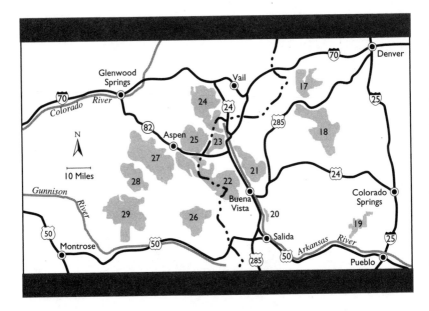

Several mountain ranges with exceptionally high peaks march through the central Colorado Rockies. The southern half of the Front Range, which runs west of the Denver–Colorado Springs metropolis, features two wilderness areas, Mount Evans and Lost Creek. Predictably, they receive a lot of use in the summer. The less-visited Beaver Creek Wilderness Study Area, administered by the BLM, lies at the southern end of the Front Range near Cañon City. Beyond South Park is the Buffalo Peaks Wilderness Area. The Arkansas River borders the BLM's Browns Canyon Wilderness Study Area; just west of the Arkansas is a cluster of established wilderness areas, including Holy Cross, Mount Massive, Collegiate Peaks, and Hunter–Fryingpan. Many of these areas encompass portions of the lofty Sawatch Range, and most feature one or more "fourteeners."

Along a corridor of peaks formed by the Elk and West Elk Mountains are the Maroon Bells–Snowmass, Raggeds, and West Elk Wilderness Areas. Situated just a few miles south of Aspen, the Maroon Bells–Snowmass area is the most heavily visited wilderness area in the state. To the south of the Elk Range is Fossil Ridge, an area of high summits.

As the heart of Colorado's rugged mountain region, the Central Mountains offer many opportunities to enjoy pristine alpine terrain.

17 Mount Evans Wilderness Area

Location: 10 mi S of Idaho Springs
Size: 74,401 acres
Status: Wilderness area (1980)
Terrain: Alpine peaks and timbered lower slopes
Elevation: 8,400' to 14,264'
Management: Pike NF, Arapaho NF
Topographic maps: Mount Evans, Hams Park, Georgetown, Idaho Springs, Meridian Hill, Mount Logan

Mount Evans is unique among Colorado "fourteeners" in that it is topped by a paved road—the highest paved highway in America. While such an intrusion may compromise the pristine characteristics of the surrounding wilderness area, it does provide convenient access to even the highest terrain. A handful of trails originate along the road and a vast expanse of alpine tundra land can be explored once it reaches timberline. Stands of bristlecone pine grow along the way. Wildlife can be readily spotted at roadside. And, despite the asphalt intrusion, there are places within the Mount Evans Wilderness that are indeed wild.

Alpine scenery in the Mount Evans Wilderness

Seasons

The summer hiking season is short in the highest reaches of Mount Evans as snow covers the terrain from mid-October through June and into July. The Mount Evans Road is closed beyond Summit Lake (a few miles from the top) after the first heavy snows of the season. Summer afternoons on Mount Evans are often racked by lightning, rain showers, and sometimes hail. Alpine flowers begin blooming in June and last into August.

Flora and Fauna

The Mount Evans Road provides many folks with an easy introduction to timberline ecosystems. Interpretive trails explain facets of the tundra to motorists who take the time to walk them. At the Mount Goliath Natural Area, for instance, visitors are treated to an up-close view of a bristlecone forest. Smaller floral species of the tundra are also discussed on signs at various pull-overs.

Motorists are often treated to the sight of mountain goats and bighorn sheep (do not feed the wildlife) from the road, and marmots and pikas are in plentiful supply. White-tailed ptarmigan inhabit the alpine reaches, being especially plentiful among the willows—a primary food source for ptarmigan—on Guanella Pass on the western border of the wilderness. Scientists have estimated that between 200 and 300 bird species migrate here in the fall, making it one of the most densely populated wintering grounds in the state.

Geology

Although it lies within the Front Range, Mount Evans is considerably older than its neighboring peaks. A batholith, Mount Evans was first formed 1.7 billion years ago when a pool of molten rock formed, pushing up layers of rock. Cooling slowly, it formed a coarse-grained granite enriched with such minerals as feldspar, mica, and quartz. Mount Evans was again pushed upward about 300 million years ago when the Ancestral Rockies were born, and once more during the more recent Laramide Orogeny 65 million years ago.

Since the last episode of mountain building, Mount Evans has been shaped by both glaciers and stream erosion. An example of extreme glacial carving is found in the Abyss Lake area, between Mount Bierstadt and Mount Evans. Alpine lakes around Mount Evans, such as Summit Lake, are situated in glacially carved depressions, and U-shaped valleys head many drainages. A fine example may be enjoyed from the Chicago Lakes Overlook along the Mount Evans Road.

History

Although miners may have climbed Mount Evans at an earlier date, the first recorded ascent came in 1863 by the famous landscape artist Albert Bierstadt. Bierstadt named the peak Rosalie after his wife-to-be, but the name was subsequently changed to commemorate an early territorial governor of Colorado. The road to the top was completed in 1930.

ACTIVITIES
Hiking

From the Mount Evans Road, a number of trails take off to penetrate drainage north slope of Mount Evans (there is a recreation fee to use the trails). The fi these, the Hells Hole Trail, begins at the West Chicago Creek Campground, 10 mil from Idaho Springs. A moderately easy route, this trail climbs less than 2,000 feet in 3.5 miles. Hells Hole itself is a meadow area situated in the bottom of a deep drainage. This trail receives heavy use on some weekends.

From Echo Lake Campground, the Chicago Lakes Trail begins its 5.5-mile climb to a pair of alpine lakes nestled in a deep canyon. The trail follows a mile of road that is closed to motor vehicles in the vicinity of the Idaho Springs Reservoir. The Chicago Lakes are clearly visible from the Chicago Lakes Overlook just north of Summit Lake on the upper end of Mount Evans Road. Again, weekends may see heavy use on the Chicago Lakes Trail.

The Resthouse Meadows Trail also begins at the Echo Lake Campground but runs from Mount Evans Road. Six miles in length, this route traverses wooded areas as well as meadows filled with wildflowers before it connects with the Beaver Meadows Trail at Resthouse Meadows. Resthouse was once a ranger station but little more than a chimney still stands.

The 7-mile Beaver Meadows Trail begins at the Camp Rock Campground on the eastern edge of the wilderness and ends at a junction with the Beartrack Trail. As the name suggests, several meadows complete with beaver ponds are found along the way. The Beartrack Trail, which also begins at the Camp Rock Campground, runs 6 miles before ending at the scenic Beartrack Lakes.

The Lost Creek Trail begins at the Bear Creek Guard Station and runs for 4.5 miles before connecting with the Cub Creek Trail. The Cub Creek Trail runs from the Beartrack Trail over Meridian Pass and south to the vicinity of Meridian Campground near Harris Park. Elevations along all of these routes are high.

The divide between the South Platte River and Clear Creek drainages slices the wilderness nearly in half. Trails south of that line fall within the Pike National Forest. Perhaps the most interesting of these is the Abyss Lake Trail. Beginning near the Burning Bear Campground, this route follows Scott Gomer Creek and then Lake Fork for a total of 8 miles to Abyss Lake. Situated at 12,650 feet in a spectacular cirque between Mount Evans and Mount Bierstadt, this jewel of a lake was once the centerpiece of a national scenic area that was superseded by the establishment of the wilderness area. The surrounding mountainsides are home to bighorn sheep and mountain goats.

At about 4 miles in, the Abyss Lake Trail intersects the Rosalie Trail. Beginning at 11,669-foot Guanella Pass, the 12-mile Rosalie Trail travels in a southeasterly direction and eventually reaches a trailhead near Deer Creek Campground a few miles north of Bailey. The hike involves a lot of elevation gain—1,280 feet from Guanella Pass to Deer Creek and 3,600 feet in reverse—but the highlights include above-timberline views of both Mount Evans and Mount Bierstadt. A hike combining the Abyss

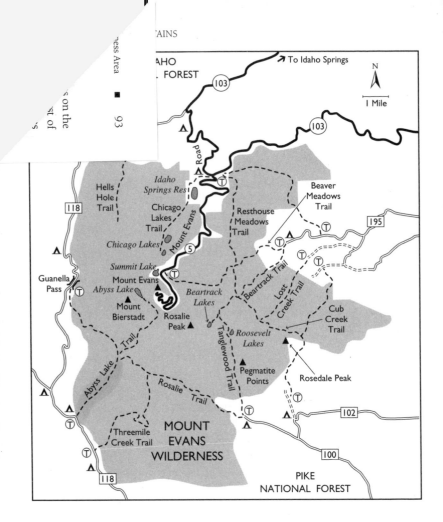

Lake and Rosalie Trails makes an interesting loop. The Threemile Creek Trail adds to the possibilities. Beginning near the Whiteside Campground on the road to Geneva Basin Ski Area, Threemile Creek roughly parallels the Abyss Lake Trail along the Scott Gomer Creek stretch. After 6.5 miles and nearly 3,000 feet of elevation gain, the Threemile Creek Trail connects with the Rosalie Trail about 2 miles southeast of the Abyss Lake Trail intersection.

Another trail that begins in the Pike National Forest, the Tanglewood Trail, is also worth investigating. Sharing the Rosalie Trail's trailhead above the Deer Creek Campground, this route cuts north to eventually enter the Arapaho National Forest. In 4 miles it climbs 2,620 feet to an 11,940-foot saddle on the divide. From there, the views in both directions are memorable. Rosalie Peak (13,575 feet) rises to the west, as do the Pegmatite Points, a series of jagged rocks. The Roosevelt Lakes lie a half-mile beyond the saddle, and a little beyond them are the Beartrack Lakes.

Cross-country Skiing

Backcountry skiing in the Mount Evans Wilderness Area can be relatively easy thanks to the fact that most approach roads are regularly plowed. Because the Mount Evans Road is clear to Echo Lake, trails that begin along it are easily reached. With its moderately sloping terrain, the first 5 miles of the Resthouse Meadows Trail makes a satisfying tour. Thanks to the fact that the road over Guanella Pass is plowed to the pass from the north, other parts of the wilderness are accessible as well. If you just want to play around, stick to the large open area just east of the pass. Avalanche danger does exist in most areas, especially on the steeper slopes, and exposure to cold and wind can be a problem.

Mountaineering

Most visitors to Mount Evans (14,264 feet) are happy just to scramble up the last hundred feet from the parking lot to the summit. Another "fourteener" that requires actual effort is Mount Bierstadt (14,060 feet). Easy by comparison to other "fourteeners," the quickest route to the top begins on Guanella Pass. After crossing a broad open area of chest-high willows, the route up the peak is self-evident. The Bierstadt summit can be reached from Abyss Lake via the south ridge. For more of a challenge, some climbers begin on the Mount Evans summit and traverse west and south along exposed ridges. This route demands considerable skill.

Another summit in the area worthy of a climb is Rosalie Peak (13,575 feet). The quickest approach is from a point on the Mount Evans Road 2 miles south of Summit Lake. From there it is a ridge walk to the summit.

Lost Creek Wilderness Area

Location: 1 mi S of Bailey
Size: 119,790 acres
Status: Wilderness area (1980)
Terrain: Alpine peaks with forested slopes and open parks
Elevation: 8,000' to 12,431'
Management: Pike NF
Topographic maps: Hacker Mountain, Tarryall, Cheesman Lake, McCurdy Mountain, Farnum Peak, Green Mountain, Windy Peak, Topaz Mountain, Observatory Rock, Bailey, Shawnee, Mount Logan

Although it has its share of alpine summits, the Lost Creek Wilderness Area is equally characterized by its lower elevations. Heavy timber covers many of its ridges while streams meander through broad meadows in the valley bottoms. Perhaps most spectacular are the granite spires and formations that crop up in many parts of the wilderness, adding variety to the landscape. The area's namesake completely disappears beneath boulders nearly a dozen times. Although not far from Denver, solitude is still a real possibility in the Lost Creek Wilderness.

Seasons

The higher reaches of the Lost Creek Wilderness may remain snowed in from October through June, but much of its lower terrain opens up as early as May, depending on the elevation and depth of the snow pack. Thunderstorms are a common occurrence on summer afternoons, and wildflowers come into bloom in June and July. Autumn is quite stimulating because of the changing color on the area's many aspen trees.

Flora and Fauna

Open parks among stands of lodgepole pine, Engelmann spruce, and subalpine fir typify this wilderness. Of course, alpine tundra prevails above timberline and stands of bristlecone pine are found near timberline. Extensive forest fires raced through the region in the late nineteenth century, leaving less-than-mature stands of timber standing today. Wildlife includes such expected species as mule deer, elk, coyotes, marmots, and chipmunks. Some sections of the Lost Creek Wilderness are noted bighorn sheep habitat.

Geology

The Lost Creek Wilderness encompasses two principal mountain chains, both part of the expansive Front Range. The Kenosha Mountains rise in the northwestern end of the wilderness, while the Tarryall Mountains run across its southern tier. Like nearby Mount Evans, both formed as batholiths nearly 2 billion years ago. The mountains were uplifted to their present height during the Laramide Orogeny. They are composed chiefly of Precambrian granite, schist, and gneiss. Crystal formations of smoky quartz and topaz are found in some bedrock.

ACTIVITIES
Hiking

Comparatively expansive, the Lost Creek Wilderness is a place where a 2- or 3-day trip is possible without running out of backcountry. Many trails follow gentle grades along valley floors, while others climb steeply to 12,000-foot ridges and summits.

The longest trail within the Lost Creek Wilderness is the Brookside–McCurdy Trail. Beginning at the Twin Eagles trailhead on County Road 77, the Brookside–McCurdy spans 31 miles, from the southern tier of the wilderness to a point on its northern border west of Bailey just off U.S. Highway 285. About midway through it leaves the wilderness long enough to touch base with the Lost Park Campground, a possible starting point. From there it follows the North Fork of Lost Creek for about 4 miles before climbing up and over a ridge to Craig Creek. It again crosses a divide to the north and then drops down into the Platte River Canyon and on to Bailey.

The Brookside–McCurdy Trail connects with several other routes that offer excellent opportunities for loop excursions. Crossing the southern tip of the wilderness, the 5-mile Hankins Pass Trail climbs up and over the pass from the Goose Creek trailhead on the eastern end of the wilderness to meet the Brookside–McCurdy Trail. The Lizard Rock Trail drops south 23 miles from the Hankins Pass Trail to the Spruce Grove Campground. The 4-mile-long Ute Creek Trail begins 6 miles northwest of the Twin Eagles trailhead on County Road 77 and hooks in with the Brookside–McCurdy near Bison Peak (12,431 feet). Although steep, this route provides the quickest access to the high point of the wilderness.

From Lost Park Campground, the Wigwam Trail heads east to follow Lost Creek through East Lost Park and Wigwam Park before exiting on the far side of the wilderness. Twelve miles in length, the trail intersects with two trails at Wigwam Park, expanding the route possibilities. Heading north is the Rolling Creek Trail, a 4.5-mile route that begins just outside the wilderness boundary near Wellington Lake. The Goose Creek Trail, 9.6 miles long, runs south from Wigwam Park to the Goose Creek trailhead near the Molly Gulch Campground. The 7.7-mile McCurdy Park Trail branches west and south off the Goose Creek Trail to connect with the Brookside–McCurdy Trail.

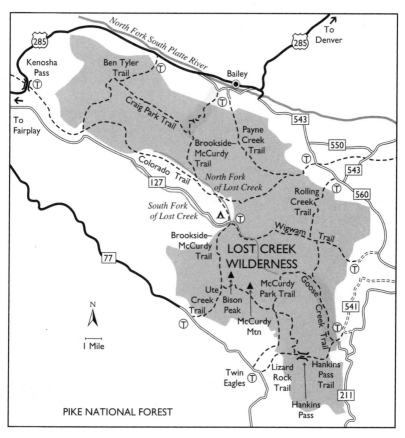

About 1.5 miles north of Lost Park Campground, the Brookside–McCurdy Trail picks up the Colorado Trail as it comes in from the east. The two trails share a corridor for nearly 2 miles before separating again. From where these two routes join, the Colorado Trail travels 15 miles to the east end of the wilderness. The Payne Creek Trail branches off from this stretch of the Colorado and heads northwest for 9 miles before ending near the town of Bailey. West of the Brookside–McCurdy, the Colorado Trail parallels the wilderness boundary for about 6 miles before reentering its western portion. From that point it is 14 miles to Kenosha Pass.

Named for a settler, the Ben Tyler Trail passes the crumbling foundations of his former homestead as it traverses the mountains in the far western part of the wilderness. Steep in spots, this route covers 10 miles and provides access to summits in the area. The Craig Park Trail cuts off to the southeast from about the midway point on the Ben Tyler and eventually connects with the Brookside–McCurdy Trail.

Cross-country Skiing

Because snow conditions are not always suitable, the opportunities for ski touring in the Lost Creek Wilderness are marginal. Access to the wilderness, however, is better than most.

If snowfall is sufficient, from Kenosha Pass it is a straight shot into the wilderness via the Colorado Trail. From the Bailey area, both the Ben Tyler and Brookside–McCurdy trailheads are within easy reach, although both follow steep climbs into the wilderness.

Along the Wigwam Trail

County Road 77, which skirts the southwestern side of the wilderness, is regularly plowed, making the trails that begin here easily accessible. One good bet is the Brookside–McCurdy Trail. Because much of the Lost Creek area is somewhat gentle, cross-country skiing can be enjoyable and safe here. Caution should always be used, of course, when skiing across steeper ground where avalanches might pose a threat.

19 Beaver Creek Wilderness Study Area

Location: 18 mi E of Cañon City
Size: 26,350 acres
Status: Wilderness study area (1980)
Terrain: Mountains and rugged canyons
Elevation: 7,000' to 9,500'
Management: BLM (Royal Gorge Field Office)
Topographic maps: Mount Big Chief, Mount Pittsburg, Big Bull Mountain, Phantom Canyon

A collection of rugged canyons that drain from the southern end of the Front Range, the Beaver Creek Wilderness Study Area (WSA) is an anomaly of sorts. Not only does it include lower-elevation BLM lands, but it is also one of the last undeveloped tracts of land in the Colorado Springs area. The Colorado Division of Wildlife owns 870 acres of streambed along Beaver Creek itself, but this corridor has been and will continue to be managed in accordance with BLM wilderness policy.

Seasons
Hiking in the Beaver Creek WSA is usually possible for all but three months of the year. Winter brings cold temperatures and some snow from December through February; summers may be hot in the lower elevations. The best times of the year to visit are in the spring and autumn.

Flora and Fauna
Plant communities within the Beaver Creek WSA include pinyon pine and juniper woodland across the lower elevations and stands of ponderosa pine, white fir, and Douglas fir higher up. Aspen are present in places, as are lush riparian growths of cottonwood and willow. Wildlife includes mule deer, bighorn sheep, mountain lions, black bears, coyotes, and wild turkeys. Beaver Creek is a prime fishery for rainbow, brown, brook, and cutthroat trout.

Geology
The Beaver Creek area is located on the southern end of the Pikes Peak batholith, a formerly molten pool of rock that pushed upward to form the Pikes Peak massif. Geologic

formations of the area include pinkish Pikes Peak granite, some schist and gneiss, and sedimentary rock dating back to the Paleozoic era. Stream erosion is responsible for Beaver Creek's rugged topography.

ACTIVITIES
Hiking

Hiking in the Beaver Creek WSA occurs mostly along canyon bottoms. A maintained trail travels 3.5 miles from the southern boundary of the WSA to where Beaver Creek divides into east and west forks. From here, it is possible to continue up either fork, but the going is rough because of underbrush and narrow canyon walls. Anglers and hikers frequent Beaver Creek.

The Skagwuay Powerline Trail traverses east 2 miles from the Beaver Creek forks to Trail Gulch along an old powerline right-of-way. Today, only scattered poles remain. Trail Gulch, popular with both horsepackers and hikers, can be followed for 6 miles or more all the way through the WSA. Trail Gulch branches east from Beaver Creek just south of the WSA boundary.

An old trail that has suffered years of neglect heads up West Mill Creek, another tributary of Beaver Creek. A hike up West Mill Creek is possible, but the trail is not easy to find in many places.

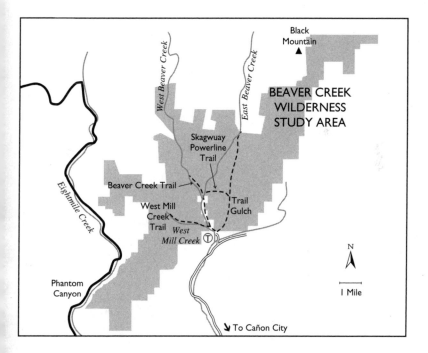

Opposite: *The ruggedly beautiful Beaver Creek drainage*

20 Browns Canyon Wilderness Study Area

Location: 7 mi N of Salida
Size: 6,614 acres
Status: Wilderness study area (1980)
Terrain: River bottom and steep canyons
Elevation: 7,500' to 8,400'
Management: BLM (Royal Gorge Field Office)
Topographic map: Nathrop

The Browns Canyon Wilderness Study Area (WSA) is a 2-mile-wide strip of BLM land directly east of the Arkansas River. The Arkansas is one of the ten most popular recreational rivers in the country, and the Browns Canyon stretch is the most used along the entire river. River running is the primary activity here, with hiking an option in some of the side canyons.

The mouth of Browns Canyon

Seasons

Except for short periods of snow cover in December and January, the terrain is usually open to hiking. Summer afternoons can be hot, but evenings cool down. The spring runoff, which occurs in May and June, raises the rapids in Browns Canyon from Class II to Class IV.

Flora and Fauna

The primary plant community is of the pinyon pine and juniper variety, though rabbitbrush, yucca, prickly pear, and various grasses also grow here. Among the fauna are great horned owls, Swainson's hawks, and golden eagles. Mule deer, coyotes, black bears, and bighorn sheep also call the area home.

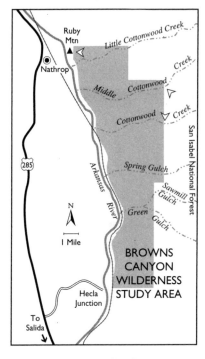

Geology

The Arkansas River has cut through the edge of the Mosquito Range, which rises just to the east. Consisting mostly of Precambrian granite, the walls of Browns Canyon are pinkish in color. River and stream erosion is the determining force that shaped the topography of the area.

ACTIVITIES
Hiking

Hikes within the Browns Canyon WSA are available mostly to boaters passing through the canyon, although access is possible by hiking around the back side of Ruby Mountain and down the eastern bank of the Arkansas River from the Ruby Mountain Recreation Site. A footbridge crosses the river at Nathrop but it is privately owned and not generally open to the public. Access is also possible from County Road 185 a few miles east of the WSA in the San Isabel National Forest. Although no trails exist in this area, the drainages of Middle Cottonwood and Cottonwood Creeks can be followed for several miles to the river. The going is rough in places and this area is quite remote.

By entering the WSA from the river, hikers can follow several drainages upstream. Besides the Middle Cottonwood and Cottonwood Creek drainages, Little Cottonwood Creek, Spring Gulch, Green Gulch, and Sawmill Gulch offer other options.

River Running

The stretch of the Arkansas River that flows through Browns Canyon is said to be the most popular white water in the Rocky Mountain West. Although the river is actually outside of the WSA, boaters can enjoy its scenery along the way. A railroad track runs between the wilderness and the river along a portion of the WSA's western boundary.

To run Browns Canyon, put in at Nathrop. Takeouts are found 8 river miles downstream at Hecla Junction and 11 river miles downstream at the Stone Bridge Recreation Site. A day-use fee is charged at both locations. Prized for both its wilderness setting and its white-water challenges, Browns Canyon is used by many commercial rafting companies. Among its rapids is the Zoom Flume, a Class III to Class IV rapid. During times of very low water, some stretches are not wide enough for rafts to pass through. Browns Canyon offers intermediate rafters a formidable experience.

21 Buffalo Peaks Wilderness Area

Location: 14 mi S of Fairplay
Size: 43,410 acres
Status: Wilderness area (1993)
Terrain: Alpine summits and heavily timbered areas
Elevation: 9,200' to 13,326'
Management: Pike NF, San Isabel NF
Topographic maps: Marmot Peak, Harvard Lakes, Jones Hill, South Peak, Mount Sherman, Leadville South

The Buffalo Peaks are a small collection of 12,000- and 13,000-foot summits that rise between the Arkansas River Valley and South Park. These peaks are not as noteworthy as the nearby Collegiates, or the rest of the Mosquito Range for that matter, but their presence is striking because of their relative isolation. The original wilderness study area was trimmed by almost 15,000 acres, mostly in the Marmot Peak area on the southern end and along both sides of the northern third.

Seasons
Hiking is usually possible between late June and October, although some patches of snow may linger year-round. The months of July and August usher in almost daily thundershowers in the higher terrain. Wildflowers bloom in July and August. Fall hikes may be highlighted by the sound of bugling elk.

Flora and Fauna
The forested lower reaches of the Buffalo Peaks Wilderness consist of Engelmann spruce, lodgepole pine, and aspen. Some ponderosa pine, Douglas fir, and blue spruce are also present. Elk and mule deer inhabit this life zone along with many smaller creatures. In addition to the expected krummholz forests, stands of bristlecone pine can be found growing near timberline. Among the creatures that inhabit this terrain are marmots,

Final rays of sun illuminate the Buffalo Peaks Wilderness.

pikas, and bighorn sheep. In fact, the Colorado Division of Wildlife identifies the Buffalo Peaks as one of the state's premier bighorn sheep habitats.

Geology

Dark in complexion, the Buffalo Peaks are the remnants of thick deposits of lava and volcanic ash that filled an ancient valley during the Tertiary period some 30 million years ago. Former lava flows also cap nearby buttes.

ACTIVITIES
Hiking

Small by comparison to other wilderness tracts, Buffalo Peaks nevertheless has a lot to offer. The 6-mile-long Rich Creek Trail and the Tumble Creek Trail both begin 1 mile

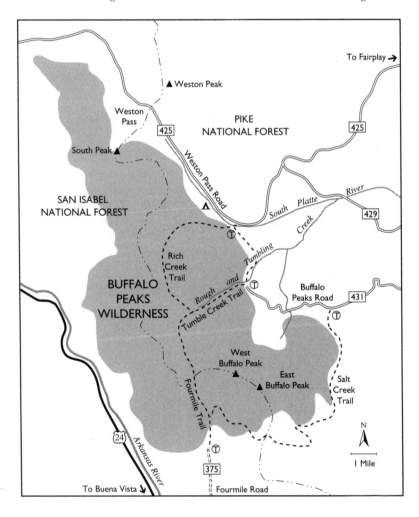

southeast of the Weston Pass Campground. They connect at Buffalo Meadows to form an 11.5-mile loop. Beyond Buffalo Meadows, the Tumble Creek Trail continues south to the top of a divide 1.5 miles west of the peaks. The Fourmile Trail continues south of this point to connect with 4WD Fourmile Road, which climbs up from the Arkansas River drainage north of Buena Vista.

The Salt Creek Trail runs just outside of the southeastern and southern boundaries of the proposed wilderness. Beginning on Buffalo Peaks Road northeast of the peaks, this trail runs 12 miles through the Pike National Forest before crossing into the San Isabel National Forest. It then continues another 2 miles or so to connect with the Fourmile Trail. Hikers can combine this route with the Fourmile and Tumble Creek Trails to make a lengthy loop around the Buffalo Peaks.

Cross-country Skiing

Since the Weston Pass Road is not regularly plowed to the forest boundary, winter access to the Rich Creek and Tumble Creek Trails is not always assured. If you do happen to reach these routes, however, the skiing can be quite enjoyable given proper snow conditions. Avalanches are not a problem until the higher meadows are reached. Beyond this point, caution should be used.

Mountaineering

The primary climbs are West Buffalo Peak (13,326 feet) and East Buffalo Peak (13,300 feet). To reach these summits, follow the ridge east from the pass on the Fourmile–Tumble Creek Trail. These summits are both walk-ups. South Peak (12,892 feet) is an easy-to-reach high point 2 miles southwest of Weston Pass in the northern end of the wilderness.

22 Collegiate Peaks Wilderness Area

Location: 8 mi W of Buena Vista
Size: 166,654 acres
Status: Wilderness area (1980)
Terrain: Alpine summits and timbered lower slopes
Elevation: 8,500' to 14,420'
Management: San Isabel NF, White River NF, Gunnison NF
Topographic maps: Aspen, Granite, Mount Elbert, Independence Pass, Hayden Peak, Italian Creek, Pieplant, New York Peak, Mount Harvard, Buena Vista

With eight of Colorado's fifty-four 14,000-foot peaks, the Collegiate Peaks Wilderness offers some of the highest terrain in the nation. Yet these mountains, despite their lofty stature, pose less of an obstacle to hikers and climbers than many other Colorado ranges. Because of this, several miles of trail run throughout the wilderness and the higher summits typically receive dozens of climbers on any given summer day. Extending between Cottonwood and Independence Passes, the Collegiate Peaks Wilderness Area does not include Mount Elbert, the state's highest point, which sits off by itself to the north.

Seasons

Hiking in the Collegiates is usually feasible between early or mid-July and October. Some lower elevations may be snow-free longer than that, however. Summers bring on a plethora of wildflowers and thundershowers. And because the range is quite exposed, winds can be dangerously fierce during the winter.

Flora and Fauna

Thick stands of lodgepole pine are common among lower elevations. Closer to timberline, around 11,500 feet, forests of Engelmann spruce and subalpine fir predominate. Herds of elk and mule deer are common among these lower haunts, as are a variety of smaller mammals such as snowshoe hares and red squirrels.

Within the alpine tundra regions, which encompass much of the wilderness, are fragile communities of slow-growing grasses and sedges. Wildflowers include sky pilot, Indian paintbrush, blue columbine, moss pink campion, and alpine sunflower, or old-man-of-the-mountain. Marmots and pikas are common in these higher reaches, and a herd of mountain goats is successfully established here. Bighorn sheep are also found in the wilderness.

Geology

Rising some 65 million years ago during the Laramide Orogeny, the Sawatch Range, which includes the Collegiate Peaks, is a good example of a faulted anticline range. A great block of Precambrian schist and gneiss were uplifted along lengthy fractures in the substrata. Volcanic intrusions occurred during the Tertiary period, spreading volcanic rock in the vicinity of La Plata, Huron, and Grizzly Peaks in the northern end of the wilderness. Glacial activity—evidenced by the many cirques found at the higher reaches and terminal moraines below—and stream erosion have given these mountains their present form.

History

The naming of the Collegiate Peaks came about during an 1869 survey of the mountains conducted by J. D. Whitney, for whom California's Mount Whitney is named. As head of the first graduating class at Harvard's School of Mining, he named the Collegiate Wilderness's highest peak Mount Harvard. Mount Yale is the second highest. The rest—Princeton, Oxford, and Columbia—received the names of other prominent schools.

ACTIVITIES
Hiking

With much of its acreage falling within the San Isabel National Forest, the eastern side of the wilderness offers the greatest number of entry points and trails, including more than 20 miles of the Colorado Trail. Entering the wilderness just south of where it crosses Clear Creek, the Colorado Trail skirts along the eastern border of the wilderness. Along the way the route dips in and out of drainages and vacillates between elevations of 8,900 and 11,900 feet. Leaving the wilderness at Harvard Lakes, the Colorado Trail reaches North Cottonwood Creek Road (County Road 365) 15 miles from the trailhead on Clear Creek Road. Traveling another 8 miles, the trail then passes through the wilderness again before crossing South Cottonwood Creek and Cottonwood Pass Road (County Road 306). This road crosses the Continental Divide over Cottonwood Pass, marking the southern end of the Collegiate Peaks Wilderness Area.

Other trails in the eastern side of the wilderness are used by climbers headed for the "fourteeners," but these routes also offer spectacular hikes for anyone who simply wants to visit the backcountry. The Browns Pass Trail begins about 1 mile west of the Collegiate Peaks Campground on the Cottonwood Pass Road (County Road 306). Climbing 2,100 feet in 4 miles, this route offers easy access to the Divide and some great scenery. From the pass, the Browns Pass Trail descends into the Texas Creek drainage in Gunnison National Forest. The North Cottonwood Creek Trail heads north and then east from Browns Pass down the North Cottonwood drainage to the eastern boundary of the wilderness; the pass is about 6 miles from the trailhead. The 3.5-mile Horn Fork Creek Trail branches off the North Cottonwood Creek Trail and runs north to the base of Mount Harvard. Connect the Browns Pass and North Cottonwood Creek Trails with an 8-mile stretch of the Colorado Trail and a 3-mile walk along Cottonwood Pass Road to make a fine 3-day loop hike.

The Pine Creek Trail begins 13 miles north of Buena Vista at the end of County Road 388. This trail accesses a large portion of the northern end of the wilderness as it follows its namesake for 10 miles, ending at Silver King Lake near the Continental Divide. From the trailhead, the route covers 2.5 miles before crossing the Colorado Trail just inside the wilderness boundary. From there it is another 2.5 miles to Little Johns Cabin, a national historical site. The cabin also marks the turnoff for the South Pine Creek Trail. The South Pine Creek Trail connects with the Harvard Trail about 3 miles to the south just east of Mount Harvard. The Harvard Trail follows 3.5 miles of 4WD road from its trailhead to the wilderness boundary. It is another mile from the wilderness boundary to the Colorado Trail, then 2.5 miles more to the trail's end. The Harvard and South Pine Creek Trails are the two principal routes up Mount Harvard.

Near its end in the Missouri Basin, the Pine Creek Trail also intersects the Missouri Gulch Trail. Beginning at Vicksburg on Clear Creek Road (County Road 390), the Missouri Gulch Trail heads south over 13,220-foot Elkhead Pass, the second highest pass in the state. This is a climb of 3,700 feet in 4 miles. The intersection with the Pine Creek Trail is 2.5 miles south of the pass.

The 3-mile-long Pear Lake Trail heads south from the Cloyses Lake area at the end of 4WD Cloyses Lake Road (FS Road 388; not passable when Clear Creek is running high) to Pear Lake on the Gunnison National Forest side of the Divide. Two short trails also enter the wilderness from the end of Clear Creek Road; one reaches Harrison Flat near the base of the Three Apostles, and the other climbs to Silver Basin. And,

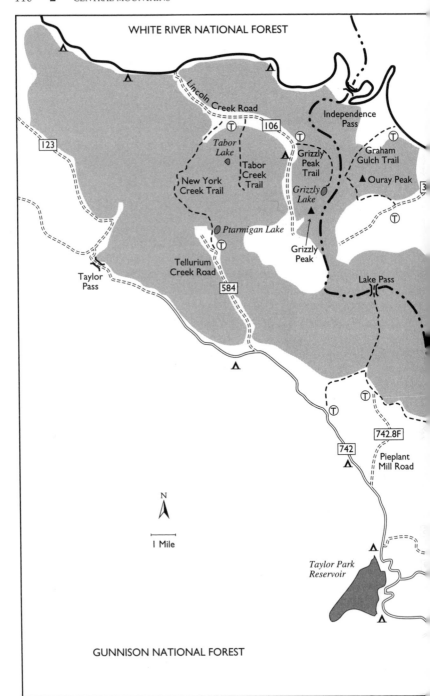

WHITE RIVER NATIONAL FOREST

Lincoln Creek Road

106

123

Independence Pass

Tabor Lake

Tabor Creek Trail

New York Creek Trail

Grizzly Peak Trail

Graham Gulch Trail

▲ Ouray Peak

3

Grizzly Lake

▲

Ptarmigan Lake

Grizzly Peak

Tellurium Creek Road

584

Taylor Pass

Lake Pass

742.8F

742

Pieplant Mill Road

N

1 Mile

Taylor Park Reservoir

GUNNISON NATIONAL FOREST

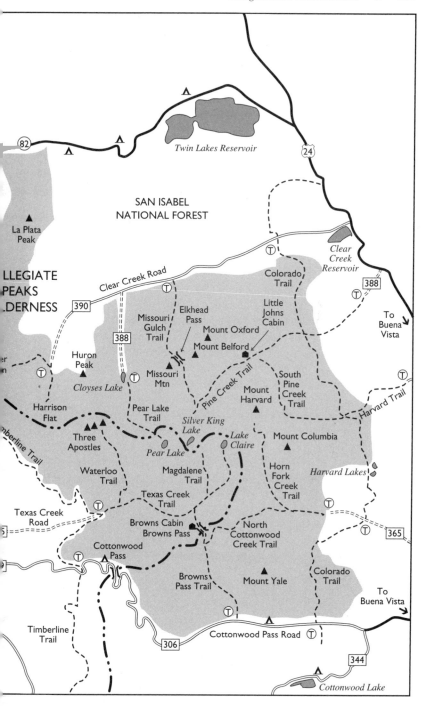

farther north, the 5-mile Graham Gulch Trail starts from a point 6 road miles east of Independence Pass and runs to South Fork Lake Creek Road (County Road 391).

West of the Continental Divide, the Collegiate Peaks Wilderness incorporates a few smaller trail systems within portions of the Gunnison and White River National Forests. The 8-mile Texas Creek Trail accesses several tributaries between Browns Pass and the Three Apostles as it runs from the end of 4WD Texas Creek Road (County Road 755) to Lake Claire. This route intersects several side trails as it climbs from 10,000 to 12,300 feet. Within a mile of the trailhead, the 3.6-mile Waterloo Trail takes off to follow Waterloo Gulch north. A less-traveled unnamed trail parallels South Texas Creek and climbs to Cottonwood Pass. The Browns Pass Trail intersects Texas Creek about 5 miles from the trailhead. Less than a mile below Browns Pass is Browns Cabin, a popular stopover for overnight hikers. Near the end of the Texas Creek Trail, the 2-mile Magdalene Trail heads north up Magdalene Gulch.

The 31-mile Timberline Trail runs along the western boundary of the wilderness. As its name suggests, this route follows the timberline along the flank of the Collegiate Peaks. Because it falls just outside the wilderness, motorcyclers and mountain bikers use it too. Conflicts are rare, however, making the Timberline Trail equally good for backpacking. Crossing Cottonwood Pass Road near the trail's midpoint, only half of the Timberline Trail is adjacent to the Collegiate Peaks Wilderness. Access points include Cottonwood Pass Road, Texas Creek Road, and Pieplant Mill Road (County Road 742.8F). From the Pieplant Road trailhead, a 6-mile side trail off the northern end of the Timberline runs north into the wilderness to Lake Pass (12,220 feet) on the Continental Divide.

A small portion of the wilderness falls within the White River National Forest and three in-and-out routes head south from a side road off State Highway 82—the road from Aspen to the Arkansas Valley via Independence Pass. All three begin along 4WD Lincoln Creek Road (County Road 106). The New York Creek Trail climbs 2,300 feet in 4.2 miles to a 12,280-foot pass between New York Creek and the headwaters of the Taylor River in the Gunnison National Forest to the south. The trail continues beyond this pass to Ptarmigan Lake and 4WD Tellurium Creek Road. The Tabor Creek Trail climbs some 2,000 feet in 4 miles to the ridge dividing Tabor and Galena Creeks; Tabor Lake lies 0.5 mile off the trail to the west. Beginning at Portal Campground, the Grizzly Creek Trail climbs a little more than 3 miles to Grizzly Lake at the base of Grizzly Peak (13,988 feet).

Cross-country Skiing

Parts of the Collegiate Peaks Wilderness Area are accessible during the winter months. County Road 306 (the Cottonwood Pass Road) is usually plowed to the Collegiate Peaks Campground, 1 mile from the Browns Pass trailhead. Because of its outstanding scenery and skiable grade, the Browns Pass Trail is excellent for day tours.

Taking any of the trails that begin on the eastern slope of the mountains means skiing several miles on unplowed road before you reach the wilderness boundary. The road up Independence Pass is regularly cleared to the Twin Lakes tunnel, about 6 miles

A small miner's cabin near Browns Pass

shy of the pass. Access is considerably more limited from the Gunnison–White River National Forest side. Avalanches pose a near constant threat on any steep terrain throughout the Collegiates.

Mountaineering

Eight of the state's elite 14,000-foot summits are found within the wilderness boundary and all can be climbed by nontechnical routes. In the southern end of the wilderness, Mount Yale (14,196 feet) is considered a great family climb. The recommended route, which follows Denny Creek from Cottonwood Pass Road, is 3 miles long and climbs 4,400 feet. A slightly longer approach is along the North Cottonwood Creek Trail. Mount Harvard (14,420 feet) and Mount Columbia (14,073 feet) can be scaled via the North Cottonwood Creek and Horn Fork Creek Trails. Mount Harvard rises at the head of the Horn Fork Basin; its broad, grassy south shoulder provides the easiest route up. From there, Mount Columbia is a 2-mile ridge walk to the south. Some scrambling is involved, but the views are excellent. To return to the basin, descend along the same route you came up.

Three other "fourteeners" are clustered in the northeast portion of the wilderness; all are accessible by the Missouri Gulch Trail. Mount Belford (14,197 feet) and Mount Oxford (14,153 feet) are considered walk-ups; Missouri Mountain (14,067 feet) offers some challenges. To reach these summits, hike into upper Missouri Gulch to Belford. Oxford is a 1.5-mile walk east. Missouri Mountain lies at the head of upper Missouri Gulch and can be climbed via the northwest ridge. An ice ax comes in handy if snow or ice is present. All three summits can also be climbed from Elkhead Pass farther up the trail.

Huron Peak (14,005 feet) sits west of Missouri Mountain and is approached from the Clear Creek Road (County Road 390) by trail or via neighboring Browns Peak and the north ridge. A high point among many 13,000-foot summits, Huron serves as an anchor for other climbs in the northern reaches of the wilderness, including the Three Apostles (13,920 feet) 2 miles to the south. The realm of technically adept climbers, these spectacular stone summits are highly visible sentinels along the Continental Divide.

La Plata Peak (14,336 feet) is off by itself in a northern extension of the wilderness. Unlike much of the Sawatch Range, La Plata is quite rugged. Technical climbers delight in the many rock pinnacles and faces, especially those along the northeast ridge, also known as Ellingwood Ridge, which was named after the first person to conquer the route. A somewhat simpler ascent follows the peak's northwest ridge, reached via La Plata Gulch or La Plata Basin.

23 Mount Massive Wilderness Area

Location: 6 mi W of Leadville
Size: 30,540 acres
Status: Wilderness area (1980)
Terrain: Alpine summits and timbered lower slopes
Elevation: 10,000' to 14,421'
Management: San Isabel NF, U.S. Fish and Wildlife Service
Topographic maps: Mount Massive, Homestake Reservoir, Independence Pass, Mount Elbert

Mount Massive is Colorado's second-highest summit. It stands out on the skyline above the headwaters of the Arkansas River. Rising to five distinct points, its crest stretches for 3 miles. Most visitors to this wilderness area are intent on either bagging the summit or following the Colorado Trail as it skirts Massive's eastern flank.

Seasons

Don't expect to find the hike to the summit free of snow until mid-July. Lower elevations are usually passable by late June. Wildflowers are in bloom in late July and early August. Watch for lightning during the frequent summer storms. The first snows of the season usually fall by early or mid-October.

Flora and Fauna

With much of the wilderness above timberline, vast stretches of alpine tundra are typical in the Mount Massive Wilderness. A variety of wildflowers—blue columbine, Indian paintbrush, alpine sunflowers, and sky pilots among them—grow among these low-

Atop Mount Massive

profile sedges and grasses. Bighorn sheep reside on the mountain, as do pikas and marmots. Below timberline, mule deer and elk are frequently seen among the Engelmann spruce and subalpine fir forests, and stands of lodgepole pine.

Geology

As part of the Sawatch Range, Mount Massive was uplifted during the Laramide Orogeny beginning 65 million years ago. Although other parts of the Sawatch Range consist of Precambrian schist and gneiss, Mount Massive is mostly granite. Large alluvial deposits of rock eroded off the mountain by streams now rest along its eastern flank. Glacial cirques are evident in the higher elevations.

History

Henry Gannett of the Hayden Geological Survey named the mountain Mount Massive in 1873. The first attempt to change its name came in 1901 when a Denver newspaper decided it should be renamed to honor recently slain President William McKinley. Local residents fought the change with a petition of more than a thousand signatures. As chairman of the U.S. Board of Geographic Names, the same Henry Gannett who originally named the peak agreed. Two decades later, a move arose to name it after Gannett, who was deceased. The locals fought the change again. In 1965, a state senator tried to rename it after Winston Churchill, but again it was to no avail.

ACTIVITIES
Hiking

Between Turquoise Lake to the north and Halfmoon Creek just south of the boundary, a 13-mile stretch of the Colorado Trail crosses a number of drainages that descend the mountain's east slope. A lot of grade changes result. At 11,280 feet, the high point comes at the intersection with the Mount Massive Trail. Several creeks are stocked with trout. Keep in mind that fishing is catch-and-release only.

Native Lake, a scenic fishing hole in the north end of the wilderness, is best reached via a 2-mile trail that heads south from Hagerman Pass Road (County Road 105). Native Lake can also be reached by following the Highline Trail for about 5 miles from the Leadville Federal Fish Hatchery. Near its midpoint, the Highline takes a short jaunt along the Colorado Trail.

Cross-country Skiing

Skiing is a popular pastime in the Mount Massive Wilderness thanks to access provided by the Leadville Federal Fish Hatchery. A pamphlet describing some routes is

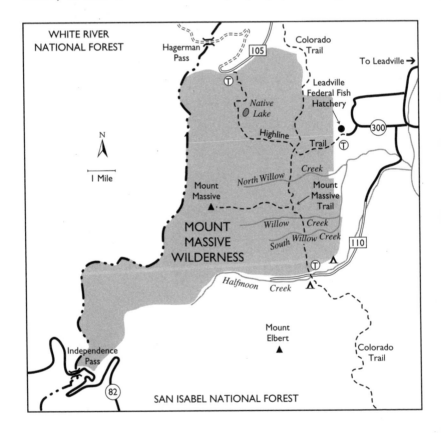

available from the hatchery. For more-experienced skiers, the slopes of Mount Massive itself offer wide-open terrain for mountaineer skiing.

Mountaineering

The climb up Mount Massive (14,421 feet) is more a hike than anything else. Climbing 4,400 feet in 7 miles, the route follows the Colorado Trail for 3 miles from a trailhead in the vicinity of the Elbert Creek Campground on Halfmoon Creek Road (County Road 110), then turns west up the Mount Massive Trail to complete the ascent. Because Mount Massive can be extremely crowded, you may want to plan your climb for a weekday or after Labor Day.

24 Holy Cross Wilderness Area

Location: 8 mi SW of Vail
Size: 122,037 acres
Status: Wilderness area (1980)
Terrain: Alpine summits and forested drainages
Elevation: 8,000' to 14,005'
Management: White River NF, San Isabel NF
Topographic maps: Grouse Mountain, Mount Jackson, Crooked Creek, Homestake Reservoir, Mount of the Holy Cross, Minturn, Fulford, Nast, Meredith

With its two intersecting crevasses that appear as an enormous white cross when filled with snow, the Mount of the Holy Cross has been the subject of countless pilgrimages by both the pious and curious for more than a century. Nevertheless, it is but one of several impressive sights in the wilderness that shares its name. Several other peaks, while not as ripe with symbolism, pose striking profiles against the sky. Deep and seemingly impassable canyons open up between treeless ridges while dozens of alpine lakes nestle among bowls and benches, forests and meadows.

Seasons

Mostly high terrain, the Holy Cross Wilderness is usually snowbound from late October through June. Some years even see snow blocking the uppermost trails well into July. Afternoon thunderstorms typically rumble through the area in the summer. Watch for wildflowers shortly after the snows melt, usually in late July.

Flora and Fauna

The forest ecosystem here consists mostly of Engelmann spruce and subalpine fir, along with intermittent stands of aspen. Some meadows are scattered about the valleys. Mule deer, elk, black bears, coyotes, bobcats, and an occasional mountain lion are key inhabitants of these timbered lands. Above timberline in a mixture of rocky areas and alpine meadows, marmots and pikas are often spotted, as well as bighorn sheep and mountain goats.

Geology

Encompassing the northern end of the Sawatch Range, the Holy Cross area was initially formed during the Laramide Orogeny as faulted anticlines or uplifted blocks of basement rock. Much of the range consists of Precambrian gneiss and schist. Periods of heavy glaciation followed, etching cirques and deep valleys into the range and depositing glacial outwash at the foot of the mountains.

The ravines that constitute the cross follow joints in the mountain's east face. Although snowbanks persisted through most summers, a succession of years with less than normal snowfall have left the cross empty by August.

History

For years, tales had been told of a great mountain with a snowy cross on it, but it did not receive wholesale attention until William Henry Jackson produced a photo in 1873 after an exhaustive search for the peak. Jackson—then a photographer for the Hayden Geological Survey—topped nearby Notch Mountain on a cloudy evening. The cross was revealed to the party on the morning of August 23, and Jackson's photo taken that day inspired thousands to pay homage to the peak. Pilgrimages and even stories of miraculous healings continued through the early part of the 1900s. A stone shelter was built on top of Notch Mountain in 1924 for the throngs of folks who made the climb. The shelter is still maintained today. The mountain was designated a national monument in 1929, but the status was withdrawn in the 1950s after interest in the shrine dwindled. Today, the peak is still revered for its natural beauty.

ACTIVITIES
Hiking

The Mount of the Holy Cross is one of the more remote "fourteeners" in the state, and views of the fabled peak are rare outside of the wilderness. For those willing to hike beyond road's end, the view of the mountain is as stirring as that of any summit in the state.

Jackson made his famous photo from the top of Notch Mountain, a 13,100-foot peak that sits directly across the Bowl of Tears from the cross. The Notch Mountain shelter is in excellent condition and offers a safe haven during lightning storms. A plaque installed in 1963 commemorates William Henry Jackson's role in popularizing the site and the sight. The Notch Mountain Trail begins at the Half Moon Campground, located at the end of 8-mile Tigiwon Road, a rough 2WD route that begins just south of Minturn. Climbing nearly 3,000 feet in 5.3 miles, this trail steepens on switchbacks as it achieves most of its elevation gain in the last 3 miles.

The first 2.5 miles of the route up Notch Mountain actually follow the Fall Creek

Opposite: A stone cabin on Notch Mountain

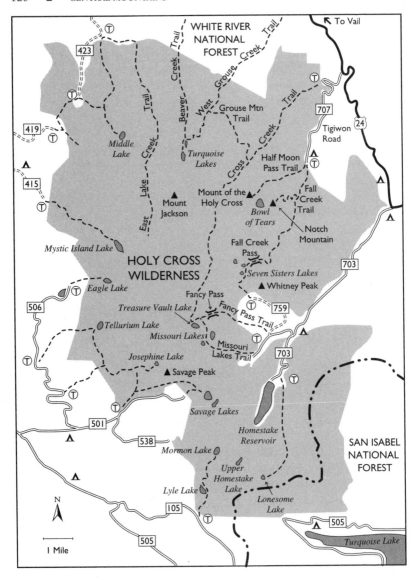

Trail. Continuing past Notch Mountain, the Fall Creek route eventually tops 12,600-foot Fall Creek Pass and terminates on a 4WD road up French Creek just out of Gold Park Campground. Nine miles long, the trail gains 2,200 feet if traveled in a southerly direction and 1,400 feet when following it north. A number of beautiful lakes are encountered along the way, including the Seven Sisters Lakes, which are arranged in a stair-step configuration.

The 15.5-mile Cross Creek Trail parallels the Fall Creek route and follows the

Cross Creek drainage to its headwaters below 12,400-foot Fancy Pass. The northern trailhead is 2 miles up Tigiwon Road, while the southern end is at Treasure Vault Lake, where the Fancy Pass and Missouri Lakes Trails branch off. The Fancy Pass Trail continues southeast over 12,400-foot Fancy Pass to Missouri Lakes Road near Gold Park Campground, 3.3 miles away. The 3-mile-long Missouri Lakes Trail crosses 11,986-foot Missouri Pass before meeting the same road. The Cross Creek Trail passes west of Holy Cross and the Fall Creek Trail passes east of it; combine these two routes for a long-distance backpacking trip.

A number of interconnected trails offer similar loop-hike possibilities in the northern half of the wilderness. The West Grouse Creek Trail follows West Grouse Creek past Grouse Mountain (12,799 feet) to the Turquoise Lakes about 9 miles in. A spur trail connects the Grouse Mountain Trail with the Cross Creek Trail 3 miles to the east. From Turquoise Lakes, the Beaver Creek Trail follows Beaver Creek north for 7 miles to the Beaver Creek Ski Resort. Farther west, the East Lake Creek Trail follows 11.5 miles of old jeep road to a historic mining district in an isolated section of the wilderness.

From the west, a number of shorter in-and-out trails enter the wilderness to lead to several alpine lakes, including Middle, Mystic Island, Eagle, Tellurium, and Josephine. To the south, trails access Savage, Lyle, Mormon, Upper Homestake, and Lonesome Lakes. Unlike those in the eastern side of the Holy Cross area, these trails typically do not interconnect.

Cross-country Skiing

Because forest roads in the area are not plowed, winter access to the Holy Cross Wilderness is limited. Those with time and stamina will not find this a problem, but for skiers interested in day tours, the possibilities are limited. One choice is the West Grouse Creek Trail, which begins on U.S. Highway 24 near Minturn. Another is the northern end of the Cross Creek Trail, which is only 1.5 miles from the highway. Even at lower elevations within the wilderness, however, you should be mindful of avalanches, especially on steep and open slopes.

Mountaineering

Most of the peak baggers who visit the Holy Cross Wilderness Area do so with the single purpose of climbing Mount of the Holy Cross (14,005 feet), the only "fourteener" in the area. Begin at the Half Moon Campground and follow the Half Moon Pass Trail over the 11,040-foot pass and into the East Cross Creek drainage. After crossing the creek, the route climbs the peak's north ridge all the way to the summit. The hike up is about 7 miles each way.

Other peaks in the Holy Cross Wilderness offer less crowded alternatives. Mount Jackson (13,657 feet) can be reached from Turquoise Lakes at the end of the West Grouse Creek Trail, from the East Lake Creek Trail, or from the Cross Creek Trail to the east. Whitney Peak (13,290 feet) is climbable from Fall Creek Pass. And Savage Peak (13,083 feet) is an easy climb from the Savage Lakes area in the southern portion of the wilderness. All of these climbs are nontechnical scrambles.

25   Hunter–Fryingpan Wilderness Area

Location: 3 mi E of Aspen
Size: 82,580 acres
Status: Wilderness area (1978)
Terrain: Alpine summits and forested lower slopes
Elevation: 8,500' to 13,845'
Management: White River NF
Topographic maps: Meredith, Nast, Aspen, Independence Pass, Thimble Rock, Mount Champion, New York Peak

The Hunter–Fryingpan Wilderness receives relatively little use, especially compared to the neighboring Collegiate Peaks and Maroon Bells–Snowmass Wilderness Areas. Encompassing several 13,000-foot peaks in a portion of the Sawatch Range that falls west of the Continental Divide and north of Independence Pass, the Hunter–Fryingpan also offers a lot of promising fishing streams. Access to its higher reaches is easy thanks to Independence Pass Road over 12,095-foot Independence Pass. The name Hunter–Fryingpan refers to two rivers with headwaters within the wilderness area. The Colorado Wilderness Act of 1993 added 8,330 acres to the Hunter–Fryingpan Wilderness along the northwest boundary,

Seasons
Hiking at lower elevations is possible by early June, but don't count on entering the higher terrain until after the first of July. A variety of alpine wildflowers bloom in late July and early August. Aspens hit their peak in September, while October usually ushers in the first major snowstorm of the season.

Flora and Fauna
Stands of Douglas fir, ponderosa pine, and aspen predominate across the lower elevations along the western edge of the wilderness. Higher up, lodgepole pine gives way to a mix of Engelmann spruce and subalpine fir. At timberline, the alpine tundra takes over with its variety of low-growing perennials, among them alpine forget-me-nots, moss pink campions, and alpine sunflowers. Thick growths of willow are also found above timberline. Mule deer, elk, coyotes, marmots, pikas, and bighorn sheep can be found here, and wildlife officials suspect that lynx and wolverines also inhabit the area.

Geology
The Sawatch Range, a faulted anticline mountain system, was uplifted during the Laramide Orogeny, which began about 65 million years ago. These mountains consist of Precambrian gneiss, schist, and some granite. Glaciers were once at work in the upper

reaches of the wilderness, shaping valleys and cirques, and carving out lake basins. The rolling nature of this high terrain was, in fact, smoothed over by glacial ice. Stream erosion still occurs today.

ACTIVITIES
Hiking

The Hunter–Fryingpan includes approximately 50 miles of hiking trails, most of which begin near Independence Pass to the south and along a trio of Forest Service roads that approach the wilderness from the north. Beginning at Lost Man Campground, 14 miles east of Aspen, the Lost Man Trail offers convenient access to the Hunter–Fryingpan high country and outstanding alpine scenery. Nearly 9 miles long, this route climbs from 10,700 feet to a high point of 12,800 feet at Lost Man Pass. From there, it drops back down to a trailhead on the Independence Pass Road, 18.5 miles from Aspen. The Continental Divide runs very near this section of the trail. Lost Man and Independence Lakes are passed along the way, and Linkins Lake is situated less than 1 mile off the route.

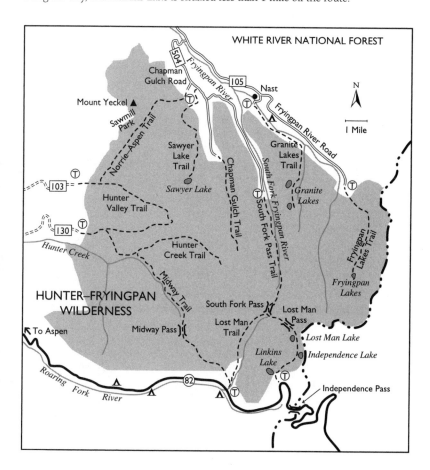

Near the halfway point of the Lost Man Trail, the South Fork Pass Trail takes off over its 11,840-foot namesake and down the South Fork of the Fryingpan River to the north end of the wilderness. It is 5 miles from the intersection with the Lost Man Trail to the trailhead at the end of Forest Road 504. To get to the northern terminus of the South Fork Trail, turn right off the road to Ruedi Dam just past the Norrie Ranger Station. With a shuttle, this traverse makes a nice weekend backpacking trip.

Beginning 0.5 mile in from the Lost Man trailhead is the 9-mile Midway Trail, which runs northwest over 11,841-foot Midway Pass before dropping into the Hunter Creek drainage. Here, it connects with the Hunter Creek Trail, which begins along the Hunter Valley Trail—in other words, the north end of the Midway Trail is still at least 5 miles from the nearest trailhead. The Hunter Valley Trail actually begins at the northern edge of Aspen, near the Aspen Community Center. To get to the Hunter Creek Trail, follow the Hunter Valley Trail for 3.3 miles to its end. Past its intersection with the Midway Trail, the Hunter Creek Trail continues another 5 miles to the headwaters of Hunter Creek where the popular trail is in faded condition.

Besides the South Fork Pass Trail, a number of other trails enter the Hunter–

Lost Man Lake

Fryingpan Wilderness from the north. From the end of Fryingpan River Road, which passes the Horseshoe Bend Guest Ranch, the Fryingpan Lakes Trail follows the Fryingpan River for 4 miles to the Fryingpan Lakes. The lakes are situated at 11,020 feet, 1,100 feet higher than the trailhead. Fishing is good in both the lakes and the river. The Granite Lakes Trail, which begins at Nast, climbs some 3,000 feet in 6.5 miles to another good fishing spot. The 5-mile Chapman Gulch Trail accesses a seldom-visited corner of the wilderness beginning off Chapman Gulch Road. It is not recommended for horsepackers because of its rough condition. The Sawyer Lake Trail, which begins along the Chapman Gulch Road, climbs 1,500 feet in 4 miles to its namesake. And the Norrie–Aspen Trail climbs up Mount Yeckel to cross Sawmill Park in the northwestern corner of the wilderness. The high point of this trail has a good view of the Fryingpan drainage and the Elk Mountains to the south.

Cross-country Skiing

Because Independence Pass is closed from November to the end of May, the trails that begin along Colorado Highway 82 are not readily accessible. Backcountry skiers can, however, follow the Hunter Valley Trail into the Hunter–Fryingpan from the northern edge of Aspen. Along the northern end of the wilderness, the road is regularly plowed to Nast, opening up the route along the Fryingpan River toward Granite Lakes. A 2-mile stretch of road can be skied to reach the northern end of the Norrie–Aspen Trail, which is marked for cross-country skiers. Throughout, skiers should be mindful of the danger of avalanches, especially on steep slopes.

26 Fossil Ridge Wilderness Area

Location: 22 mi NE of Gunnison
Size: 33,060 acres
Status: Wilderness area (1993)
Terrain: Alpine summits and river valleys
Elevation: 8,800' to 13,254'
Management: Gunnison NF
Topographic maps: Almont, Crystal Creek, Fairview Peak, Cumberland Pass, Matchless Mountain, Taylor Park Reservoir

Fossil Ridge is named for a ridge of sedimentary limestone filled with fossils. High peaks, alpine lakes, and streams characterize the area and trail access is good. But many routes are popular with motorbike and mountain bike riders. Because of this, the original wilderness study area proposed by the Forest Service was pared down by nearly 40 percent and the remaining area was designated as a recreation management area, which permits use of motorized vehicles.

Entrance sign to the Fossil Ridge Wilderness

Seasons

Hiking trails at lower elevations are usually free of snow by late May or early June. At higher elevations, snow can persist well into July. Lightning is a frequent hazard on exposed ridges and summits in the summer months. Expect the first heavy snows by mid-October. Seasonal happenings include the wildflower season in July and the turning of aspen leaves in September.

Flora and Fauna

Forests at the lower elevations include stands of aspen and lodgepole pine. Engelmann spruce and subalpine fir are most common higher up. Much of the terrain above timberline is rocky and bears little vegetation. Game species include mule deer, elk, bighorn sheep, mountain goat, mountain lion, coyote, bobcat, pine marten, red fox, and marmot.

Geology

Much of the Fossil Ridge Wilderness consists of sedimentary rocks that overlie a mix of Precambrian granite, schist, and gneiss. These sedimentary formations include limestone and sandstone dating back to the Paleozoic era, 300 million to 600 million years

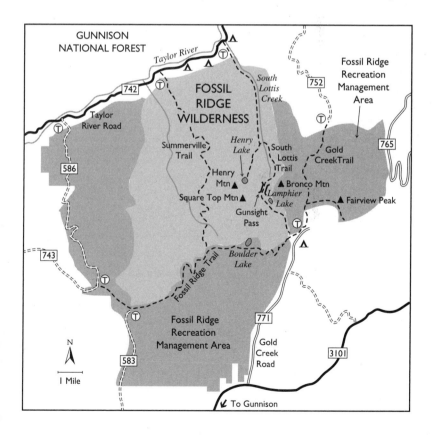

ago. Many fossils of marine invertebrates are found here. Uranium deposits have led to the filing of claims and, consequently, some opposition to wilderness consideration. Small volcanic intrusions such as dikes are also seen in the area. Glacial activity is evident at higher elevations.

ACTIVITIES
Hiking
Good access to the Fossil Ridge Wilderness Area is from Gold Creek Road, specifically in the vicinity of Gold Creek Campground where the trailhead for the Fossil Ridge Trail is located. Heading west toward its namesake ridge, this route traverses a number of small drainages and passes near Boulder Lake before topping the ridge. From end to end, the Fossil Ridge Trail is 13 miles long and has several elevation changes. Because the boundary for the actual wilderness falls just north of this trail, motorbikes are permitted along its entire length.

At about 6 miles in the Fossil Ridge Trail connects with the southern end of the Summerville Trail, a 12-mile route that cuts north to the Taylor River Road. This route is off-limits to bikes because it is within wilderness land. The elevation is nearly 12,000 feet where the Summerville and Fossil Ridge Trails meet, and the views are splendid.

The South Lottis Trail begins within 0.5 mile of the Gold Creek Campground along the Fossil Ridge Trail. Heading north, this trail makes the 2,000-foot climb to Lamphier Lake in 3 miles, and reaches Gunsight Pass (12,167 feet) 1 mile after. North to the pass, the trail is quite rugged and impassable to horses. From the pass it drops down Brush Creek and then down South Lottis Creek to the Lottis Creek Campground on Taylor River Road. The entire trail is 11 miles long and would make a nice 2-day trip with a shuttle. Six miles from the Gold Creek trailhead is a turnoff for Henry Lake, which lies 2 miles off the South Lottis Trail. Situated at 11,704 feet, Henry Lake commands some outstanding views, including Henry Mountain (13,254 feet), the high point of the wilderness area.

Cross-country Skiing
Taylor River Road is the only regularly plowed road near the Fossil Ridge Wilderness. It allows access to the north ends of the Summerville and South Lottis Trails. To reach the Gold Creek area south of the wilderness, you must ski 6 miles of road before encountering the first trailhead. Watch for avalanches on steep and open slopes in all areas.

Mountaineering
Fossil Mountain (12,760 feet), Henry Mountain (13,254 feet), and Square Top Mountain (13,012 feet) are grouped together and can be climbed from Gunsight Pass. Bronco Mountain (12,845 feet) lies 0.5 mile east of the pass. Fairview Peak (13,214 feet) can be approached by a side trail that branches off the Gold Creek Trail near Shaw Ridge.

27 Maroon Bells–Snowmass Wilderness Area

Location: 3 mi SW of Aspen
Size: 181,138 acres
Status: Wilderness area (1980)
Terrain: Alpine peaks and timbered lower slopes
Elevation: 7,500' to 14,265'
Management: Gunnison NF, White River NF
Topographic maps: Aspen, Hayden Peak, Pearl Pass, Highland Peak, Maroon Bells, Gothic, Basalt, Capitol Peak, Snowmass Mountain, Mount Sopris, Redstone, Marble

Situated very close to Aspen, the Maroon Bells–Snowmass Wilderness has more visitors than any other Colorado wilderness area administered by the Forest Service. From downtown Aspen, it is a 15-minute drive up paved Maroon Creek Road to Maroon Lake, which lies in the virtual heart of the highest peaks. This area is so popular that summer visitors are often forced to leave their cars at the Aspen Highlands Ski Area parking lot and ride a shuttle bus up. However, trailheads such as one at Snowmass Village and more along Castle Creek Road make other areas of the Maroon Bells–Snowmass readily accessible.

Many trails within this wilderness are overcrowded and should by avoided during high-use seasons, but the Maroon Bells–Snowmass area still has much to offer. With more than 100 miles of trails, many routes offer a fair amount of solitude. Much of the wilderness is above timberline, making it one of the most visually spectacular mountain areas in the state. Alpine lakes and streams abound, and countless challenging climbs await the skilled mountaineer.

Seasons

Across the highlands here, the summer hiking season usually does not begin until early July. After the winter snows melt, a quick growing season in late July ushers in a plethora of wildflowers in the alpine reaches. The region's plentiful aspen trees show their fall colors in September. And winter returns by mid-October with the first heavy snowfalls of the season. Be wary of almost daily thunderstorms in the summer and unexpected snow squalls in the fall.

Flora and Fauna

Above the forests of aspen, Engelmann spruce, subalpine fir, and ultimately alpine tundra predominate. Wildflowers such as blue columbine, Indian paintbrush, and alpine sunflowers treat hikers to showy splashes of color. Smaller blossoms are equally fascinating. Among these are American bistort, moss pink campion, alpine sandwort, and alpine forget-me-not. Because of the extensive use that the wilderness receives, backpackers should avoid camping in sensitive alpine meadows.

Of the animals that make their home in the Maroon Bells–Snowmass, the larger species include mule deer and elk, black bears, mountain lions, and coyotes. Bighorn sheep can be spotted in several areas, a band of mountain goats lives in the Mount Sopris area, and marmots and pikas animate most high meadows and tundra expanses.

Geology

More than any other aspect, geology is what attracts people to the Maroon Bells–Snowmass Wilderness. Maroon and North Maroon Peaks are said to be the most photographed mountains in the state. Rising dramatically above Crater Lake, the well defined layers of Paleozoic sediment that make up these summits are reflected perfectly in the still water of early morning.

Although classified as faulted anticline mountains, much more went into the shaping of the Elk Mountains than mere uplifting during the Laramide Orogeny. Tinted red, the Maroon Formation occurred when iron-bearing sands and mud eroding from the ancestral Uncompahgre Range collected in layers. These, in turn, metamorphosed by heat and pressure. The resulting quartzite and slate, still red, now covers much of the wilderness.

Other parts of the Maroon Bells–Snowmass Wilderness exhibit different geologic processes. In the western end, Mount Sopris is a large intrusion of quartz monzonite. Other igneous intrusions are found west and southeast of the Maroon Bells. Evidence of glacial carving such as U-shaped valleys and alpine lakes is widespread and rock glaciers are found in many locations. Like those composed of ice, rock glaciers—large accumulations of scree and boulders—actually move en masse downhill.

History

The Elk Mountains got their name in 1853 when the Gunnison Survey found so many bleached elk horns in the vicinity that they whitened the hills. Years later, beginning in the late 1870s, miners established small camps in the range. One of these camps became the town of Aspen in 1880. Mining fizzled out in the early 1900s. However, ski troopers from Camp Hale discovered recreational possibilities in the hills above Aspen, and skiing was firmly established in the town by the late 1940s. As for the peaks themselves, first ascents of many came around the turn of the twentieth century.

ACTIVITIES
Hiking

The most heavily used trails—those nearest Aspen—boast spectacular scenery. Beginning at the end of Maroon Creek Road, the Crater Lake Trail runs 1.75 miles to Crater Lake. A quick and easy hike, Crater Lake is the most popular trail in the forest. Camping within 0.25 mile of the lake is prohibited.

The trails split at Crater Lake with one route leading to Snowmass Lake and the other toward West Maroon Pass. Snowmass Lake is slightly less than 7 miles from Crater Lake and the trail tops 12,462-foot Buckskin Pass along the way. The climb up and over is difficult and can be very crowded. Fires are prohibited at Snowmass Lake. A right turn at a junction near Buckskin Pass leads over Willow Pass to Willow Lake, another popular backpacking destination. Willow Lake, which sits at nearly 12,000 feet, is 6.25 miles from the trailhead at Maroon Lake. The East Snowmass Trail branches north from the Willow Lake route over a 12,690-foot pass and then drops down East Snowmass Creek to a trailhead 2 miles east of Snowmass Village. Covering a little more than 8 miles, this less-traveled path to Willow Lake is quite rugged in places.

From Snowmass Lake, the less-difficult and overused Snowmass Lake Trail continues along Snowmass Creek for 8.5 miles to a trailhead just beyond the start of the East Snowmass Trail to Willow Lake. A loop hike is possible using the Snowmass Lake, East Snowmass, and Willow Lake Trails. With a shuttle, you can begin at Maroon Lake and wind up near Snowmass Village. Either hike requires 2 or 3 days of travel time.

The West Maroon Pass Trail begins at Crater Lake and heads south toward its namesake some 5 miles away. It continues over the 12,500-foot pass into Schofield

The Maroon Bells tower above Crater Lake.

Basin, eventually connecting with 4WD Schofield Pass Road between the town of Crystal and Gothic Campground in Gunnison National Forest. About 1 mile west of West Maroon Pass, the Fravert Basin Trail comes in from the northwest. Crossing over 12,380-foot Frigid Air Pass, this 8-mile route begins about 1.5 miles north of Crystal on a 4WD road. Scenic Fravert Basin is on the back side of the Maroon Bells but receives significantly less traffic. The Geneva Lake Trail, which shares a trailhead with the Fravert Basin route, runs 4 miles over 10,950-foot Trail Rider Pass to Snowmass Lake. It too is well used by those visiting the wilderness from Aspen. Beginning with either the West Maroon Pass Trail or the Fravert Basin Trail, a 2- or 3-day circle hike around the Maroon Bells is feasible.

While the Maroon Lake trailhead conducts many visitors into the Crater Lake area, the East Maroon Creek Trail, which also begins on Maroon Creek Road, is not quite as popular. Following the East Maroon Creek to its headwaters, this 10-mile trail accesses two passes situated on the White River–Gunnison National Forest boundary. The trail forks a little more than 8 miles in; a right turn leads to 11,820-foot East Maroon Pass and a left turn accesses 12,580-foot Copper Pass. The trails connect again beyond the passes to become the Copper Creek route, which drops down to a trailhead on Copper Creek 4 miles from Gothic, a cluster of buildings north of Crested Butte. From the top of Copper Pass, another route crosses over Triangle Pass less than 1 mile southeast and then drops down Conundrum Creek. Thirteen miles in length, the Conundrum Creek Trail begins 5 miles south of Aspen and 1.5

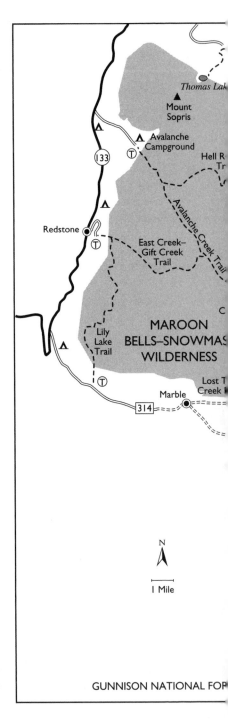

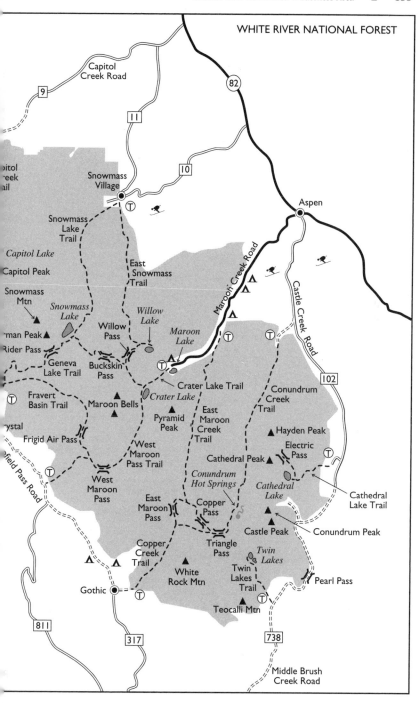

WHITE RIVER NATIONAL FOREST

Capitol
Creek Road

82

9

11

10

Snowmass
Village

Aspen

Snowmass
Lake
Trail

Capitol Lake

Capitol Peak

East
Snowmass
Trail

Snowmass
Mtn

Snowmass
Lake

Willow
Lake

Maroon
Lake

102

rman Peak

Willow
Pass

Rider Pass

Geneva
Lake Trail

Buckskin
Pass

Crater Lake Trail

Conundrum
Creek
Trail

Fravert
Basin Trail

Maroon Bells

Crater Lake

rystal

Frigid Air Pass

Pyramid
Peak

East
Maroon
Creek
Trail

Hayden Peak

Electric
Pass

West
Maroon
Pass Trail

Cathedral Peak

eld Pass Road

West
Maroon
Pass

Conundrum
Hot Springs

Cathedral
Lake

Cathedral
Lake Trail

East
Maroon
Pass

Copper
Pass

Copper
Creek
Trail

Triangle
Pass

Castle Peak

Conundrum Peak

White
Rock Mtn

Twin
Lakes

Twin
Lakes
Trail

Gothic

811

317

Teocalli Mtn

738

Pearl Pass

Middle Brush
Creek Road

miles off Castle Creek Road (County Road 102). Use of this trail is heavy, in part because of the Conundrum Hot Springs, which are 8.5 miles in from the trailhead. For a 24-mile hike, walk up Conundrum Creek, traverse Triangle and Copper Passes, and descend East Maroon Creek, but be sure to arrange a shuttle beforehand.

Outside the Maroon Bells area, other corners of the wilderness offer somewhat less crowded spaces. For instance, the Cathedral Lake Trail is farther up Castle Creek Road. Scenic Cathedral Lake sits at 11,866 feet a little more than 2 miles in. It shares its name with nearby Cathedral Peak (13,943 feet). Camping within 0.25 mile of the lake is prohibited. A side trail continues north from the lake for 3 miles to 13,500-foot Electric Pass, which overlooks the Conundrum Creek drainage.

Off 4WD Middle Brush Creek Road (County Road 738, the approach from Crested Butte to Pearl Pass), the Twin Lakes Trail leads for 2.5 miles to Twin Lakes, which sit at 11,800 feet. The area is very scenic and not many people hike this out-of-the-way route.

West of the Maroon Bells area, several trails run independently of the network that interconnects Maroon, Crater, and Snowmass Lakes. Beginning along 4WD Lost Trail Creek Road (County Road 315) east of Marble, the Silver Creek Trail climbs 1,200 feet in 6 miles to meet the Avalanche Creek Trail in the vicinity of Capitol Peak. The Avalanche Creek Trail then runs another 15 miles north to the Avalanche Campground off Colorado Highway 133. From south to north this route climbs 4,400 feet. Because Capitol Peak is a "fourteener," the Avalanche Creek Trail sees a lot of foot traffic, but the Silver Creek Trail does not. Vistas of Capitol, other peaks, and some beautiful alpine lakes make this area well worth the visit. Two other trails—9.3-mile Capitol Creek Trail, which begins at the end of Capitol Creek Road (County Road 9), and 9-mile Hell Roaring Trail—connect with either end of the Avalanche Creek route, making a 31-mile loop hike. The East Creek–Gift Creek Trail also connects with the Avalanche Creek Trail. Climbing 4,400 feet in 8 miles, this route is considered one of the most difficult in the wilderness and is seldom used. It begins at a trailhead just northeast of the small town of Redstone off Colorado Highway 133.

Also taking off from Redstone is the Lily Lake Trail, a 10-mile route that is quite popular with horsepackers. Heading south from Redstone, this trail crosses several drainages before reaching Lily Lake on the road to Marble. Because of these traverses, more than one climb should be anticipated. Although the uphill grade change totals about 3,000 feet, the highest point is only 10,300 feet, making it a trail of only moderate difficulty.

Cross-country Skiing

Because most approach roads are not regularly plowed, backcountry skiing in the Maroon Bells–Snowmass Wilderness usually means an overnight excursion. You can ski 9 miles on Maroon Creek Road to Maroon Lake and enter the wilderness from there. More practical access points are found up Castle Creek Road, which is plowed to Ashcroft. The start of the Conundrum Creek Trail is along this road, as is the trail to

Cathedral Lake. To get to the Cathedral Lake trailhead, you must ski about 1 mile beyond Ashcroft on Castle Creek Road. Because of steep slopes and heavy snow accumulations, the avalanche threat is great throughout the Maroon Bells–Snowmass. Use extreme caution.

Mountaineering

With six "fourteeners" among its ranks, the Maroon Bells–Snowmass Wilderness has long lured climbers. But because the weather can change suddenly and because many of its peaks consist of rotting and crumbling rock, that lure has often proved deadly.

For all their beauty, Maroon Peak (14,156 feet) and North Maroon Peak (14,014 feet) have earned the nickname Deadly Bells. To tackle these two difficult summits, climbers usually begin from Maroon Lake and follow the trail that heads toward Buckskin Pass for 0.5 mile before turning south up a prominent gully. The route crosses beneath the north face of North Maroon Peak before following a series of couloirs and ledges to the summit of North Maroon Peak. A slow traverse to the higher Maroon Peak is possible with a return route down the south ridge. Ropes and helmets are recommended as loose rock and exposure abound throughout the climb. Be observant of both the weather and the timing of your climb.

Pyramid Peak (14,018 feet) is another very difficult climb, probably more so than the Maroon Bells. Like the Bells, it is reached from Maroon Lake via the trail into Crater Lake. About halfway to the lake, turn south up a prominent couloir that climbs the peak's north face. This route is quite exact and any wrong turn cannot be compensated for later. After reaching a large amphitheater, the route splits to contour up either the west or east ridge. Both routes involve following ledges and some exposed drop-offs. First-time visitors should check locally for an exact description of the routes or, better yet, climb with someone who knows the way.

In the western end of the wilderness, Capitol Peak (14,130 feet) can be approached from either Snowmass Lake or Capitol Lake on the Capitol Creek Trail. The climb from the Snowmass Lake Trail involves conquering a knife-edge ridge of uncommonly solid rock. The ascent from Capitol Lake is similarly technical and exposed in places. Both are considered difficult. Check in Aspen for specific routes.

Climbing Snowmass Mountain (14,092 feet) requires an approach walk of 8.5 miles. It is, in fact, the most remote of all of Colorado "fourteeners." From Snowmass Lake the accepted route continues around the southeast shore of the lake and then climbs up a steep basin that is covered with snow until late in the summer. It gains the rugged southeast ridge before finally topping out at the summit. Some scrambling over rock is required, but it is mostly sound. Nearby Hagerman Peak (13,841 feet) also offers skilled climbers several challenging routes.

The highest summit in the Maroon Bells–Snowmass area, Castle Peak (14,265 feet) is a relatively easy walk-up from Montezuma Basin. Two routes are possible, one through a bowl and over Conundrum Peak and the other up the northeast ridge of Castle Peak itself.

Though under 14,000 feet, other summits also provide climbers with a variety of challenges and rewards. Cathedral Peak (13,943 feet), which sits above Cathedral Lake, is a bit of a scramble, as is Hayden Peak (13,561 feet). On the Gunnison National Forest side of the wilderness, Teocalli Mountain (13,208 feet) is usually climbed from the Twin Lakes Trail. It was named for its resemblance to the Aztec pyramid. White Rock Mountain (13,500 feet) is climbed from the Copper Creek Trail out of Gothic.

Mount Sopris (12,823 feet), the prominent summit overlooking the town of Carbondale, can be attempted from Dingle Lake Picnic Ground a couple of miles north of the wilderness boundary. The trail climbs to Thomas Lakes and to timberline beyond.

Raggeds Wilderness Area

Location: 11 mi W of Crested Butte
Size: 65,019 acres
Status: Wilderness area (1980)
Terrain: Alpine peaks and forested lower slopes
Elevation: 8,000' to 13,528'
Management: Gunnison NF, White River NF
Topographic maps: Snowmass Mountain, Marble, Chair Mountain, Marcellina Mountain, Oh-Be-Joyful, Paonia Reservoir

Separated from the West Elk Wilderness to the south by Kebler Pass Road, and from Maroon Bells–Snowmass by a 4WD route over Schofield Pass to the north, this smaller wilderness fills a void in the rugged and beautiful west end of the Elk Range. Although few in number, trails in the Raggeds offer outstanding scenery. Established in 1980, the original wilderness boundary was pushed eastward toward Gunsight Pass when the Oh-Be-Joyful area was added as part of the Colorado Wilderness Act of 1993.

Seasons
Usually arriving by mid- to late October, winter snows render trails impassable until late June or July. Watch for almost daily thunderstorms in the summer. Wildflowers bloom in July and early August; September brings on the elk rutting season and the spectacular turning of aspen stands in the area.

Flora and Fauna
The lowest elevations in the Raggeds mostly feature stands of aspen and Douglas fir. Engelmann spruce and subalpine fir forests become more common above 9,500 feet. Above timberline, which starts around the 11,500-foot mark, stretches of alpine tundra alternate with rocky ridges and summits. Among the fauna that reside in this wilderness

are elk, mule deer, bobcats, coyotes, mountain lions, bighorn sheep, and, thanks to a transplant program in the 1970s, mountain goats.

Geology

As part of the Elk Range, the Raggeds consist mostly of uplifted sedimentary and metamorphic rock. The Ruby Range, a small chain of mountains along the eastern edge of the wilderness, offers an example of the colorful Maroon Formation. Laid down during the Paleozoic era, the Maroon Formation consists of sand and mud tinted red by traces of iron. Ragged Mountain and other summits in the western portion of the wilderness consist mostly of sedimentary rock.

Whitehouse Mountain, on the northern flank of the wilderness, yields fine white marble. Stone from a nearby quarry was used to build the Lincoln Memorial and the Tomb of the Unknown Soldier. But the quarry was closed in 1940 because it was too far from the markets. A smaller operation opened up in recent years.

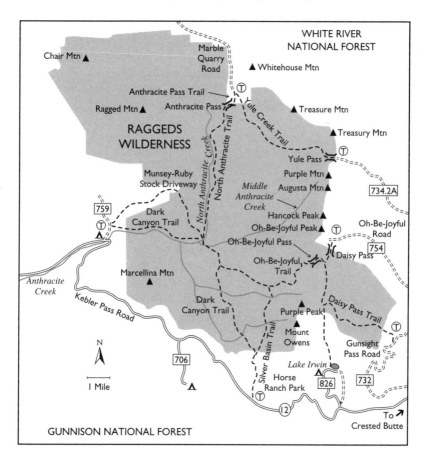

ACTIVITIES
Hiking

Although most trails within the Raggeds begin on the Gunnison National Forest side, a few start within the White River National Forest in the vicinity of Marble. Two routes begin 2.75 miles up the 4WD Marble Quarry Road, which is best walked because parking is limited beyond the old marble mill site. The Yule Creek Trail begins 0.25 mile before the quarry and travels 5.5 miles to 11,700-foot Yule Pass on the eastern boundary of the wilderness. A gradual climb from 9,000 feet and a tricky stream crossing along the way make this a moderately difficult hike.

The Anthracite Pass Trail also begins 0.25 mile before the quarry but climbs steeply for 1 mile to Anthracite Pass, which is more than 10,000 feet in elevation. Just inside the wilderness, the North Anthracite Trail accesses Anthracite Pass from the south. From Anthracite Pass this route drops down North Anthracite Creek for 6.4 miles to where it meets Middle Anthracite Creek. At this point the trail encounters the Dark Canyon Trail, which crosses the Raggeds Wilderness.

Sixteen miles long, the Dark Canyon Trail offers good access to the heart of the area. Beginning near the Erickson Springs Campground on the western edge of the wilderness, the route first follows Anthracite Creek through a steep-walled canyon where the fishing is good and waterfalls add to the scenery. Five miles in, the North Anthracite Trail is reached. An alternate trail to this point is the 6.7-mile Munsey–Ruby Stock Driveway. Although it begins near the start of the Dark Canyon Trail, it instead cuts northeast over Lightning Ridge. Receiving little use, this route is difficult to follow and grade changes are very steep in places. Upon reaching the North Anthracite Trail junction, the Dark Canyon Trail then climbs to the Devils Stairway, a series of switchbacks that gain 1,200 feet in less than a mile. The trail tops out on a plateau between drainages before dropping to Horse Ranch Park on the Kebler Pass Road. Plan on taking 2 or 3 days to complete the entire Dark Canyon Trail.

The Silver Basin Trail begins and ends along the Dark Canyon Trail, offering the possibility of a loop hike. Beginning 2 miles north of Horse Ranch Park, the Silver Basin Trail covers 5.4 miles before reconnecting with the Dark Canyon Trail above the Devils Stairway. Extending along the base of the Ruby Range, this route is very scenic. Near the halfway point, it connects with the western end of the Oh-Be-Joyful Trail, which crosses the Ruby Range via 11,740-foot Oh-Be-Joyful Pass. At its eastern end, the Oh-Be-Joyful Trail meets the Daisy Pass Trail, an 11.4-mile route that runs north–south. Access to the Daisy Pass Trail is possible via Gunsight Pass Road (County Road 732), Oh-Be-Joyful Road (County Road 754), or Baxter Basin Road—all 4WD routes out of the Crested Butte area.

Cross-country Skiing

While skiing within the Raggeds Wilderness Area is possible, poor access makes it unfeasible for casual tours. The Dark Canyon Trail, which is accessible via plowed road, is extremely dangerous because of avalanches and should be avoided. Gentler terrain exists from Kebler Pass Road, but the road is not plowed and skiers must share the route with snowmobilers.

Mountaineering

The area's highest summit, Treasure Mountain (13,528 feet), and nearby Treasury Mountain (13,462 feet), both lie along the Raggeds' northeast boundary and are accessible from the Crystal area and from Yule Creek. Purple Mountain (12,958 feet) can easily be approached from Yule Pass.

Farther south along the Ruby Range several 12,000-foot summits offer a variety of climbs and a wealth of scenery. Augusta Mountain (12,559 feet) is climbed from the end of the Baxter Basin Road. Four peaks—Hancock Peak (12,410 feet), Oh-Be-Joyful Peak (12,400 feet), Afley Peak (12,646 feet), and Purple Peak (12,800 feet)—rise just to the south of Oh-Be-Joyful Pass. Ruby Peak (12,644 feet) and Mount Owens (13,058 feet) round out the southern end of the Ruby Range; they are reached via Lake Irwin, a few miles north of Kebler Pass.

In the northwestern reaches of the wilderness, Ragged Mountain (12,094 feet) and Chair Mountain (12,721 feet) top a rugged stretch of peaks. Access is from the road into Marble, but count on an overnight stay if you want to bag both summits.

29 West Elk Wilderness Area

Location: 8 mi SE of Crested Butte
Size: 176,092 acres
Status: Wilderness area (1964)
Terrain: Alpine peaks and forested lower slopes
Elevation: 7,000' to 13,035'
Management: Gunnison NF
Topographic maps: Minnesota Pass, West Beckwith Peak, Anthracite Range, Mount Axtell, Mount Guero, Big Soap Peak, West Elk Peak, Squirrel Creek, Little Soap Park, West Elk Peak SW, McIntosh Mountain

With more than 200 miles of hiking trails, the West Elk Wilderness is one of the larger wilderness areas in Colorado. It is the kind of place where you can hike for days on end without running out of backcountry. Several drainages allow passage for many of these routes, and high, rugged summits add to the lure. The West Elk also offers plenty of solitude thanks to few visitors.

Seasons

Snow-covered from October through June, the high country of the West Elk Wilderness does not open up until early July. Lower elevations may be accessible by the first

of June. Thunderstorms are a near-daily occurrence in the summer months; watch out for them on exposed terrain. Wildflowers bloom a week or two after the last snowbanks melt, usually in mid- or late July. Aspens take on the vivid hues in September, and the elk rutting season also occurs at this time.

Flora and Fauna

The lower elevations of the West Elk Wilderness are covered by pinyon pine and juniper, oak brush, mountain mahogany, serviceberry, and other shrubs. These areas offer valuable winter range for big game species such as mule deer and elk. Higher up, forests of Engelmann spruce and subalpine fir are typical, as are glades of aspen. Above timberline, around 11,500 feet, stretches of alpine tundra intermix with rock outcrops and boulder fields. Wildflowers include blue columbine, Indian paintbrush, and alpine sunflower.

In addition to deer and elk, the West Elks are home to bighorn sheep. Marmots and pikas reside above timberline and snowshoe hares inhabit the forested regions. Black bears, mountain lions, and coyotes also are sighted here.

Geology

The West Elk Mountains consist of a broad dome smothered with intrusive volcanic rock. Beginning 35 million years ago, volcanic activity deposited a layer of material thousands of feet thick over what are now the West Elk Mountains. An interesting by-product of this geologic activity is the West Elk Breccia, a series of stunning outcrops along the southern edge of the mountains. Consisting of coarse volcanic tuff, these formations have been eroded into dramatic spires and cliff faces to form the beautiful palisades that overlook the Blue Mesa Reservoir west of Gunnison.

ACTIVITIES
Hiking

A handy access point for the West Elk Wilderness is at the Lost Lake Campground off Kebler Pass Road to the north. Within its first 2.5 miles, the 10.5-mile Beckwith Pass Trail enters the wilderness and continues over its namesake before dropping into the headwaters of Cliff Creek. The trail eventually ends at an intersection with the Soap Creek Trail deep within the northern half of the wilderness.

Six miles in length, the Cliff Creek Trail also begins off Kebler Pass Road. It joins the Beckwith Pass Trail just outside the wilderness. About 2 miles farther is the Lowline Trail, which departs from the Beckwith Pass Trail for Swampy Pass. On top of 10,200-foot Swampy Pass, the Lowline branches to become the Swampy Pass Trail, which runs 6 miles to Ohio Creek Road. Although elevations along the Beckwith Pass, Lowline, and Swampy Pass Trails are not very high, panoramas often open up thanks to subalpine meadows.

Opposite: *The Castles*

The Castle Pass Trail crosses over 11,057-foot Castle Pass as it follows a 5.5-mile route from the Cliff Creek Trail to the end of Castle Creek Road. Because this road is closed to the public, access to the trail's eastern end is gained by hiking to Swampy Pass and then following a 3-mile southern extension of the Lowline Trail.

The Little Robinson Trail begins at the end of Coal Creek Road to the north and runs south for 4.6 miles. It in turn connects with the Soap Creek Trail, which follows its namesake drainage south to Big Soap Park at the end of 4WD Soap Creek Road. These two routes follow streams most of the way, completing a 15-mile traverse of the wilderness that is easy to moderate in difficulty. The Soap Basin Trail offers an alternate route to part of the Soap Creek Trail. Branching eastward 1 mile inside the wilderness, the Soap Basin Trail joins back up with the Soap Creek Trail 7 miles later.

The Coal Mesa Trail, which is a little more than 14 miles long, begins at the Soap

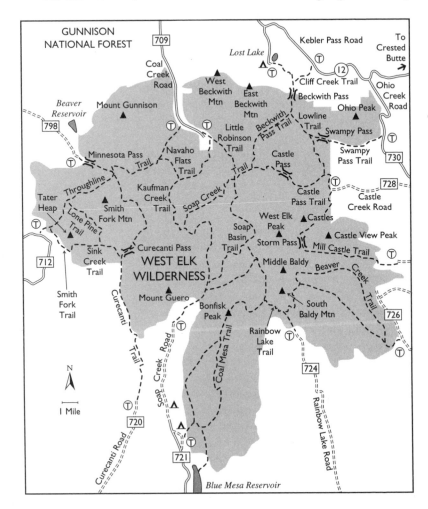

Creek Campground at an elevation of 7,740 feet and runs up a southern extension of the wilderness, topping Bonfisk Peak (11,629 feet) before descending into the West Elk Creek drainage. While following West Elk Creek, the Coal Mesa route picks up the end of the 4.5-mile Rainbow Lake Trail, which begins at the end of Rainbow Lake Road.

The 11-mile Beaver Creek Trail heads north and then east from the Rainbow Lake Trail to eventually connect with the Mill Creek Road outside the wilderness, skirting east of South Baldy (12,380 feet) and Middle Baldy (12,598 feet) Mountains in the process.

The 14.3-mile Mill Castle Trail begins at the end of Mill Creek Road. Heading west along Mill Creek, it then cuts north over 12,460-foot Storm Pass before reaching Castle Creek Road, which is closed to the public. Siding up to North Baldy Mountain (12,850 feet) and West Elk Peak (13,035 feet), this scenic trail meets the Castle Pass and Lowline Trails in the vicinity of Castle Creek Road, making possible several long-distance hikes of 4 days or more. The best trailheads for such an adventure are at the end of Mill Creek Road or at the start of the Cliff Creek Trail on Kebler Pass Road.

Another network of trails in the western half of the wilderness also allows for several long-distance treks. The Kaufman Creek Trail branches off the Little Robinson Trail near its end at Coal Creek Road. Eight miles long, this route climbs from 7,800 feet to nearly 11,000 feet on Kaufman Ridge. The views are nice, as open parks are plentiful. The trail's southern end is along the Soap Creek Trail.

Also beginning on Coal Creek Road is the 13-mile Throughline Trail. While not a particularly high trail (elevations range from 7,200 feet to just over 9,000 feet), this trail offers vistas of surrounding summits and good fishing in the creeks it encounters. From Coal Creek Road, the Throughline travels southwest to meet the road up Smith Fork east of Crawford. The 2.6-mile Navaho Flats Trail offers a little-used connector between the Throughline and Kaufman Creek Trails. With a shuttle, hiking the length of the Throughline Trail makes a nice 2- or 3-day trek. Several trails intersect the route, adding to the options. About halfway in, the Throughline intersects the 22-mile-long Curecanti Trail. Beginning at Beaver Reservoir southeast of Paonia, the Curecanti route cuts south across the entire western end of the West Elk Wilderness to finally end on Curecanti Road, accessing some good fishing streams and crossing Minnesota (9,993 feet) and Curecanti (10,400 feet) Passes along the way. Just south of Curecanti Pass, the 6.6-mile Sink Creek Trail takes off toward the west to eventually reach the wilderness boundary. The Lone Pine Trail branches from Sink Creek and eventually meets the Smith Fork Trail along the western boundary of the wilderness. Because the Smith Fork connects with the western end of the Throughline Trail, you can make a loop hike by following the Curecanti Trail to the Throughline Trail, and then heading south again via either the Lone Pine or Smith Fork–Sink Creek routes.

Cross-country Skiing

Because wintertime access to the West Elk Wilderness is very limited, the opportunities for single-day ski tours are nonexistent. No roads are plowed to the boundary in the western and eastern reaches of the wilderness. Similarly, the road to Kebler Pass is not plowed.

Mountaineering

The West Elk Wilderness offers quite a few attractive peaks, but access often requires lengthy hikes along a network of trails. Ohio Peak (12,271 feet), the high point of a ridge line known as the Anthracite Range, is one summit that is less than 3 miles from Kebler Pass Road. There is no trail; instead make your way cross-country to the summit. Other peaks relatively close to Kebler Pass Road include West Beckwith Mountain (12,185 feet) and East Beckwith Mountain (12,432 feet). Both are on the ridge that runs west from Beckwith Pass.

Farther south in the vicinity of Castle and Mill Creeks rise the best-known summits within the West Elks. West Elk Peak (13,035 feet), the highest point in the range, is reached via the Mill Castle Trail. The nearby Castles—a group of spires of volcanic rock around 12,000 feet in elevation—pose technical challenges that only skilled climbers should tackle. They do offer a fine backdrop for those climbing Castle View Peak (12,544 feet) to the south. High summits that are reached from the Beaver Creek and Rainbow Lake Trails include South Baldy Mountain (12,380 feet), Middle Baldy Mountain (12,598 feet), another Middle Baldy (12,709 feet), and North Baldy Mountain (12,850 feet). The panoramas from all of these summits are breathtaking.

In the western half of the wilderness climbers will find the likes of Mount Gunnison (12,719 feet), which is usually approached by a bushwhack up Hoodoo Creek from the Beaver Reservoir area. Smith Fork Mountain (11,230 feet) lies between the Throughline and Curecanti trails. The Tater Heap (10,984 feet) is accessible from the Lone Pine Trail and Mount Guero (12,052 feet) is about 1 mile off the Sink Creek Trail.

Opposite: *Alpine scenery near San Luis Pass*

chapter 3 **Southern Mountains**

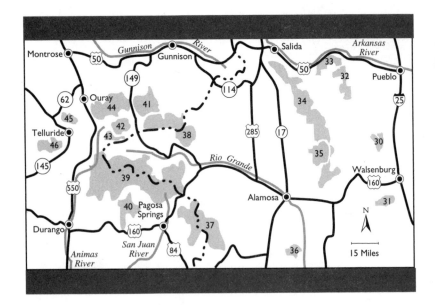

Characterized by sweeping valleys and scattered snowcapped ranges, Colorado's southern mountains region is dominated by the San Juan Mountains—not only the most extensive range in the U.S. Rockies but also the highest assemblage of peaks in North America with a mean elevation of 10,400 feet. The region includes the state's largest wilderness area, the Weminuche at nearly a half million acres. Smaller wilderness areas in the San Juans include the South San Juan, Uncompahgre, La Garita, Mount Sneffels, and Lizard Head areas. The Colorado Wilderness Act of 1993 added the Powderhorn Wilderness and the Piedra Area to the list. Additionally, two BLM wilderness study areas include the Redcloud Peak and Handies Peak areas.

Stretching east from the San Juans is the San Luis Valley, which includes Great Sand Dunes National Monument and Preserve. The lofty spine of the Sangre de Cristo Range provides an immediate backdrop to the park's 700-foot dunes. An elongated wilderness encompasses most of the Sangre de Cristos. Dotting the southern end of the San Luis Valley is the BLM's San Luis Hills WSA.

Three BLM wilderness study areas clustered just south of the Arkansas River—McIntyre Hills, Upper Grape Creek, and Lower Grape Creek—encompass rugged canyon areas south of the Arkansas River Gorge near Cañon City. The Greenhorn Mountain Wilderness is found within the last ripple of mountains before the plains begin. And the Spanish Peaks Wilderness is the region's newest inductee into its impressive docket of federally protected wildlands. A bill signed by President Bill Clinton and endorsed by the state's congressional delegation established an 18,000-acre wilderness among the impressive twin summits.

Location: 20 mi SW of Pueblo
Size: 22,040 acres
Status: Wilderness area (1993)
Terrain: Mountains and steep canyons
Elevation: 7,600' to 12,367'
Management: San Isabel NF
Topographic maps: San Isabel, Rye, Badito Cone, Hayden Butte

The Greenhorn Mountain Wilderness Area covers the southern end of the Wet Mountain Range. The high point of the Wet Mountains, Greenhorn's 12,367-foot summit rises above timberline. From there, rugged canyons fall away to the high plains stretching in from the east. Views from the top include the Sangre de Cristo Mountains to the west and the start of the Great Plains to the east.

Seasons

Many trails in this area are clear of snow by June and usually remain so until late October. Lightning storms often crop up on summer afternoons. Wildflowers bloom during June, July, and August.

Flora and Fauna

Forests within the Greenhorn Mountain Wilderness include stands of pinyon pine, ponderosa pine, aspen, Engelmann spruce, and subalpine fir. Alpine tundra is found in the highest reaches of Greenhorn Mountain. Important tracts of winter range for mule deer, elk, and bighorn sheep are found within the area, and a stretch of South Apache Creek is home to the threatened greenback cutthroat trout.

Geology

Like most of the Wet Range, Greenhorn Mountain consists of Precambrian granite. The block was pushed up as a faulted anticline during the Laramide Orogeny. Similar to the Front Range, the Wet Mountains dive into the plains along their eastern facade, but instead of trending north–south, they run northwest to southeast.

ACTIVITIES
Hiking

A few trails penetrate the Greenhorn Mountain Wilderness, and a Forest Service road approaches the top of Greenhorn Mountain itself. The road is reached by driving Greenhorn Mountain Road (Forest Road 403) in from the Ophir Campground. The last 2 miles are closed to vehicles.

Greenhorn Mountain Wilderness

Beginning from a trailhead 1.5 miles south of Rye on Forest Road 427, the 5.5-mile Bartlett Trail climbs from 7,720 to 11,660 feet. This hike is difficult, especially in the summer when it can be hot and dry. The Bartlett Trail ends on the closed road near the top of Greenhorn Mountain. The South Apache Trail branches off from the Bartlett Trail and drops eastward down South Apache Creek. Because the South Apache Trail ends at private land, the trailhead can not be accessed from below.

The Greenhorn Trail begins at the western end of Rye and climbs 9.5 miles to Greenhorn Mountain Road. Following Greenhorn Creek for a ways, the route then enters the wilderness before topping out at 12,050 feet. This hike climbs nearly 5,000 feet in all, making it a real grind.

The Santana Trail ascends Greenhorn Mountain from the west. Six miles long, this route begins at 8,200 feet and ends at the 11,600-foot level, where it joins the Bartlett Trail 0.5 mile from the end of the closed Greenhorn Mountain Road.

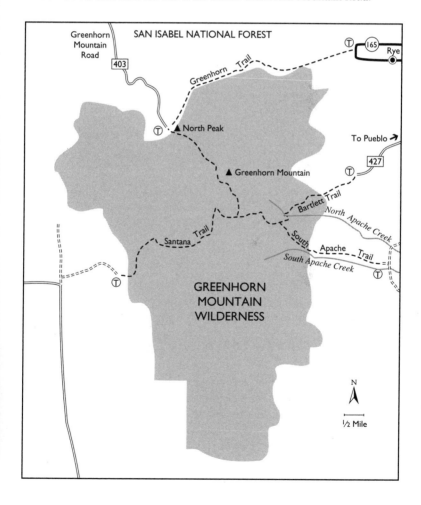

31 Spanish Peaks Wilderness Area

Location: 10 mi S of La Veta
Size: 18,000 acres
Status: Wilderness area (2000)
Terrain: Mountains and steep canyons
Elevation: 8,400' to 13,626'
Management: San Isabel NF
Topographic maps: Cuchara, Cucharas Pass, Spanish Peaks, Herlick Canyon

The Spanish Peaks rise as twin sentinels above the edge of the high plains. Volcanic in origin, these 12,000- and 13,000-foot peaks are strikingly steep and picturesque. The Indians called them *Huajatolla* or "Breasts of the World." Early Spanish explorers used them as easily identifiable landmarks marking the northern frontier of their American conquest. This newest of Colorado's wilderness areas is small, but the promise of enjoying a fair amount of solitude and grand vistas at nearly every turn makes it an ideal destination for hikers. Drawing support from the state's congressional delegation, President Bill Clinton signed a bill establishing the wilderness in November 2000.

Seasons

Trails in the Spanish Peaks Wilderness are usually snow free from late June or early July into October. Wildflowers offer trailside treats during the summer months, as do the colorful aspen leaves in the fall. Watch for lightning on most summer afternoons and for sudden changes in the weather at any time of the year.

Flora and Fauna

Stands of pinyon pine and ponderosa pine, as well as Douglas fir, are common in the lower elevations. In the higher elevations expect to find mostly Engelmann spruce, subalpine fir, and aspen. Ancient bristlecone pines grow along timberline locations. The Spanish Peaks provide critical habitat for bighorn sheep, elk, and mule deer.

Geology

Formed as a volcanic intrusion in sedimentary rock, the Spanish Peaks include hundreds of volcanic dikes that radiate out from the summits themselves. These knife blade formations formed when molten rock filled fissures in the surrounding strata, and then cooled. The sedimentary rock has since eroded away. These mountains are so unique they were added to the National Register of Natural Landmarks in 1977.

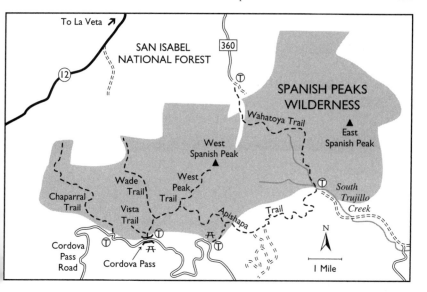

ACTIVITIES
Hiking

A number of short trails and one longer route are found within the Spanish Peaks Wilderness. Most are accessible from Cordova Pass Road, an improved gravel road over 11,005-foot Cordova Pass.

The Chaparral Trail begins a mile west of Cordova Pass and travels 3.5 miles before reaching a dead end at private property on the range's north slope.

A developed trailhead with a fee for parking is located at Cordova Pass. From here the 2.5-mile West Peak Trail sets off to climb West Spanish Peak, the taller of the two peaks. Steep and rocky, especially above timberline, this is one of the most scenic hikes to be found in the state. The 0.75-mile, handicapped-accessible Vista Trail branches off of the West Peak Trail 0.25 mile from the trailhead. As its name suggests, the Vista Trail proffers an overview of the Cucharas River Valley to the north. The Wade Trail also branches off of the West Peak Trail to dead end at some private property 3.5 miles from the start.

Farther east on the Cordova Pass Road, the 3-mile Apishapa Trail starts at the Apishapa Creek Picnic Ground. It climbs 1,200 feet to meet the West Peak Trail above. The considerably longer Wahatoya Trail branches off the Apishapa Trail 1.5 miles north of the trailhead. The Wahatoya Trail continues east to traverse the South Trujillo Creek drainage. It then turns north to top the 10,350-foot saddle between West and East Spanish Peaks. From this high point it drops to the Wahatoya Creek Road (County Road 360). It is more than 14 miles from the Apishapa Creek Picnic Ground to the northern end of the Wahatoya Trail.

Mountaineering

As mentioned above, the 2.5-mile West Peak Trail climbs the taller West Spanish Peak. East Spanish Peak (12,683 feet) is reached via a ridge from the 10,350-foot saddle on the Wahatoya Trail.

Grape Creek Wilderness Study Area

Location: 17 mi SW of Cañon City
Size: 21,525 acres
Status: Wilderness study area (1978)
Terrain: Deep canyons and forested ridges
Elevation: 6,400' to 8,200'
Management: BLM (Royal Gorge Field Office)
Topographic maps: McIntyre Hills, Curley Peak, Royal Gorge, Iron Mountain, Westcliffe, Mount Tyndall

There are actually two Grape Creek Wilderness Study Areas (WSAs): 11,295-acre Lower Grape Creek WSA and 10,230-acre Upper Grape Creek WSA. They are separated in part by County Road 143. Embracing their namesake drainage, these WSAs provide a wonderful look at a lengthy and rugged canyon system within the Front Range. Such pristine drainages are a rarity in this part of the state, and hiking in Grape Creek's envi-

Grape Creek is a beautiful waterway throughout.

rons is a real treat. The delight of visiting this 12-mile corridor is further enhanced by an old narrow-gauge railroad grade, which now serves as an ideal hiking route.

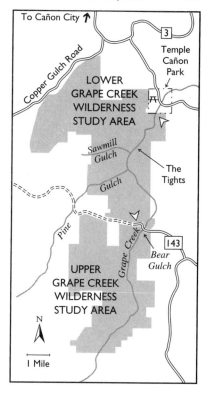

Seasons

Snow occasionally falls within the lower reaches of the Grape Creek drainage, but it rarely accumulates. Additionally, while summertime temperatures at these lower elevations may seem hot, especially when compared with mountainous reaches of Colorado, the canyon bottom is cooled a bit by the perennial flow of Grape Creek itself. Access to upper elevations of the WSA is typically blocked by snow from November to May.

Flora and Fauna

Given its pristine character and impressive selection of ecosystems, the Grape Creek WSA offers a wonderful blend of flora and fauna. Hikers will enjoy the fine riparian ecosystem found along Grape Creek itself. Forests of pinyon pine and juniper are plentiful beyond the confines of the canyon bottom, and higher reaches are dominated by stands of ponderosa pine, Douglas fir, and Colorado blue spruce. Aspen glades are also found in places. Wildlife includes mule deer, elk, black bears, and a sizeable number of mountain lions. Grape Creek supports a thriving trout population.

Geology

Exposed rock within Grape Creek drainage is mostly Precambrian gneiss and schist. This rock was once part of an ancestral highland known as Frontrangia.

History

A narrow-gauge railroad was constructed in 1881 to serve Westcliffe and the surrounding mines. It ran the length of the Grape Creek drainage, but the route was long ago cleared of rails, ties, and other rubble to form a broad trail.

ACTIVITIES
Hiking

Many hikers visiting the Grape Creek WSA take advantage of the old railroad bed. From Temple Cañon Park it is possible to follow the path or the canyon bottom upstream for

12 miles to the WSA's southern end. The Tights is an interesting feature found a few miles in. This is a stretch of the drainage that narrows down considerably before opening up where Sawmill Gulch drains in from the west. Upstream from Sawmill Gulch, other drainages add to the hike possibilities. Temple Cañon Park can be reached by turning on County Road 3 (the road to Royal Gorge) from U.S. Highway 50 and continuing 7 miles south.

Separating Upper and Lower Grape Creek WSAs, County Road 143 provides ready access to the middle portion of the Grape Creek drainage. Dropping down Bear Gulch, this graded 2WD road is closed at Grape Creek itself. As with the lower portion of the drainage, hiking is easy here when following the canyon bottom, and a number of side drainages only add to the exploration possibilities. The Bear Gulch access is 14 miles south of Cañon City.

33 McIntyre Hills Wilderness Study Area

Location: 12 mi W of Cañon City
Size: 17,210 acres
Status: Wilderness study area (1978)
Terrain: Forested ridges, summits and canyons
Elevation: 5,900' to 8,100'
Management: BLM (Royal Gorge Field Office)
Topographic maps: McIntyre Hills, Echo, Hillside

Siding up to U.S. Highway 50 in the Arkansas River Gorge west of Cañon City, the McIntyre Hills Wilderness Study Area (WSA) includes a broken topography typified by rugged canyons and forested uplands. No established trails exist in the area but drainage bottoms do offer possible hiking routes.

Seasons

Generally snow-free, the McIntyre Hills WSA is usually accessible throughout the year. Winter does bring some snow, but it mostly melts off quite quickly. Shaded canyon bottoms offer protection from the heat of summer afternoons.

Flora and Fauna

Lower elevation forests include pinyon pines and junipers, while ponderosa pines and Douglas firs are common higher up. Gambel oak is also plentiful. Cottonwoods and willows lend a verdant touch to riparian areas along drainage bottoms. Mule deer live here year-round. Bighorn sheep have been transplanted to the area, which is also prime habitat for black bears and numerous mountain lions.

Opposite: *Five Point Gulch is a rugged drainage.*

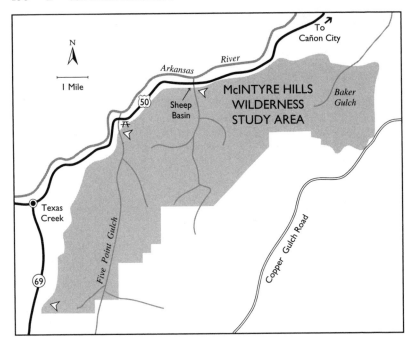

Geology

Thanks to the erosive powers of the Arkansas River, numerous rock outcrops characterize the northern front of the WSA. These faces include Precambrian granite, gneiss, and schist.

ACTIVITIES

Hiking

No trails exist in the McIntyre Hills WSA, but a handful of drainage bottoms are easily accessible thanks to its close proximity to U.S. Highway 50. Five Point Gulch offers the best access. It starts from the Five Point Recreation Site 4 miles northeast of Texas Creek along U.S. Highway 50. A use fee is charged. Heading south, Five Point Gulch penetrates the heart of the WSA for several miles. The canyon bottom is a bit rough in places but wholly passable. Shady cottonwoods add to the pleasure of the route.

Another drainage heads south from the highway about 2 miles east of Five Point at Sheep Basin. Still farther east is Baker Gulch, which dissects the eastern portion of the WSA. Not as lengthy as Five Point Gulch, these two drainages are steeper and more rugged.

Access to the western end of the McIntyre Hills WSA is possible along State Highway 69 (the Texas Creek Road) about 2 miles south of its intersection with U.S. Highway 50. But, because no obvious hiking routes exist here, expect the going to be strictly rugged cross-country travel.

34 Sangre de Cristo Wilderness Area

Location: 8 mi S of Salida
Size: 226,455 acres
Status: Wilderness area (1993)
Terrain: Rugged peaks and ridges
Elevation: 8,200' to 14,345'
Management: Rio Grande NF, San Isabel NF
Topographic maps: Wellsville, Howard, Bushnell Peak, Coaldale, Cotopaxi, Electric Peak, Beckwith Mountain, Horn Peak, Crestone Peak, Beck Mountain, Medano Pass, Mosca Pass, Red Wing, Blanca Peak

Like the mountain range it encompasses, the Sangre de Cristo Wilderness Area is long and narrow, some 70 miles from end to end and varying in width from 2 to 10 miles. Despite its unusual dimensions, however, this is a premier section of the wilderness system. Spectacular mountains rise as much as 7,000 feet above the valley floor. Eight summits top 14,000 feet, while several others are slightly lower. Alpine lakes nestle in this high terrain, and a variety of wildlife makes a home in these mountains.

Seasons
The summer hiking season in the Sangre de Cristo Mountains usually begins by June in the lower elevations and in early or mid-July up high. Summer showers almost always include lightning. Conditions can turn cold and nasty in a very short time. Wildflowers in late July and August add to the spectacle of this stunning mountain terrain. Scattered patches of aspen change color in September. Winter arrives in force by mid- or late October.

Flora and Fauna
Ponderosa pines are scattered across the slopes of the Sangre de Cristo Mountains. Lower elevations host thick stands of lodgepole pines and aspen, while Engelmann spruce and subalpine fir are found higher up. Bristlecone pines are also present. Alpine tundra covers most of the range's crest. Mule deer, elk, and bighorn sheep inhabit the Sangre de Cristos, as do pine martens, coyotes, black bears, mountain lions, marmots, and pikas.

Geology
Like other Colorado ranges, the Sangre de Cristos are a faulted block range, formed when an elongated block of substrata was pushed upward along adjacent faults. Parts of the range, however, consist of sedimentary rocks such as sandstone, shale, and

Rugged peaks above the North Crestone Trail

fossil-bearing limestone. Not metamorphosed, these formations have been considerably folded and faulted. The northern end of the range features some Precambrian granite and metamorphic rocks. Blanca Peak at the southern tip is made of granite. Although uplifting began during the Laramide Orogeny, the range continued to rise well into the Pliocene epoch, less than 10 million years ago. Some evidence such as triangular facets at the base of the range suggests that it may be still rising even today. Signs of glaciation, including U-shaped valleys, cirques, and glacially carved lakes, abound in the upper reaches.

History

The name Sangre de Cristo, Spanish for "Blood of Christ," refers to the deep red hue that the mountains sometimes take on at dusk. Spanish missionaries and settlers moved into the nearby San Luis Valley in the early eighteenth century. Remains of stone fortresses built by the early Spaniards have been found near the Crestone Needle. In the 1850s an American expedition found a skeleton dressed in Spanish armor in Sangre de Cristo Cave.

ACTIVITIES
Hiking

Trails in and about the Sangre de Cristo Wilderness mostly reflect the rugged stature of the mountains. No trail follows the crest of the range for very far, but some parallel it along the slopes below. Several rugged 4WD tracks reach the top of the range, severing the wilderness area into four parcels, and many trails follow drainages to their headwaters along the mountain crests. Trail administration falls into the jurisdiction of the Rio Grande National Forest on the west slope and the San Isabel National Forest to the east.

The 100-mile-long Rainbow Trail runs adjacent to the northeastern boundary of the Sangre de Cristo Wilderness. The Rainbow, which dates to the beginning of the 1900s, is so named for the crescent it forms as it runs southeast between the Salida area and Music Pass. This trail was excluded from the wilderness area because it is popular with motorized trail users. Nevertheless, it offers fine backpacking opportunities, and many trails that enter the wilderness from this side are reached via the Rainbow.

When following the Rainbow Trail, remember that the trail drops in and out of drainages for its entire length. Elevations typically vacillate between 7,500 and 9,500 feet along all stretches of the trail. The trail does not top 10,000 feet, however, which makes these grades more manageable. From the trailhead at Bear Creek near the northern end of the wilderness area, the Rainbow covers 12 miles to the next access point at Stout Creek. About midway, a 3-mile trail climbs up to Hunts Lake inside the wilderness. Stout Creek ushers a 4-mile trail to Stout Creek Lakes just shy of the range crest. The Stout Creek trailhead lies at the end of Kerr Gulch Road.

From Stout Creek it is 5 miles via the Rainbow Trail to the vicinity of the Hayden Creek Campground. A little more than 2 miles south from Stout Creek, a side trail climbs to Bushnell Lakes. From the Hayden Creek Campground, a 4WD road climbs

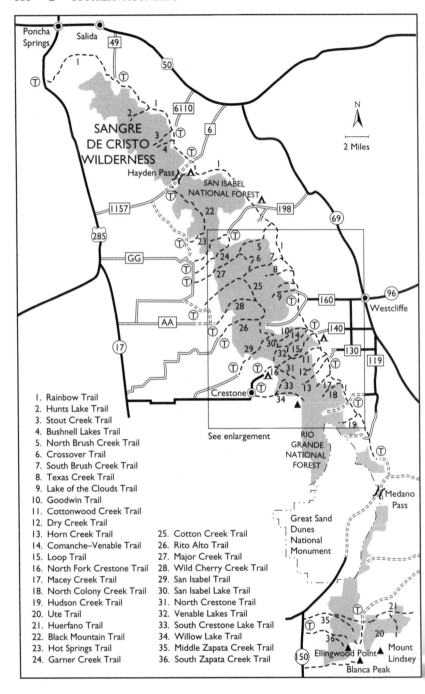

1. Rainbow Trail
2. Hunts Lake Trail
3. Stout Creek Trail
4. Bushnell Lakes Trail
5. North Brush Creek Trail
6. Crossover Trail
7. South Brush Creek Trail
8. Texas Creek Trail
9. Lake of the Clouds Trail
10. Goodwin Trail
11. Cottonwood Creek Trail
12. Dry Creek Trail
13. Horn Creek Trail
14. Comanche–Venable Trail
15. Loop Trail
16. North Fork Crestone Trail
17. Macey Creek Trail
18. North Colony Creek Trail
19. Hudson Creek Trail
20. Ute Trail
21. Huerfano Trail
22. Black Mountain Trail
23. Hot Springs Trail
24. Garner Creek Trail
25. Cotton Creek Trail
26. Rito Alto Trail
27. Major Creek Trail
28. Wild Cherry Creek Trail
29. San Isabel Trail
30. San Isabel Lake Trail
31. North Crestone Trail
32. Venable Lakes Trail
33. South Crestone Lake Trail
34. Willow Lake Trail
35. Middle Zapata Creek Trail
36. South Zapata Creek Trail

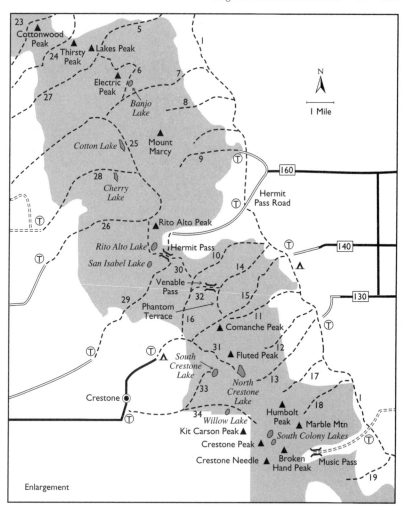

to Hayden Pass (10,709 feet) before dropping down the other side. This motorized route severs the northern quarter of the wilderness from the rest.

From Hayden Creek to Big Cottonwood Creek is 8.5 miles along the Rainbow; another 7 miles brings you to Lake Creek. A 4WD road that climbs Lake Creek pushes the wilderness boundary all the way to the crest of the range. After another 5 miles south, the Rainbow Trail crosses North Brush Creek. From here, the North Brush Creek Trail climbs to the Brush Creek Lakes and an intersection with the Crossover Trail. The Crossover Trail skirts the high peaks south of the lakes and continues southward to Banjo Lake at the foot of Electric Peak. Just south of Banjo Lake, this high route connects with the South Brush Creek Trail near the crest. The South Brush Creek route drops 6 miles back down to the

Rainbow Trail. It also crosses a 12,820-foot saddle into Horsethief Basin on the Rio Grande National Forest side. Following the North Brush Creek, Crossover, South Brush Creek, and Rainbow Trails makes a nice 2- or 3-day hike totaling 20 miles.

From South Brush Creek, the Rainbow Trail continues southeast for another 9 miles before crossing Hermit Pass Road at Middle Taylor Creek. Two trails in this stretch—the Texas Creek and Lake of the Clouds—each climb about 4 miles into the higher reaches of the range. Hermit Pass Road forces another incongruity in the wilderness boundary.

A number of short in-and-out trails are found along the 7.5-mile stretch of the Rainbow Trail between Hermit Pass Road and Horn Creek. One allows access to the west slope of the range. Among the routes that do not cross the range are the Goodwin, Cottonwood Creek, Dry Creek, and Horn Creek Trails. Typically, these trails are less than 5 miles in length, but the climbs are formidable. Beginning at the Alvarado Campground 8 miles southwest of Westcliffe, the Comanche–Venable Trail climbs along Venable Creek to Venable Pass. From there it traverses the Phantom Terrace for 1 mile before dropping back down to the campground. This route connects with two trails on the Rio Grande National Forest side of the range: the Loop Trail near Comanche Peak and the North Fork Crestone Trail at Venable Pass.

From Horn Creek it is another 14.5 miles to the Rainbow Trail's end at Music Pass Road. The Macey Creek, North Colony Creek, and Hudson Creek Trails climb up drainages to the foot of the crest along this stretch, and South Colony Creek ushers in a 4WD road to within a mile of the South Colony Lakes. Situated at the base of Crestone Needle and Crestone Peak (both "fourteeners"), the South Colony Lakes are a favored destination for off-road vehicle enthusiasts.

A 4WD route climbs most of the way to Music Pass, and south from there the wilderness boundary runs either along the range crest or very close to it. A 4WD road over Medano Pass severs the wilderness again, and below that another jeep route cuts off the area's southeastern wing tip. Within that wing tip the Ute and Huerfano Trails form a small loop visiting the headwater streams of the Huerfano River. Most hikers who visit this area head toward Mount Lindsey (14,125 feet), which lies just south of the forest boundary on the Sangre de Cristo Land Grant.

Along the northwest end of the wilderness, the Rio Grande National Forest features several short in-and-out trails, as well as a few lengthier routes with loop possibilities. One longer trail is the 10-mile Black Mountain Trail, which runs from the top of Hayden Pass (4WD Forest Road 790 follows the pass over the range) south to the mouth of Black Canyon. Because the route begins and ends around the 10,000-foot mark and the high point is 11,600 feet, the climbs are not particularly difficult. Some stretches run through thick timber. Both trailheads are accessible only by 4WD road.

South of Black Canyon, the 5-mile Hot Springs Trail climbs up Hot Springs Canyon and ends just shy of Cottonwood Peak (13,588 feet). The Garner Creek Trail follows the next drainage south for 6.5 miles to the crest. With its trailhead at 8,860 feet and its high point at 12,700 feet, this route poses quite a climb. The 11-mile Cotton Creek Trail begins at the end of a 4WD road up Cotton Creek and climbs toward the crest before turning south at Horsethief Basin. A branch trail continues 2.5 miles up the basin to the crest where it meets the South Brush Creek Trail on the other side. Continuing south from Horsethief Basin, the Cotton Creek route encounters both Cotton and Teacup Lakes—both of which offer good fishing—before ending on the Rito Alto Trail.

Seven miles long, the Rito Alto Trail begins at the forest boundary a few miles south of the Cotton Creek trailhead, continuing on to Rito Alto Lake and a junction with the North Fork Crestone Trail just beyond. The Rito Alto Trail climbs from 8,600 to 11,920 feet. With a shuttle, a 16-mile hike of the Cotton Creek and Rito Alto routes is possible. The Wild Cherry Creek Trail, which climbs 4.6 miles to Cherry Lake, is also of interest. An in-and-out route, this trail penetrates the interior of the Cotton Creek–Rito Alto loop but does not connect with it. Its grade runs from 8,600 to 11,770 feet.

In the vicinity of the town of Crestone, a network of trails improves the opportunities for extended hiking trips. Beginning 3 miles north of Crestone, the San Isabel Trail follows San Isabel Creek for 5 miles before meeting the San Isabel Lake Trail, which climbs 3,200 feet to access San Isabel Lake, a popular fishing hole. The San Isabel Lake Trail also connects with the above mentioned Rito Alto and North Fork Crestone Trails.

Starting at the North Crestone Creek Campground, the North Crestone Trail climbs some 3,000 feet in 6 miles before ending at North Crestone Lake. Along the way, other trails branch off to the north and east. One, the North Fork Crestone Trail, branches north near the edge of the wilderness to travel 7 miles to Hermit Pass, where it meets the Hermit Pass Road from the San Isabel side. The North Fork Crestone Trail also intersects the Rito Alto Trail about 1 mile before reaching Hermit Pass. The Venable Lakes Trail branches off the North Fork Crestone Trail to climb 2 miles to 12,800-foot Venable Pass where it meets the Comanche–Venable Trail.

East of Crestone, a pair of trails access the South Crestone Lake and Willow Lake areas. A little more than 5 miles long, the South Crestone Lake Trail climbs from 9,200 to 11,840 feet. Fishing is popular in both the lake and South Crestone Creek, and bighorn sheep live in the area. Beginning at the same trailhead, the Willow Lake Trail is 6 miles long and climbs to 11,600 feet. Peak baggers use this route to access some of the "fourteeners" in the area.

The western slope of the range south of Crestone was formerly part of the large Baca Land Grant but has since become part of the Great Sand Dunes National Monument and Preserve. Trails in this area are discussed in the Great Sand Dunes National Monument and Preserve description to follow. South of the park, however, a pair of in-and-out trails access Middle Zapata Creek Lake and South Zapata Creek Lake. And, just outside of the wilderness boundary, the 8-mile ascent to the top of Blanca Peak climbs from 7,800 to 14,345 feet.

Cross-country Skiing

The eastern slope of the Sangre de Cristo Wilderness offers ski tour possibilities during winters of sufficient snow, as do several stretches of the Rainbow Trail and some of the routes that climb from it. Access points are found on the Bear Creek Road (County Road 49), Hayden Creek Road (County Road 6), Lake Creek Road (County Road 198), and Horn Creek Road (at the end of County Road 130), and on the road leading into the Alvarado Campground. Typically, these roads are plowed to the forest boundary within 1 or 2 miles of the Rainbow Trail. Watch for avalanche conditions, especially on steep terrain.

Mountaineering

With eight "fourteeners" plus dozens of slightly lesser peaks, the Sangre de Cristo Range is a mountain climber's dream. Several summits are technical in nature, but others are walk-ups.

Rising just south of the wilderness boundary, Blanca Peak (14,345 feet) is the fourth-highest mountain in the state. The usual route up is from the west along an 8-mile stretch of very rugged 4WD road that turns to trail near Como Lake. Other peaks in the area include Ellingwood Point (14,042 feet; considered part of Blanca) and Little Bear Peak (14,037 feet). Ellingwood is reached by a traverse from Blanca Peak or from below via the peak's south face. Little Bear is usually approached from the summit's rugged west ridge. Mount Lindsey (14,042 feet) lies east of the wilderness area in the Sangre de Cristo Land Grant. It can be climbed from the Huerfano drainage to the north.

In the Crestone area (the middle of the range), four "fourteeners" attract many climbers, but these rugged summits pose some of the most difficult climbs in the state. Crestone Needle (14,197 feet), Crestone Peak (14,294 feet), Humboldt Peak (14,064 feet), and Kit Carson Peak (14,165 feet) are grouped together at the heads of Cottonwood Creek to the west and South Colony Creek on the east. Crestone Peak and Crestone Needle are located on the crest of the range, while Humboldt Peak sits just to the east. Kit Carson Peak, which is actually within the Great Sand Dunes National Monument and Preserve, rises a mile west of the crest.

The most popular approach to these summits is from South Colony Lake on the eastern slope. Humboldt is 1.5 miles north of the lake and is a simple scramble up. Its summit permits spectacular views of the Crestones. Crestone Needle is 1 mile southwest of South Colony Lake and is climbed by the southeast ridge. Crestone Peak, which was the last "fourteener" in the state to be climbed, is 0.25 mile west of the needle. Experienced climbers often climb the two together by traversing a tricky ridge between. Unstable rock conditions and exposure make these two summits unsuitable for inexperienced climbers. To reach Kit Carson Peak, cross the crest of the range north of Crestone Peak and traverse another mile west to the summit. Here again, loose rock and steep terrain make for a difficult ascent. Some climbers approach these peaks from the west via either the Willow Creek or Spanish Creek drainages—but the last pitches up the summits are generally the same as for routes from the east.

Several 13,000-foot peaks also offer spectacular climbs in the Sangre de Cristo Range. In the Crestone area, Marble Mountain (13,266 feet) and Broken Hand Peak (13,573 feet) are accessible from the South Colony Creek drainage. A few miles north along the crest of the range sit Mount Adams (13,931 feet) and Fluted Peak (13,554 feet); both are climbed from North Crestone Lake. Rito Alto Peak (13,794 feet) is a short scramble north from Hermit Pass. Mount Marcy (13,510 feet) is a 2-mile walk northeast from Cotton Lake. Looming near Horsethief Basin, Electric Peak (13,621 feet) can be climbed via the Major Creek Trail. Three other prominent summits—Lakes Peak (13,382 feet), Thirsty Peak (13,217 feet), and Cottonwood Peak (13,588 feet)—complete this section of the range.

North of Cottonwood Peak, the mountains relax a bit, with a couple of "thirteeners" and some 12,000-foot summits that stand more as high points along the crest of the range than as prominent peaks. Climbing them is a matter of following the nearest trail and then scrambling up ridge lines.

35 Great Sand Dunes National Monument and Preserve

Location: 30 mi NE of Alamosa
Size: 150,000 acres
Status: National monument and preserve (2000)
Terrain: Sand dunes and alpine mountains
Elevation: 7,900' to 14,165'
Management: NPS
Topographic maps: Liberty, Zapata Ranch, Sand Camp

Nestled at the base of the Sangre de Cristo Mountains and standing up to 750 feet high, the dunes of the Great Sand Dunes National Monument and Preserve are the tallest in the Western Hemisphere. Ever changing with the shifting winds, the topography within the dunes is filled with surprises.

Celebrating the uniqueness of the dunes and their surrounding topography, the Great Sand Dunes National Park and Preserve Act of 2000 transformed a fairly small national monument into a much larger national monument and preserve. Encompassing the original 38,659-acre monument, the congressional act added a portion of the adjacent Rio Grande National Forest to the monument and directed the purchase of the privately owned, 100,000-acre Baca Land Grant, which sides up to the original monument on the northwest. When this land purchase is complete (a process that could take some years), the unit will become a national park and preserve. Much of the land grant acreage, which includes 14,165-foot Kit Carson Peak, will become a 92,000-acre wildlife refuge. The new configuration of monument and preserve showcases an ecosystem unique to the nation.

Seasons

Summer temperatures in the lower elevations can climb into the 80s, but nights are almost always cool. Thundershowers occur with some frequency in the summer and the sun reflecting off the sand can be intense. Winters often bring subzero temperatures and snow. In the park's higher elevations, winter comes much earlier, usually in mid-autumn, and stays into July. Nevertheless, hiking is usually possible throughout the year in the lower elevations. The winds—the very force that formed the dunes—can be strong.

Flora and Fauna

Few plants and animals can survive in the sterile conditions within the dunes themselves. An exception is the Great Sand Dunes tiger beetle, which is found only at Great Sand Dunes. A number of small rodents, bobcats, coyotes, mule deer, and pronghorn antelope live within the grasslands and stands of pinyon pine and juniper that grow adjacent to the dunes.

A variety of life zones ranging from upper Sonoran to alpine tundra are encountered in the park's montane reaches. Hikers may encounter elk, marmots, and pikas in the higher elevations.

Geology

Three key factors led to the formation of the sand dunes: wind, sand, and a suitable place for the wind to deposit the sand, which was the base of a low spot in the mighty wall of the Sangre de Cristo Mountains. The winds pick up sand as they blow across the expansive San Luis Valley (it's as big as Connecticut). Funneling through the break in the mountains, the winds then drop their load. Scientists estimate that 4.8 billion

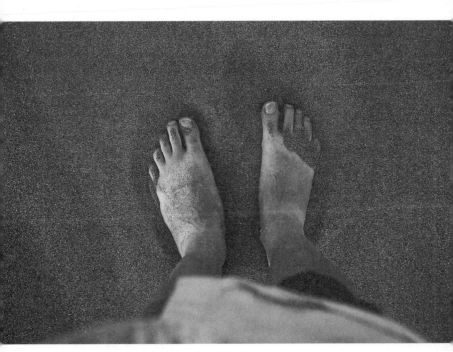

Walking barefoot is perfectly acceptable in the dunes.

cubic meters (1.3 cubic miles) of sand have been deposited so far. They also believe that the process is ongoing. The dunes change constantly and reverse winds prevent them from piling up on the mountains.

History

Archaeological evidence suggests that Folsom Man lived in the area 10,000 years ago, followed by bands of Utes many years later. Zebulon Pike climbed the dunes in 1807. A short while later he built a stockade in the San Luis Valley, where the Spanish arrested him for trespassing.

ACTIVITIES
Hiking

Hiking in the dunes is a matter of setting off in any direction and exploring the ever-shifting sands. No trails exist and maps are useless. Try walking the crest of the dunes and then bounding down their faces, freeform. The best times to visit are close to dawn or dusk, when the light is especially beautiful, and under the eerie cast of a full moon. Watch for lightning when storm clouds roll in, and wear shoes when surface temperatures become hot. The highest dune is about a 1-hour walk from the Dunes parking area. Hardcore skiers have been known to schuss down the dunes on skis. Don't use your best boards for this trick, though, as the sand is abrasive.

East of the dunes, the 5.5-mile Little Medano Creek Trail begins at the campground, near campsite 62. Roughly paralleling the 4WD Medano Pass Road much of the way, this trail eventually winds up at an overlook just north of Little Medano Creek. Watch for mule deer along the way.

A shorter hike is the 0.75-mile jaunt to Escape Dunes–Ghost Forest, an area where relatively new dunes have partially buried tall trees and turned the area into a forest of dead timber. The 0.5-mile Pinyon Flats Trail traverses grasslands that grow near the base of the dunes north of the Dunes parking area. And the Mosca Pass Trail climbs 1,400 feet in 3.5 miles to the top of nearby Mosca Pass in the Sangre de Cristo Mountains.

Jutting north from the original monument boundary, a portion of the Great Sand Dunes Preserve encompasses the Sand Creek drainage, which was formerly part of the Rio Grande National Forest. The Sand Creek Trail loops 12 miles up Sand Creek and into Cottonwood Creek to the north, passing very near the crest of the range. From the Sand Creek Trail, a number of smaller trails branch off to various destinations. The rugged (this trail has not been maintained and conditions may be extremely difficult) Cottonwood Trail climbs 1,600 feet in 1 mile to a lake situated at the foot of Crestone Needle (14,197 feet). The 2.5-mile Little Sand Creek Trail accesses the 12,000-foot-high Little Sand Creek Lakes. A 1-mile trail climbs to Lower Sand Creek Lake, while a 0.5-mile route accesses Upper Sand Creek Lake. It is necessary to cross private property in the vicinity of Liberty (the access area for the lower end of the Sand Creek drainage), so obtain permission before entering.

Mountaineering

Access to Kit Carson Peak is possible from South Colony Lake on the eastern slope of the range in the San Isabel National Forest. From the lake, cross the range crest north of Crestone Peak and traverse another mile west to the summit. Climbers also approach the peak from the west via the Willow Creek drainage. Loose rock and steep terrain along either route make for a difficult and dangerous ascent.

Other peaks rise along the boundary of the preserve portion of the monument, including Milwaukee Peak, Music Mountain, and Tijeras Peak, all of which head the Sand Creek drainage to the west. These 13,000-foot-plus summits can be approached from Upper and Lower Sand Creek Lakes.

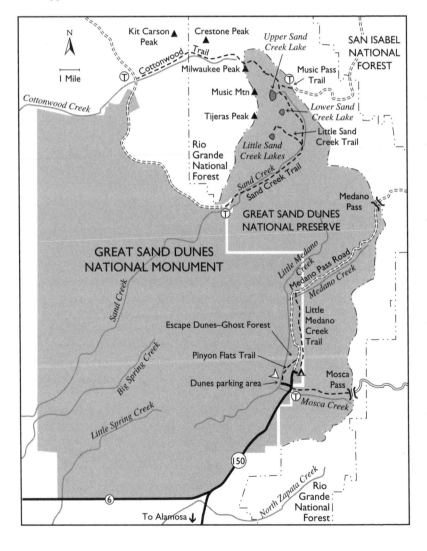

San Luis Hills Wilderness Study Area

Location: 25 mi S of Alamosa
Size: 10,240 acres
Status: Wilderness study area (1978)
Terrain: Open and forested hills
Elevation: 7,700' to 9,476'
Management: BLM (San Luis Field Office)
Topographic maps: Kiowa, Manassa NE

Situated in the southern end of the San Luis Valley near the border with New Mexico, the San Luis Hills Wilderness Study Area (WSA) encompasses more than 10,000 acres of mostly open hills. Its attractions include expansive views in all directions. The sparsely vegetated terrain is conducive to hiking, and canyon systems add to the exploration possibilities. The San Luis Hills fan out across a wide portion of the southern San Luis Valley, but the WSA encompasses just one section known as the Piñon Hills.

Seasons

Given the relatively low elevation, visiting the San Luis Hills area can be a year-round activity. Winter snows are sparse, and those that do fall quickly melt off. Summer temperatures can be uncomfortably high, and there are no perennial sources of water.

Flora and Fauna

Lower elevations in the San Luis Hills feature grasslands and low profile shrubbery, such as bitterbrush, rabbitbrush, and sagebrush. Stands of pinyon pines and junipers are typical in higher elevations. Mule deer and pronghorn antelope are common in the San Luis Hills, especially in the wintertime. And a variety of raptors may be spotted there.

Geology

The geology of the San Luis Hills reflects the volcanic origins of the entire San Luis Valley. The hills consist of debris deposited during past episodes of volcanic activity. The surrounding valley lands have eroded away, often along faults that constitute the Rio Grande Rift.

ACTIVITIES
Hiking

To access the San Luis Hills from Alamosa drive south on U.S. Highway 285 to State Highway 142. Turn left and drive east to the small town of Manassa. Continue another 2.4 miles east to where Road 20 turns south. Drive 1.8 miles and turn left on

The San Luis Hills WSA features a lot of open terrain.

Road M. Turn right in another 0.9 mile and drive 2.2 miles to BLM Road 5015. This road is technically closed to vehicles but climbs to the high point of the WSA (9,476 feet). While off-road vehicles occasionally find their way around roadblocks below, this road makes a sensible approach route to the top.

To reach the southern side of the WSA, continue south on Road M from BLM Road 5015. Follow this south and then southeast. Here, again, open terrain is an ideal conduit for hikers interested in entering the hills. A dirt road skirts along the WSA's

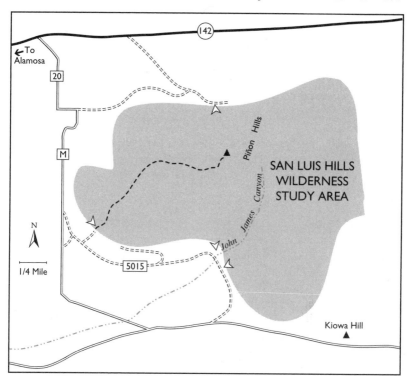

southwest boundary to access the mouth of John James Canyon. This impressive abyss can be followed for a mile or two before climbing steeply to the hills above.

37   South San Juan Wilderness Area

Location: 12 mi E of Pagosa Springs
Size: 158,785 acres
Status: Wilderness area (1980)
Terrain: High summits and forested valleys
Elevation: 8,200' to 13,300'
Management: San Juan NF, Rio Grande NF
Topographic maps: Blackhead Peak, Summit Peak, Platoro, Wolf Creek Pass, Elwood Pass, Hams Lake, Elephant Rock, Victoria Lake, Spectacle Lake, Chama Peak, Archuleta Creek, Cumbres

Straddling the Continental Divide between Wolf Creek Pass and the New Mexico border, the South San Juan Wilderness includes some of the more remote reaches of the San

Juan Mountains. Perhaps in part because there are no "fourteeners" here, the South San Juans have considerably fewer visitors than other Colorado wilderness areas. Nevertheless, the rewards are many for those who venture into this wilderness. With several peaks rising above 13,000 feet, skylines are impressive. As if to underscore the pristine character of the area, a female grizzly bear was killed near the head of the Navajo River in September 1979—nearly three decades after the "last" grizzly bear in the state was taken.

Seasons

Covering mostly high, mountainous terrain, the South San Juan Wilderness is best visited between the months of June and October. Higher elevations may not open up until early July. Watch for wildflowers in July and early August, and for the change of aspen leaves in September.

Flora and Fauna

The mountainous terrain of this wilderness area contains several ecosystems. Lower elevations feature stands of ponderosa pine and patches of gambel oak. Aspen forests usually grow at elevations between 8,000 and 10,000 feet, often in areas disturbed by fires. In subalpine meadows, wildflower species include blue columbine, Indian paintbrush, marsh marigolds, and cinquefoil. Above timberline look for pink moss campions and alpine sunflowers.

The 1979 discovery of a grizzly bear in the South San Juans took wildlife experts by surprise and kindled hope that others might be living in the area. While no others have turned up, proponents remain excited by the possibility that these mountains can, in fact, support grizzlies. Mammals that are found in established numbers include black bears, elk, mule deer, and bighorn sheep. River otters have been successfully transplanted into waterways of the South San Juan, and pikas and marmots enliven the alpine reaches of the wilderness with their high-pitched chirping. Raptors, including great horned owls and golden eagles, also live in these mountains.

Geology

Initially rising as a broad dome during the Laramide Orogeny, the San Juan Mountains were further shaped by a lengthy period of volcanic activity as evidenced in the dark basalt found in the South San Juan region. Lasting about 30 million years, this geologic episode saw huge calderas form among the peaks. One of these was the Platoro Caldera near Conejos Peak. After the mountains finally fell silent, glaciers formed in the range's higher reaches and began grinding away at the terrain, resulting in classic U-shaped valleys, glacial cirques, lakes, and terminal moraines.

History

Before the arrival of Europeans in southwestern Colorado, the Ute Indians occupied the San Juan Mountains—including the higher terrain of the South San Juan Wilderness. Zebulon Pike wintered near the confluence of the Conejos River and the Rio Grande in 1807 while exploring the newly acquired Louisiana Purchase. Land grants

Quartz Lake in the South San Juan Wilderness

lured settlers to the region after Mexico was liberated from Spain in 1821. A mining boom in the 1880s led to quite a bit of activity along the headwaters of the Conejos River. The San Juan National Forest was established in 1907, followed by the Rio Grande National Forest a year later. Adjacent to the South San Juan Wilderness, the Tierra Amarilla Land Grant is a tract of private land that may have provided an undisturbed home for the last known grizzly bear in Colorado.

ACTIVITIES
Hiking
Approximately 35 miles of the interstate Continental Divide Trail run south to north through the South San Juan Wilderness. Mostly above timberline, the views from the trail are spectacular. With a shuttle, the route can be a wonderful 4- or 5-day hike. Some stretches are difficult to follow, so bring along topographic maps and a compass. The Continental Divide Trail parallels the actual crest of the range quite closely, occasionally dipping into the headwaters of several drainages. Although the route never drops below 11,000 feet, it does include several descents and climbs that add to the difficulty of the hike. Elwood Pass is a convenient access point to the north. To the south, the trail can be picked up near the parking area at the Cumbres–Toltec Railroad way station. Between these two points, the Continental Divide Trail covers 49 miles.

Several trails, many of which follow stream drainages, reach the Continental Divide. On the San Juan National Forest side, the Quartz Creek Trail begins near the end of Quartz Meadows Road (FS Road 684), 12.5 miles from U.S. Highway 160, and climbs from 9,000 to 12,200 feet in 7 miles before topping out on the Divide. Easily confused with the Quartz

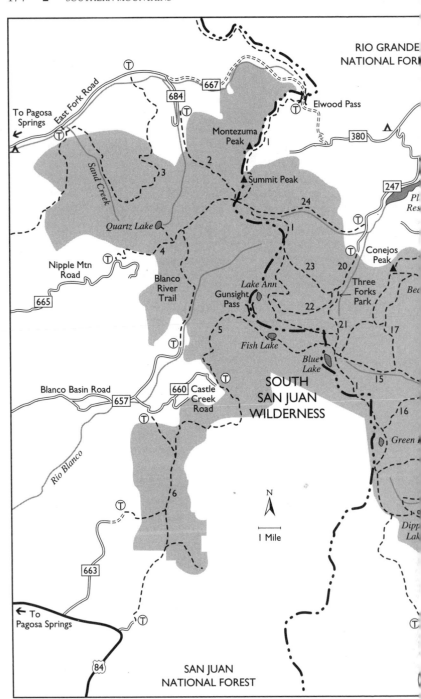

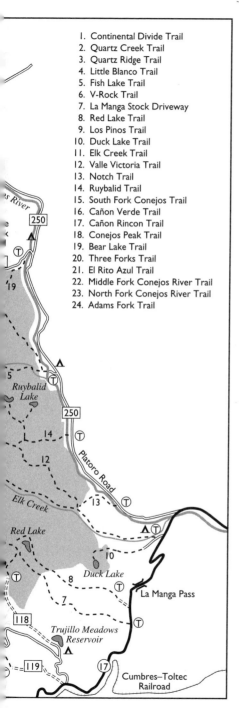

Creek Trail is the Quartz Ridge Trail, which runs for 15 miles independent of the Continental Divide in the western-most reaches of the wilderness. Climbing along Sand Creek from East Fork Road, the Quartz Ridge Trail ascends 3,000 feet to a high point of 10,900 feet. Although steep, this trail makes a nice 2-day trip. Four miles of road separate its beginning and end.

From where the Quartz Creek Trail tops the Continental Divide, the 8-mile Little Blanco Trail follows a ridge south-west from the Divide before dropping 2,160 feet to meet Nipple Mountain Road (FS Road 665) on the Rito Blanco. It passes within 1 mile of Quartz Lake and, near its midpoint, intersects the upper end of the Blanco River Trail. Also 8 miles long, the Blanco River Trail drops from a high point of 10,400 feet south to Blanco Basin Road (FS Road 657) 2,800 feet below.

From Blanco Basin, the 10-mile Fish Lake Trail begins at the end of Castle Creek Road, 17 miles from U.S. Highway 84. Beginning at 9,040 feet, this trail follows Fish Creek down-stream then turns up the North Fork of Fish Creek and climbs some 2,800 feet before topping out near Gunsight Pass. Fish Lake is six miles in and Blue Lake is a bit beyond the trail's end on the Continental Divide Trail. Heading south from the end of Castle Creek Road, the Fish Creek Trail connects with the V-Rock Trail 9 miles away.

The Rio Grande National Forest side of the Continental Divide offers a higher concentration of hiking trails. Because many of these routes connect with the Continental Divide Trail, this is a good area for circle hikes. Access to most of these trails is along Colorado Highway 17 (the highway over Cumbres Pass) or Platoro Road (FS Road 250), which follows the upper Conejos River.

Crossing Colorado Highway 17 a mile south of La Manga Pass, the La Manga Stock Driveway covers 10 miles before intersecting with the Continental Divide Trail near Dipping Lakes. Beginning at the end of a 1-mile spur road, also near La Manga Pass, the Red Lake Trail heads northwest toward the crest of the range. It reaches Red Lake in 6 miles and ends 1 mile farther on the La Manga Stock Driveway. Along its 7-mile course, the Red Lake Trail climbs from 10,300 to 11,700 feet. With excellent fishing, Red Lake is quite popular and often crowded. The Los Pinos Trail is a quicker route to the Dipping Lakes area. It begins 4 miles beyond the Trujillo Meadows Reservoir and climbs nearly 1,000 feet in 2 miles to an intersection with the La Manga Stock Driveway.

Beginning 1.5 miles past the Elk Creek Campground, the 5-mile Duck Lake Trail climbs about 2,000 feet to dead-end at Duck Lake, which is situated on a bench above Elk Creek. Like Red Lake, Duck Lake is popular with anglers. The 13.5-mile Elk Creek Trail follows Elk Creek upstream to Dipping Lakes and an intersection with the Continental Divide Trail. Also beginning near the Elk Creek Campground and climbing to an elevation of 11,750 feet, this route encounters a series of beautiful meadows and virgin stands of Engelmann spruce. From Dipping Lakes, it is a 3-mile walk along the Continental Divide Trail to Trail Lake, another popular fishing hole.

The 12-mile Valle Victoria Trail ends near Trail Lake. To find it from below, follow the Notch Trail from its start on Platoro Road; the Valle Victoria begins 3 miles in. Combine the Valle Victoria, Continental Divide, and Elk Creek Trails for a loop hike of nearly 30 miles. About 5 miles in, a spur trail takes off from the Valle Victoria Trail to reach Ruybalid Lake in 2 miles and No Name Lake in 3 miles. A connecting trail known as the Ruybalid Trail drops 2 miles to Platoro Road.

The major drainage system along the eastern slope of the South San Juans, the Conejos River and its tributaries conduct many hiking routes into the wilderness. The South Fork Conejos Trail runs 10 miles from Platoro Road to the Blue Lake area on the Continental Divide. It climbs from 8,950 feet to 11,400 feet, revealing a spectacular, glacier-carved canyon system. The Cañon Verde Trail branches off from the South Fork Conejos Trail to run 4 miles southwest to Green Lake, also along the Continental Divide Trail. The distance between Green and Blue Lakes is about 5 miles. Branching north from the South Fork Conejos Trail is the Cañon Rincon Trail; it reaches Glacier Lake in 3 miles and in another 3 miles it intersects with the Conejos Peak Trail.

The Conejos Peak Trail shares a trailhead with the South Fork Conejos Trail, but instead of ascending a drainage it loops to the north over Conejos Peak (13,172 feet) before reaching the Blue Lake area in 12.5 miles. Combining this hike with the South Fork Conejos Trail makes a 23-mile loop through the heart of the wilderness. The Bear Lake Trail is an additional point of access for the Conejos Peak Trail. Bear Lake is 3 miles from the trailhead on Saddle Creek Road (FS Road 105) and about 1 mile from the Conejos Peak Trail.

The Conejos River has its headwaters in the northeast quadrant of the wilderness west of Platoro Reservoir. Following the Conejos River from the end of the road that skirts the north shore of the reservoir, the Three Forks Trail runs 2 miles to a junction with the El Rito Azul Trail. This 3.5-mile trail climbs 1,100 feet, making it the quickest route to Blue Lake. Continuing from Three Forks Park, the Middle Fork Conejos River Trail is 4.4 miles long and climbs about 1,000 feet to the Lake Ann area on the Continental Divide Trail. Meanwhile, the North Fork Conejos River Trail climbs 3.4 miles to the Continental Divide a few miles north of Lake Ann. All three spurs of the Three Forks connect with the Continental Divide Trail, making a number of loop hikes possible. The Adams Fork Trail—a 6.5-mile route that begins near Platoro Reservoir—adds more loop options in this area. It can be combined with the Quartz Creek and Little Blanco Trails on the west slope of the wilderness, making a traverse of the entire wilderness feasible.

Cross-country Skiing

Winter access to the South San Juan Wilderness is limited because forest roads in the area are not plowed regularly. The handiest entries into the wilderness are in the Cumbres Pass area, especially the Red Lake Trail and the La Manga Stock Driveway. The Red Lake, Elk Creek, and Valle Victoria Trails are all suitable for an overnight ski trip. Because slopes are steep and because the San Juans receive some of the heaviest snow accumulations in the state, avalanches pose a constant threat to backcountry travelers in the winter and early spring. Exposure to high winds and extreme cold are possible in the higher reaches of the South San Juan.

Mountaineering

Summits in the South San Juan are not as lofty as those in the nearby Weminuche Wilderness, so climbers are not as apt to explore the uplands of this section of the range. This area is home to several 13,000-foot peaks, but most are simple walk-ups. Montezuma (13,150 feet) and Summit (13,300 feet) Peaks are two high points along the Continental Divide Trail.

La Garita Wilderness Area

Location: 5 mi N of Creede
Size: 129,626 acres
Status: Wilderness area (1964)
Terrain: Alpine summits with forested drainages
Elevation: 9,000' to 14,014'
Management: Gunnison NF, Rio Grande NF
Topographic maps: Stewart Peak, Elk Park, Creede, Bristol Head, Mineral Mountain, Cannibal Plateau, Half Moon Pass, Wagon Wheel Gap, Pool Table Mountain

Extending along the Continental Divide in the northern reaches of the San Juan Mountains, the La Garita Wilderness offers sublime alpine scenery, the "fourteener" San Luis

Peak, and a trail system that allows for many fine overnight hikes. Yet it is one of the least-visited wilderness areas in the state. The Colorado Wilderness Act of 1993 added 25,640 acres south of the original wilderness boundary in the vicinity of the Wheeler Geologic Area.

Seasons

The hiking season usually begins in June across most lower elevations and in early July up high. Summer is the season for thunderstorms—a very real danger to hikers above timberline. Watch for wildflowers in late July and early August. After Labor Day, the aspen begin to change color and elk start their rutting season. Heavy snows usually preclude hiking by mid-October.

Flora and Fauna

Mixed Engelmann spruce and subalpine fir dominate the forests below timberline (around 11,500 feet). Patches of aspen and lodgepole pine occasionally grow here and subalpine meadows are plentiful. In the timbered regions, residents include mule deer, elk, coyotes, black bears, bobcats, mountain lions, and snowshoe hares. More than half of the La Garita area is above timberline, however. Bighorn sheep, marmots, and pikas haunt this lofty terrain. And a plethora of wildflowers grow in these higher reaches of the wilderness, including blue columbine, Indian paintbrush, moss pink campion, and sky pilot.

Geology

As part of the San Juan Range, the mountains of the La Garita mostly resulted from deposits of volcanic ash and debris during the Tertiary period. Some evidence of glacial carving exists, but conspicuously absent is the steep and broken terrain that characterizes other sections of the San Juans. Conical-shaped and light gray in color, the formations of the Wheeler Geologic Area are composed of tuff, a rock made from compacted cinder and ash. Quite soft, these deposits have eroded into such unusual shapes that the area was once declared a national monument. Because of its remote locale, however, it was withdrawn from monument status in 1938.

ACTIVITIES
Hiking

The premier hike in the La Garita Wilderness is the Skyline Trail, which extends 20 miles across the length of the wilderness. Following the Continental Divide for much of the way, the Skyline forms part of the interstate Continental Divide Trail. It also picks up a 17-mile stretch of the Colorado Trail. To the east, the Skyline Trail begins near the end of Stewart Creek Road at the Eddiesville trailhead. This road can be reached by following Colorado Highway 114 through Cochetopa Canyon and then turning right on the access road to Dome Lakes. Turn right again after the Upper Dome Reservoir and continue south on Forest Road 794, then turn right on Stewart Creek Road and drive 5 miles to the trailhead.

The Wheeler Geologic Area features fascinating rock formations.

From the trailhead, the Skyline Trail follows Cochetopa Creek to its headwaters near the Continental Divide. A bushwhack across the eastern flank of San Luis Peak (14,014 feet) leads to the upper end of the Stewart Creek Trail, making a 14-mile loop that takes in a "fourteener" along the way. Upon reaching the Continental Divide, the Skyline Trail stays above 10,000 feet the rest of the way across the wilderness. San Luis Pass lies near the Skyline's halfway point and the headwaters of Tumble Creek are found near Baldy Cinco (13,383 feet). The route follows Tumble Creek out to the western edge of the wilderness. To find this end of the Skyline Trail, turn off Colorado Highway 149 onto Gardner Ridge Road and follow it 2 miles to the Tumble Creek trailhead.

The Cebolla Trail also crosses part of the La Garita Wilderness. Branching off from the Skyline Trail less than 1 mile from the Tumble Creek trailhead on the western border of the wilderness, the Cebolla Trail cuts east across several drainages that flow north from the Continental Divide. The Rough Creek Trail intersects the Cebolla Trail 5 miles from the Tumble Creek trailhead. Beginning along Los Pinos–Cebolla Road, the Rough Creek route runs 7.5 miles south and climbs some 3,000 feet to join the Skyline Trail near Baldy Cinco. A 2- or 3-day loop trip is possible by following the Cebolla, Rough Creek, and Skyline Trails. Four miles east of Rough Creek, the Cebolla Trail intersects the Mineral Creek Trail. Slightly longer than the Rough Creek Trail, this route begins on a spur off Los Pinos–Cebolla Road and eventually ends on the Skyline Trail. The Cebolla Trail crosses this route 9 miles in.

Fourteen miles from the Tumble Creek trailhead, the Cebolla Trail temporarily drops out of the wilderness to cross 4WD Spring Creek Road (FS Road 592). From the end of this road, two short, unnamed trails head south into the wilderness; one climbs up Cascade Creek to San Luis Pass, and the other follows Spring Creek to meet the Skyline Trail east of the pass. After reentering the northeastern corner of the wilderness, the Cebolla Trail crosses over to Big Meadows Road, where it ends, 18 miles from its start.

Extending south of the Continental Divide, an arm of the La Garita Wilderness stretches into the headwaters of Saguache Creek in the Rio Grande National Forest. This area can be reached from either the north via the road that extends beyond the Stone Cellar Campground, or from the Creede area to the south on Forest Road 600, the road to the Wheeler Geologic Area.

From the north, two major drainages, the middle and south forks of Saguache Creek, usher most routes into the wilderness. Following the middle fork to its head-waters at Machin Lake, the 7.5-mile Middle Fork Trail climbs 2,300 feet to an elevation of 12,400 feet. It connects with the Machin Basin Trail at Machin Lake. This trail runs alongside a high ridge for most of the way. The Machin Basin Trail runs southeast for 5 miles before ending at Halfmoon Pass (12,700 feet); north from Machin Lake, it crosses the Continental Divide into Gunnison National Forest and follows the Lake Fork (10 miles from Machin Lake), eventually ending at Stewart Creek Road. Because of rough trail conditions, the Machin Basin Trail is not recommended for horses.

The Halfmoon Pass Trail also begins along the middle fork of Saguache Creek, but it cuts a more direct route to the pass, which is 7 miles and a 2,200-foot elevation gain away. Slightly shorter, the South Saguache Trail connects with the Halfmoon Pass Trail after following the South Fork of Saguache Creek for much of the way. After climbing 1,600 feet, it reaches a high point of 12,000 feet before dropping a little to join the Halfmoon Pass Trail not far from the pass.

The Whale Creek Trail begins within 0.25 mile of where the South Saguache Trail starts. Climbing 2,000 feet in 4.6 miles, this route accesses Palmer Mesa, which is paralleled by the La Garita Stock Driveway. Staying high, the La Garita Stock Driveway in turn continues northwest along the Divide to Halfmoon Pass. Given the number of interconnecting trails (six trails converge on Halfmoon Pass alone), several overnight loop trips are feasible in this section of the La Garita. Deciphering which route to follow may take some time and thought.

Five trails enter the Wheeler addition, most of which converge at the Wheeler Geologic Area. Because the 4WD road to the Wheeler Geologic Area is very rugged and impassable when wet, its strange rock formations are best reached by hiking in. The East Bellows Trail begins on Pool Table Road east of Creede and travels 8.4 miles to Halfmoon Pass, reaching the Wheeler Geologic Area in about 6 miles. The route follows a 4WD road for part of the way. The 4-mile West Bellows Creek Trail offers a shorter route to the geologic area from La Garita Ranch Road (FS Road 502), but the road is private and permission to use it must first be obtained from the guest ranch. Climbing 2,400 feet, the West Bellows Creek Trail joins the East Bellows Creek Trail 0.3 mile south of the Wheeler Geologic Area.

The 10.7-mile Wason–Wheeler Trail begins in Creede and also connects with the East Bellows Creek route. It climbs from 8,900 to 11,200 feet; highlights include the view from Inspiration Point about 2 miles in. The 7.2-mile Farmers Creek Trail joins the Wason–Wheeler Trail at Wason Park, about 7 miles from Creede. To reach the Farmers Creek Trail, drive 0.25 mile north of the Wason Guest Ranch. A continuation of the La Garita Stock Driveway can be accessed by a trailhead on 4WD Phoenix Park

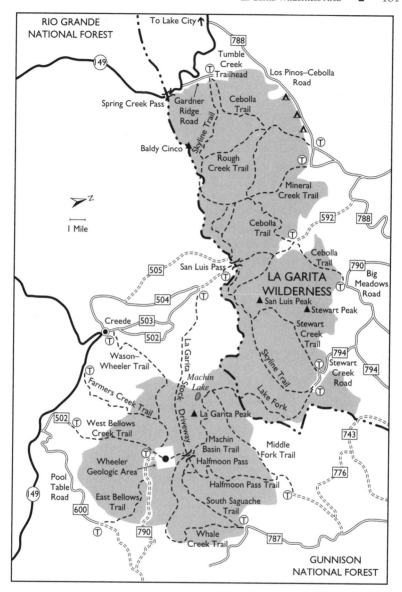

Road north of Creede. Covering 6.8 miles, this seldom-used segment climbs 2,400 feet to Halfmoon Pass.

Cross-country Skiing

The La Garita Wilderness is not easily accessible during the winter months. Colorado Highway 149, which runs from Lake City to Creede over Spring Creek Pass, is plowed and allows access to within 2 miles of the western end of the Skyline and Cebolla Trails. Deep snow could make this a difficult route to follow, though. An overland route from Spring Creek Pass itself toward Baldy Cinco along the Continental Divide might be possible, but this country is very rugged and avalanches pose an almost constant hazard.

While wintertime access to the Wheeler addition is limited, some overnight ski trips can be enjoyed. The best routes are the Farmers Creek and Wason–Wheeler Trails. West Bellows Creek follows a narrow canyon, making ski conditions difficult. The Wason Park area offers excellent touring, and the formations of the Wheeler Geologic Area are spectacular under a blanket of snow.

Mountaineering

San Luis Peak (14,014 feet) is ranked fifty-first in the state and is considered a walk-up. Climbers can reach the summit from the Spring Creek, Stewart Creek, or Cochetopa Creek drainages. At 6 miles each way, the Stewart Creek route is the shortest. Stewart Peak (13,983 feet) is another climb in the La Garita Wilderness. Once considered a "fourteener," Stewart was dropped from the list after being re-surveyed. Connected to San Luis Peak by a ridge, these two summits are often climbed together. La Garita Peak (13,718 feet) rises above the Machin Lake area and is also a walk-up. In the western end of the wilderness, high points along the Continental Divide include Baldy Cinco (13,383 feet), which is a 4-mile climb from Spring Creek Pass (10,898 feet).

Weminuche Wilderness Area

Location: 20 mi NE of Durango
Size: 488,544 acres
Status: Wilderness area (1975)
Terrain: Alpine peaks and ridges, forested drainages and lower slopes
Elevation: 8,000' to 14,084'
Management: San Juan NF, Rio Grande NF
Topographic maps: Mountain View Crest, Lemon Reservoir, Snowdon Peak, Columbine Pass, Storm King Peak, Howardsville, Silverton, Vallecito Reservoir, Emerald Lake, Granite Peak, Rio Grande Pyramid, Pole Creek Mountain, Weminuche Pass, Finger Mesa, Granite Lake, Little Squaw Creek, Cimarrona Peak, Hermit Lakes, Bristol Head, Workman Creek, Palomino Mountain, Pagosa Peak, South River Peak, Spar City, Saddle Mountain, Wolf Creek Pass, Mount Hope, Lake Humphreys, Electra Lake, Engineer Mountain

At nearly half a million acres, the Weminuche is Colorado's largest wilderness area. It spans the heart of the San Juan Mountains, the largest range in the U.S. Rockies and, at an average elevation of 10,400 feet, the highest mountain chain in North America as well.

A vast array of alpine terrain is found within the Weminuche. The Needles, a group of granite peaks considered among the most rugged in the lower forty-eight states, rise in the west. Running east from the Needles, 12,000- and 13,000-foot summits carry the Continental Divide for many miles before reaching U.S. Highway 160 on Wolf Creek Pass. The headwaters of two major rivers—the Rio Grande and the San Juan—originate on either side of this geographical boundary. Streams and lakes are plentiful throughout, and sawtooth summits pile up along the horizon.

The Colorado Wilderness Act of 1993 added 28,740 acres to the Weminuche. The bulk of this lies west of the Animas River Gorge in the West Needle Mountains, leaving a corridor through the wilderness for the Durango and Silverton Narrow Gauge Railroad (D&SNGR).

Seasons

Because the San Juan Mountains receive the brunt of many heavy snowstorms throughout the winter, their statistics are astounding. Nearly 500 inches of snow falls each year in several strategic spots. Consequently, in some years the hiking season in the high country does not get into full swing until mid-July. Sudden snow squalls can occur in any month, and thundershowers accompanied by lightning are an almost daily occurrence in the high country during the summer months. Wildflowers reach their peak in late July and early August, and September ushers in some of the most vivid displays of aspen leaves in the state. Late October usually brings the first heavy blankets of snow.

Flora and Fauna

Below 8,500 feet, the transitional zone is home to stands of ponderosa pine, gambel oak, and Douglas fir. Next, the Canadian zone with its glades of aspen reaches up to about the 10,000-foot level. Up to timberline, which in the San Juans is around 11,500 feet, the Hudsonian zone displays thick forests of Engelmann spruce and subalpine fir. In the alpine zone opportunistic forbs utilize a short growing season by blooming at a moment's notice.

Because so many different habitats are found in the San Juans, it is home to many species. Some, like the mule deer and elk, range freely between zones. The San Juans, in fact, are known for their herds of elk. Other species, like bighorn sheep, mountain goats, moose, marmots, and pikas live at or above timberline. Coyotes, black bears, bobcats, and mountain lions also inhabit these mountains. Efforts to re-introduce lynx have been partially successful.

Geology

During the Laramide Orogeny, when other mountain chains were being pushed skyward, a broad dome 100 miles across was slowly forming where the San Juans now stand. Erosion exposed parts of this bubble of Precambrian rock and then, beginning 40 million years ago, the region exploded in volcanic eruptions. Ash, rock, and lava accumulated to form a layer of debris more than a mile thick in spots. Erosion again stripped some areas down to the Precambrian core, but most of the San Juan highlands still bear dark gray volcanic rock. With volcanic activity coming to an end

5 million years ago, Pleistocene glaciers eventually went to work, giving the San Juans their final shape. Cirques, U-shaped valleys, sharply angular peaks, moraines, and glacial lakes are all components of modern San Juan topography.

History

The Ute Indians frequented the high country of the Weminuche. In fact, the word Weminuche was the name of a particular band of Utes. Spanish explorers passed through the area during the eighteenth and early nineteenth centuries, and the explorer John Fremont attempted to lead an expedition across the San Juans in December 1848.

During the 1860s, a few prospectors entered the San Juans, which was then Ute territory, in search of gold. Although they were not overly successful, their tales did ignite an unquenchable interest in the San Juans that eventually led to the Brunot Treaty—an 1873 document that ceded most of the San Juan Range to the U.S. government. Thousands of miners made their way into the region within days of its signing. Few corners of the San Juans escaped their diggings and many areas did prove profitable. One such area was Chicago Basin in the heart of the Needles Range. Mine shafts and accompanying tailings piles are plentiful in the basin, and a few cabins still stand. The trail from Needleton into Chicago Basin was once a wagon road. Running along the bottom of the Animas River Gorge, the century-old Durango and Silverton Narrow Gauge Railroad still makes daily runs—albeit for tourists—in the summer.

ACTIVITIES
Hiking

Nearly 500 miles of trails crisscross the Weminuche Wilderness Area. Some routes follow drainage bottoms to their headwaters, while others stick primarily to the tops of alpine ridges. Lakes lure hikers, and the views are seldom ordinary. Because of its beauty, however, the Weminuche can be crowded. Find solitude by steering clear of 14,000-foot peaks and popular fishing streams and lakes.

Located in the western third of the wilderness, the Needles is the most heavily used area of the Weminuche. Three summits within the range—Eolus, Sunlight, and Windom—are part of Colorado's elite corps of "fourteeners" and dozens of other peaks top out just shy of that. The grades in this part of the Weminuche are considerable and elevations are high.

The two established routes that penetrate the Needle Mountains follow the Elk Creek and Needle Creek drainages from the west. Beginning at the old townsite of Needleton and running into Chicago Basin is the Needle Creek Trail. Because Needleton is a stop on the D&SNGR, many backpackers preface their hikes with a ride on the steam-powered train. The ease and romanticism make this trail the busiest in the wilderness, especially from July 1 through Labor Day weekend. An 11-mile walk down the Purgatory Creek Trail and up the Animas River bypasses the train ride. The hike

Opposite: *Wildflowers are plentiful in the San Juan Mountains.*

from Needleton to Chicago Basin climbs nearly 3,000 feet in 7 miles. Fires are banned in the Needle Creek drainage because of overuse. Once in the Basin, you may want to follow climbers to Twin Lakes, another 1,000 feet or so above Chicago Basin. Hundreds of people tackle one or more of three neighboring "fourteeners" each year starting from the lakes. Camping is prohibited in the Twin Lakes Basin, however.

At the head of Chicago Basin, the Needle Creek Trail climbs up and over 12,680-foot Columbine Pass before dropping into the Johnson Creek drainage. The pass is 9 miles from Needleton and 4,400 feet above it. Johnson Creek eventually spills into Vallecito Creek, 14.25 trail miles east of Needleton. From the top of Columbine Pass, the Endlich Mesa Trail traverses south over 12,840-foot Trimble Pass and then heads south across Silver Mesa to City Reservoir, the source of drinking water for the city of Durango. The trail continues south from City Reservoir to an obscure trailhead at the end of a logging road northwest of Lemon Reservoir, 13 miles from Columbine Pass. The City Reservoir Trail begins at City Reservoir and heads west for 8 miles to a seldom-used trailhead on Lime Mesa at the end of Missionary Ridge.

Like the Needle Creek Trail, the Elk Creek Trail follows a drainage east into the Needles range and is accessed by the D&SNGR. From Elk Park along the Animas River, this route climbs 3,760 feet in 9 miles before reaching the Continental Divide Trail. If you want to bypass the train, hike down the Molas Trail from Molas Pass on U.S. Highway 550. The detour covers 4 miles and drops 1,700 feet.

Stretching east from the Needles, the Continental Divide dominates the rest of the Weminuche Wilderness. The Continental Divide Trail follows the Divide quite closely, picking up the upper ends of more than half of the remaining trails in the Weminuche. South of the Divide, all streams eventually drain into the Pacific via the San Juan River. The trails on this side are administered by the San Juan National Forest. North of the Divide, all waters drain into the Rio Grande and eventually the Gulf of Mexico. This side falls under the auspices of the Rio Grande National Forest.

Running from Stony Pass to Wolf Creek Pass (the entire length of the wilderness), the Continental Divide Trail covers some 80 miles within the Weminuche. Indeed, it is a dream hike for those with a week or more to devote to a backpack trip. It dips below timberline in only three places, and, while it is seldom level, the grades are often easy once you are on top. Spectacular scenery is nonstop as you rarely lose that "on-top-of-the-world" feeling.

For those unable to walk the entire Continental Divide Trail, segments of the route can be hiked separately. Just follow one drainage up to the Divide, follow the Divide Trail to another drainage, and follow that one back down. Such a configuration often puts you in close proximity to your starting point, making the logistics easier. In some cases, you may even wind up at the same trailhead from which you started.

Beginning a few miles north of the Vallecito Reservoir, the popular Vallecito Creek Trail follows a mostly easy grade for 17 miles to 12,493-foot Hunchback Pass on the Divide. This trail accesses two other interesting trails: The Johnson Creek Trail, which is 8.5 miles from the trailhead, and the Rock Creek Trail, which climbs to Rock Lake, a popular fishing hole. The turnoff for the Rock Creek Trail is about 14 miles from the trailhead. After climbing 4 miles to Rock Lake (situated at about 12,000 feet) the trail continues on to meet the Continental Divide Trail in the vicinity of Twin Lakes.

Just south of Hunchback Pass, the Vallecito Creek Trail connects with the Continental Divide Trail near Kite Lake. The Colorado Trail crosses this area, dropping over the Divide and down Elk Creek as it heads toward Durango. From Kite Lake it is about 1 mile to the Divide and then another 9 miles down Elk Creek to Elk Park, where it intersects the D&SNGR tracks. From there the Colorado Trail follows the Molas Trail 4 miles up to Molas Pass.

From the head of Elk Creek, the Continental Divide Trail follows high ridges 6.5 miles to 12,588-foot Stony Pass on the northern end of the wilderness. A 4WD road tops the pass, providing a wilderness entry point. If you don't mind a climb of about 1,000 feet, you can gain the Continental Divide from the end of 2WD Cunningham Gulch Road via the 2.5-mile Cunningham Gulch Trail. This trailhead also serves the Highland Mary Lakes Trail. Popular with fishermen and day hikers, the Highland Mary Lakes are surrounded by beautiful verdant tundra in the northern end of the wilderness. It is 2.5 miles and 1,860 vertical feet to the first lake.

From the Hunchback Pass area, the Continental Divide Trail stays below the actual Divide as it crosses the head of West Ute Creek, a tributary of the Rio Grande. At Middle Ute Creek the trail gains the crest of the mountains again and then passes near Twin Lakes, Flint Lakes, and Ute Lake before topping out near Ute Peak. You can pick up the Rock Creek Trail at Twin Lakes. From Flint Lakes, the Flint Creek Trail drops 7 miles before intersecting the Pine River Trail, passing such imaginatively named landmarks as the Popes Nose and Bare-bottom Park.

Like the Vallecito Creek Trail, the Pine River Trail is popular with horsepackers and hikers alike. Use is heavy, often making the trail muddy and slippery. Following the Pine (or Los Pinos) River for 22 miles, this route begins at the end of Forest Road 602 and eventually tops out on 10,622-foot Weminuche Pass, about midway through the wilderness. Here it intersects the Continental Divide Trail. To the east, the Divide Trail climbs gradually above timberline again as it heads toward Wolf Creek Pass. To the west, the trail travels 11 miles to the Twin Lakes area (different than the Twin Lakes in the Needles section), passing in the shadow of the Rio Grande Pyramid (13,821 feet) and the Window, a 140-foot cut in a rock wall that Spanish sheepherders called the Devil's Gateway. North of Weminuche Pass, a relatively short trail drops down Weminuche Creek to the Rio Grande Reservoir just outside of the wilderness.

The Pine River Trail encounters several side trails. Nearly 6 miles from the trailhead, the Emerald Lake Trail branches off to the northwest, siphoning off many backpackers in the process. Emerald Lake is Colorado's second-largest natural lake and is favored by anglers. Camping within 0.25 mile of the lake is prohibited due to its popularity. Emerald Lake is 4 miles from the Pine River Trail. Beyond Emerald Lake, the trail climbs to Moon Lake, a total of 9 miles and 3,260 vertical feet from the Pine River Trail. An unofficial cross-country route continues north for 2 miles from Moon Lake over a saddle

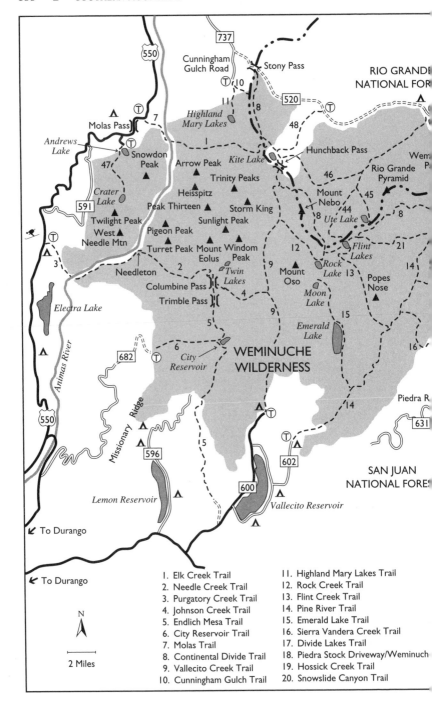

1. Elk Creek Trail
2. Needle Creek Trail
3. Purgatory Creek Trail
4. Johnson Creek Trail
5. Endlich Mesa Trail
6. City Reservoir Trail
7. Molas Trail
8. Continental Divide Trail
9. Vallecito Creek Trail
10. Cunningham Gulch Trail
11. Highland Mary Lakes Trail
12. Rock Creek Trail
13. Flint Creek Trail
14. Pine River Trail
15. Emerald Lake Trail
16. Sierra Vandera Creek Trail
17. Divide Lakes Trail
18. Piedra Stock Driveway/Weminuch
19. Hossick Creek Trail
20. Snowslide Canyon Trail

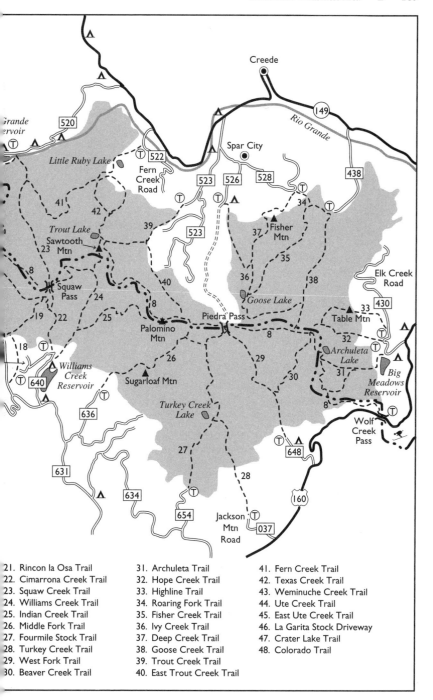

21. Rincon la Osa Trail
22. Cimarrona Creek Trail
23. Squaw Creek Trail
24. Williams Creek Trail
25. Indian Creek Trail
26. Middle Fork Trail
27. Fourmile Stock Trail
28. Turkey Creek Trail
29. West Fork Trail
30. Beaver Creek Trail

31. Archuleta Trail
32. Hope Creek Trail
33. Highline Trail
34. Roaring Fork Trail
35. Fisher Creek Trail
36. Ivy Creek Trail
37. Deep Creek Trail
38. Goose Creek Trail
39. Trout Creek Trail
40. East Trout Creek Trail

41. Fern Creek Trail
42. Texas Creek Trail
43. Weminuche Creek Trail
44. Ute Creek Trail
45. East Ute Creek Trail
46. La Garita Stock Driveway
47. Crater Lake Trail
48. Colorado Trail

and past Half Moon Lake to Rock Lake. Given its high and rugged nature, this route is not suited for horse traffic and is usually not passable before mid-July.

After reaching the Flint Creek Trail 12 miles from its trailhead, the Pine River Trail meets the Sierra Vandera Creek Trail, a 10-mile route that gains a high, alpine ridge to the east and then drops to Piedra Road outside of the wilderness. This route begins with a crossing of the Pine River and continues across some rather rugged topography.

At 15.5 miles the Pine River Trail passes the Granite Peak Guard Station, a Forest Service patrol cabin built in 1916. A bit farther on, the Divide Lakes Trail leads nearly 2 miles east to connect with the Piedra Stock Driveway along Weminuche Creek—a different Weminuche Creek than the one that flows north from Weminuche Pass. The Piedra Stock Driveway is a 10.5-mile route that connects Poison Park Road near Williams Creek Reservoir with the Pine River Trail, 3.5 miles upstream from the Divide Lakes Trail. Climbing south out of the Weminuche Valley, the Piedra Stock Driveway—also known as the Weminuche Trail—soon meets the Hossick Creek Trail, which climbs 4,000 feet in 7.5 miles to Squaw Pass on the Continental Divide. The Piedra Stock Driveway also accesses a 4.75-mile trail that dead-ends in the spectacular canyon of the East Fork of Weminuche Creek. In its last miles the Piedra Stock Driveway meets the Snowslide Canyon Trail, which climbs 4 miles through subalpine terrain, eventually topping out at 1,700 feet on the Continental Divide east of Weminuche Pass.

The Rincon la Osa Trail branches west from where the Pine River Trail and the Piedra Stock Driveway intersect. Following its namesake creek for 6 miles, this route meets the Continental Divide Trail in the vicinity of Flint and Ute Lakes, a favored fishing area.

East of the Pine River area lies the Piedra River drainage with its many wilderness access routes, the Piedra Stock Driveway, Cimarrona Creek Trail, and Hossick Creek Trail among them. Like the Hossick Creek route, the Cimarrona Creek Trail climbs steeply—3,200 feet in 6.5 miles—to gain the Continental Divide. The two routes—Hossick Creek and Cimarrona Creek—join together 2 miles shy of Squaw Pass. From the pass the Squaw Creek Trail drops 10 miles down the other side to a trailhead near the Rio Grande Reservoir.

A mile beyond the Cimarrona Creek trailhead is the start of the 9.5-miles-long Williams Creek Trail, which ascends 3,500 feet to the Continental Divide. Breaking ranks with the Williams Creek Trail about 2 miles in is the Indian Creek Trail, an 8-mile route that follows two side drainages of the Piedra before topping out on the Continental Divide. From the Williams Creek Trail–Continental Divide Trail intersection, it is a little more than 5 miles west to Squaw Pass along the Continental Divide Trail. The Middle Fork Trail follows the Middle Fork of the Piedra for less than a mile before heading up Lean Creek. After a few miles the route gains a high ridge behind Sugarloaf Mountain. Ten miles from the trailhead the route reaches the Continental Divide Trail very near the summit of Palomino Mountain (12,230 feet). Two lakes—Window and Monument—are accessed along this route. Rugged in places, this trail is for the more adventurous at heart.

Somewhat less arduous are the Fourmile Stock and Turkey Creek Trails, which begin north of Pagosa Springs. The Fourmile Stock Trail runs 7 miles before joining the Turkey Creek Trail near Turkey Creek Lake. The fishing is good at Turkey Creek Lake so the trail experiences heavier-than-normal use. There are two impressive waterfalls along the way. The Turkey Creek Trail, which begins 5 miles outside the wilderness on the Jackson Mountain Road, starts out at 8,240 feet, 1,000 feet lower than the Fourmile trailhead. It passes high walls of volcanic rock before reaching the end of the Fourmile Stock Trail 9 miles in. From there it breaks out above timberline, reaching 11,700 feet in the process. Farther on, the route drops into the head of the East Fork of the Piedra River, where a fork in the trail offers a choice. To the left, a 1.5-mile spur connects with the top of the Middle Fork Trail; to the right it is 1.5 miles along the final stretch of the Piedra River to 11,400-foot Piedra Pass.

The final approach from the south to the Continental Divide is along the West Fork Trail, which starts near the West Fork Campground just below Wolf Creek Pass, on FS Road 648. The West Fork Trail follows a major tributary of the San Juan River for 13 miles northwest to Piedra Pass. The going can be rough along this route, although the first 5 miles are well traveled. The Beaver Creek Trail branches off from the West Fork 4.5 miles in and eventually gains the Continental Divide near Sawtooth Mountain, 9 miles from its start. From Piedra Pass it is 19 miles to Wolf Creek Pass and U.S. Highway 160 via the Continental Divide Trail. It is 11 miles from the head of Beaver Creek. With 3 or more days and a shuttle, one could devise a trip that follows the Continental Divide Trail west and then drops down the Beaver Creek, West Fork, or Turkey Creek Trails.

Although smaller in acreage than the San Juan side of the Continental Divide, the Rio Grande side also features many trails. One of the most popular—the Archuleta Trail—is a few miles north of Wolf Creek Pass. Beginning at the Big Meadows Reservoir a little more than 1 mile off U.S. Highway 160, the Archuleta Trail climbs 2,400 feet up the Archuleta Creek drainage to Archuleta Lake, 7 miles in. A favorite of weekend fishermen, this lake can be crowded at times. A less-used trail breaks from the Archuleta Lake Trail to head southwest up the South Fork of the Rio Grande, reaching the Continental Divide Trail a few miles south of Archuleta Lake.

From Elk Creek Road (FS Road 430), 1.5 miles beyond the Big Meadows Reservoir, the Hope Creek Trail follows a beautiful wooded canyon for 6 miles before ascending Sawtooth Mountain, 2 miles north of Archuleta Lake. On the eastern flank of Sawtooth it joins the 6.5-mile Highline Trail, which begins farther up Elk Creek Road. Rather than following a drainage, this route gains 12,688-foot Table Mountain and then stays above timberline the rest of the way to the Continental Divide Trail. The Hope Creek Trail junction is less than 1 mile from the Continental Divide Trail.

The Roaring Fork Trail begins at the head of Lime Creek above Spar City. Only 3 miles long, this trail serves as an access to two longer trails, which in turn reach the Continental Divide to the south. The first of these routes, the 8-mile-long Fisher Creek Trail, follows the Fisher Creek drainage to Goose Lake, Little Goose Lake, and then

In the heart of the Needles

the Continental Divide Trail. The Ivy Creek Trail joins this route at Goose Creek. Eight miles long, the Ivy Creek Trail offers a shorter alternative to the Fisher Creek route. From Goose Lake to the Divide it is 3 miles of open, alpine terrain. Another route, the 7.75-mile Deep Creek Trail, begins near the Roaring Fork trailhead and eventually connects with the Ivy Creek Trail south of Fisher Mountain. It climbs 1,800 feet.

The other trail that takes off from the Roaring Fork Trail, the Goose Creek Trail, follows Goose Creek for 13 miles before connecting with the Fisher Creek Trail at Little Goose Lake. From Little Goose Lake it is 1.5 miles around the summit of South River Peak (13,149 feet) to the Continental Divide Trail. Goose Creek is known for its trout fishing and the trail is easy to follow. Goose Creek turns west 7.5 trail miles from its start, to parallel the Continental Divide the rest of the way. At this point, a 3.5-mile spur trail links up with the Continental Divide Trail near Sawtooth Mountain.

West of the Ivy, Fisher, and Goose Creek drainages, the wilderness boundary dips south to the Continental Divide, excluding the Red Mountain and Middle Creek drainages in the process. Not until Trout Creek does the wilderness extend northward again to encompass more headwater streams of the Rio Grande. Following Trout Creek for 5 miles and then turning up West Trout Creek is the 9-mile Trout Creek Trail. Although its grade is not severe, this route crosses the stream several times, posing possible hazards during periods of high snowmelt. Near trail's end is Trout Lake and farther south on the Continental Divide Trail is an intersection with the Williams Creek Trail. The East Trout Creek Trail branches southeast 5 miles in from the Trout Creek trailhead and covers 7 miles before reaching the Continental Divide Trail near Palomino Mountain. At this point, the head of the Middle Fork Trail is to the south.

The Fern Creek Trail offers a scenic high route into the heart of the Weminuche. Beginning 1.25 miles off Colorado Highway 149 on Fern Creek Road (FS Road 522), this route reaches Little Ruby Lake in 3.5 miles. Shortly after, the trail passes Fuchs Reservoir and Ruby Lake; then, after entering the wilderness, it crosses over to Little Squaw Creek. Finally, 15 miles from its start, the Fern Creek Trail ends at the Squaw Creek Trail almost due east of where it started. From Ruby Lake, the Texas Creek Trail heads south for 5.5 miles before joining the Trout Creek Trail at Trout Lake. This route offers an above-timberline alternative to following drainage bottoms to the Continental Divide.

In the vicinity of the Rio Grande Reservoir, the Continental Divide swings northward to within a few miles of the Rio Grande itself. Two trails—one short and one long—head south from the reservoir to meet the Continental Divide Trail. The Squaw Creek Trail runs for 10 miles up its namesake and eventually tops out on Squaw Pass where it meets the Cimarrona Trail from the San Juan side. The 5.5-mile Weminuche Creek Trail reaches the Continental Divide at Weminuche Pass, 12 trail miles northwest of Squaw Pass. These two trails share the same trailhead at Thirtymile Campground, making a pleasurable 26-mile loop possible by using the Continental Divide Trail.

Ute Creek is the remaining major drainage system between Weminuche and Hunchback Passes. Extending southwest from the upper end of the Rio Grande Reservoir, this basin is accessed by the 12-mile Ute Creek Trail, which splits into three branches at 7.5 miles. The Ute Creek Trail picks up Middle Ute Creek and eventually tops out in the Twin Lakes area; the 3.5-mile East Ute Creek Trail hits the Continental Divide between Ute Peak and the Window; and the La Garita Stock Driveway follows West Ute Creek for just over 3 miles to find the Continental Divide Trail near Kite Lake. A nice loop trip follows Ute Creek and West Ute Creek before picking up the Divide and returning along Middle or East Ute Creek.

Extending west of the Animas River and the D&SNGR, the Weminuche Wilderness takes in the West Needles, which is home to one trail of note. Crater Lake Trail begins at Andrews Lake just off Molas Pass, and travels 5 miles to pristine Crater Lake. The elevation gain is negligible. A saddle just above the lake provides a fantastic view of the Animas River Gorge and the Needles. Crater Lake is popular among local and visiting hikers, so weekends can be crowded.

Cross-country Skiing

Reaching trails within the Weminuche Wilderness during winter can be difficult because most approach roads are not plowed regularly. An expedition-style trip into the Weminuche is one option, but such a trip requires a lot of planning and time to execute, and the threat of avalanches is ever present.

Perhaps the handiest wintertime access to the Weminuche is afforded on Wolf Creek Pass. By following the Continental Divide north, you can enjoy powdery wilderness slopes in no time. Since the Continental Divide Trail is covered with snow, you will have to rely on topographic maps to stay properly oriented. If you are adept at skiing among trees, you might also try entering the wilderness at Big Meadow Reservoir.

With the road plowed to the dam on the Rio Grande Reservoir, trails beginning at the Thirtymile Campground are readily accessible. These include the Squaw Creek and Weminuche Creek Trails. The latter route—only 5.5 miles long—provides strong skiers with access to the Continental Divide at Weminuche Pass. From there, overnight trips can go in either direction along the Divide—exposure to avalanche conditions pose a threat, however. From Thirtymile Campground you can also ski the 5.5 miles of road to the Ute Creek trailhead on the far end of the reservoir. From there you can ski a few miles farther before entering avalanche-prone topography.

The Crater Lake Trail in the West Needles is also easily accessed in the winter thanks to U.S. Highway 550, which tops Molas Pass. Several open slopes make this a fine area to practice telemark turns. The Purgatory Creek Trail stays mostly in thick forest, making it suitable only for experienced skiers.

Mountaineering

With three "fourteeners" and several dozen peaks over 13,000 feet, the Weminuche is one of the premier mountaineering areas in the Rockies. At the center of all the attention is the Needle Range with its cluster of impressive summits. Mountaineers flock to the Needles in droves each summer. Unfortunately, some lose their lives to falls, lightning strikes, or other hazards. Be prepared for a variety of conditions when visiting the Needles and know your climbing abilities.

The primary goals of most climbers who trek into the Needles are Mount Eolus (14,084 feet), Sunlight Peak (14,059 feet), and Windom Peak (14,082 feet). Crowning the skyline surrounding Twin Lakes above Chicago Basin, these mountains are often climbed together. Mount Eolus, which sits west of Twin Lakes, poses the most difficult challenge. The standard route up gains the ridge between Eolus and North Eolus before climbing the northeast ridge (a bouldering route with some exposure). North Eolus (14,039 feet) is often bagged by climbers but is not considered a separate peak.

Sunlight and Windom Peaks, which head the Twin Lakes basin to the east, are both self-explanatory scrambles to the top. To reach Windom, climb up the drainage directly east of the lakes and then pick your way up the peak's talus-covered west slope. For Sunlight, turn up a chute on the north side of the drainage and then follow rock cairns along the crest of the ridge. This takes the guesswork out of finding the way through the large boulders on top.

Other popular peaks in the Needles include Pigeon Peak (13,972 feet) and Turret Peak (13,835 feet). Rising directly above the Animas River Gorge, these are the two most visually prominent summits in the range. Both are approachable from Ruby Creek to the north. Pigeon has two principal routes, the northwest basin and the north face, while Turret is climbed via the saddle between it and Pigeon. Both climbs are technical in nature.

Monitor Peak (13,695 feet), Peak Thirteen (13,705 feet), Animas Mountain (13,786 feet), and the Index (13,420 feet) rise along the ridge north of Ruby Creek. Among the many challenging technical climbs in this group is the 1,200-foot east face of Monitor. The Index is also shrouded with sheer rock faces.

As the Needles stretch north, the Knife Point (13,265 feet), Leviathan Peak (13,528 feet), Peak Four (13,410 feet), the Heisspitz (13,262 feet), Peak Six (13,705 feet), and Peak Seven (13,682 feet) round out the summits in the isolated heart of the Needles Range. These require technical climbing abilities for the most part.

Rising north of the Needles along the Elk Creek drainage is a group of mountains known as the Grenadiers. Collectively, they constitute one of the highest concentrations of technical climbs in the state. One of their ranks, Arrow Peak (13,803 feet), is considered one of the hardest summits in the state. Nearby Vestal Peak (13,664 feet) has a number of challenging routes, including Wham Ridge. West, Middle, and East Trinity Peaks (all above 13,700 feet) form an attractive cluster of peaks, and Storm King (13,752 feet), Mount Silex (13,628 feet), and the Guardian (13,617 feet) round out the Grenadiers' eastern front. All of these summits are strictly for skilled technical climbers.

Although the topography relaxes a bit east of the Needles, the San Juans still produce a variety of mountaineering challenges. Mount Oso (13,684 feet) is east of Vallecito Creek; approach it from Vallecito Creek, Rock Lake, or Moon Lake. Northwest of Rock Lake is Mount Nebo (13,205 feet), which makes an impressive cap along the Continental Divide and is best climbed via the southeast ridge. Constituting the high point of this stretch of the San Juans, the Rio Grande Pyramid (13,821 feet) is a scramble that is hard to pass up once you have reached its remote locale.

The highest summit in the West Needles, Twilight Peak (13,158 feet), is approached from Crater Lake. The route is a self-explanatory scramble. Other peaks that share this ridge include North and South Twilight, and West Needle Mountain. All are over 13,000 feet and are reached from Crater Lake. (Technical climbers can discover more challenging routes up each.) Snowdon Peak (13,077 feet), which was first climbed in 1874 by the Hayden Survey, rises directly above Andrews Lake. Two routes up the northeast and west ridges access the summit. Both walk-ups involve some exposure and scrambling.

River Running

The upper Animas River, which cuts off the West Needles from the rest of the Weminuche, is an expert kayaker's delight. For rafters, however, the river's near-constant rapids have proved very difficult and even deadly. Putting in at Silverton (one of the highest put-ins in the state at 9,300 feet), kayakers can float 28 miles to Rockwood. Beyond this point the river drops at a rate of 250 feet per mile and is wholly impassable because of a logjam. Boaters must carry their crafts 2 miles from the Rockwood pullout. Parts of the Upper Animas provide continuous Class III and IV water, while some drops pose Class V challenges in high water.

40 Piedra Area

Location: 45 mi E of Durango
Size: 62,550 acres
Status: Special area (1993)
Terrain: Heavily timbered canyons and river bottoms
Elevation: 6,800' to 10,500'
Management: San Juan NF
Topographic maps: Devil Mountain, Baldy Mountain, Oakbrush Ridge, Bear Mountain, Granite Peak

An anomaly among Colorado's montane wild lands, the Piedra Area encompasses mostly lower-elevation timberlands. Absent are the spectacular high peaks so often associated with the Colorado Rockies—instead, the area is rich with the beauty of virgin forests

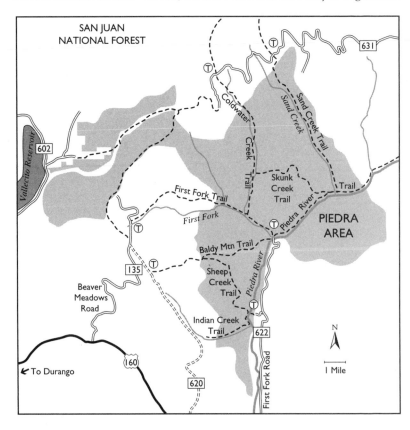

and pristine river bottoms. The entire area falls within the drainage of the Piedra River, itself a possible addition to the national Wild and Scenic River System. Principally because of water rights, the Piedra missed actual wilderness designation in the Colorado Wilderness Act of 1993 and instead garnered status as a special management area.

Seasons

Thanks to its lower elevation, the Piedra Area is relatively accessible for up to seven months a year beginning in late April or early May. Snowfall is moderate in the winter, but the spring runoff is considerable because of the river's high headwaters.

Flora and Fauna

Approximately 95 percent of the Piedra is forested. Douglas fir is predominant across lower elevations, while spruce and fir cover the upper reaches. Glades of aspen are widely scattered and occasional open meadows can be found. Riparian ecosystems consisting mostly of willow brush and cottonwoods are found along the river and streambeds. Wildlife includes mule deer, elk, coyotes, black bears, and mountain lions. River otters were successfully reintroduced to the area. The waterways within the Piedra area are considered excellent fish habitat.

Geology

Characterized by a network of deep canyons, the terrain here was shaped by stream erosion. The underlying geologic formations consist mostly of sedimentary rock, especially limestone, sandstone, and shale. This bedrock is exposed in several places, especially along the Piedra River itself.

ACTIVITIES
Hiking

Hiking trails in the Piedra Area mostly follow drainage bottoms; consequently, the grades are easy. The Piedra River Trail, for instance, begins at the end of First Fork Road and follows the Piedra River upstream for 12 miles to the upper trailhead along Piedra Road. In that distance it climbs from 7,200 to 7,700 feet—a total gain of 500 feet. The route passes through box canyons along the way and opens up to vistas of the Piedra River. To reach the end of First Fork Road, turn north from U.S. Highway 160 and drive 12 miles along the narrow gravel road.

Four miles in on the Piedra River Trail, the Sand Creek Trail branches north to follow its namesake for 8 miles before reaching improved Forest Road 631. From there it continues north into the Weminuche Wilderness Area. The Skunk Creek Trail also branches off the Piedra River Trail but crosses west to the Coldwater Creek Trail about 5 miles away.

Two other trails also begin from the end of First Fork Road. The First Fork Trail follows the First Fork of the Piedra River west for 8 miles before reaching Beaver Meadows Road. About 2 miles in from the trailhead the Coldwater Creek Trail turns north from the First Fork Trail. Like the Sand Creek Trail, it crosses into the Weminuche

Wilderness. Beginning at the First Fork trailhead, the Baldy Mountain Trail runs 5.5 miles west to a 4WD spur off the Beaver Meadows Road.

The 5-mile-long Sheep Creek Trail begins at a trailhead approximately 5 miles south of the end of First Fork Road (7 miles from U.S. 160) and connects with the Baldy Mountain Trail. The Indian Creek Trail also begins from the Sheep Creek trailhead and covers 4 miles before reaching a dead end up its namesake stream. All trails within the Piedra Area are easy to follow.

River Running

With First Fork Road as the halfway point, two stretches of the Piedra River can be run. The Piedra is recommended only for experienced kayakers, however, because of water levels and some difficult stretches. It is approximately 10 river miles from the Piedra Road Bridge, which is upstream from the wilderness, to First Fork Road. Some Class IV water is included. This stretch is not runnable in low water. From First Fork Road south, the Piedra covers another 10 miles to U.S. Highway 160, with a number of tight squeezes, sheer canyon walls, and formidable drops along the way. Plenty of Class IV rapids are found in this stretch. A rock slide in 1979 created the Eye of the Needle—a hole barely wide enough for a kayak in low water—and a portage around a 7-foot waterfall in high water. The entire 20 miles from the Piedra Road Bridge to U.S. Highway 160 can be run in 1 or 2 days.

41 Powderhorn Wilderness Area

Location: 10 mi NE of Lake City
Size: 60,100 acres
Status: Wilderness area (1993)
Terrain: Alpine plateaus and stream valleys
Elevation: 8,800' to 12,644'
Management: BLM (Gunnison Field Office), Gunnison NF
Topographic maps: Powderhorn Lakes, Rudolph Hill, Lake City, Cannibal Plateau, Mineral Mountain, Alpine Plateau, Powderhorn

The Powderhorn Wilderness Area encompasses the BLM's preexisting Powderhorn Primitive Area and the adjacent Cannibal Plateau Further Planning Area, which falls under the jurisdiction of the Gunnison National Forest. Exceptional high terrain is the primary feature here, as the Powderhorn area includes the largest alpine mesas in the lower forty-eight states. Several headwater streams drain off the Cannibal and Calf Creek Plateaus and a handful of beautiful lakes dot the high country.

Opposite: *The Piedra River*

Seasons

Winter usually arrives by mid-October in the Powderhorn Wilderness and lasts well into June; trails in higher terrain may not open up until early July. Thundershowers are likely on summer afternoons. Wildflowers bloom most heavily in July and August. Aspens change color and elk are heard bugling in September.

Flora and Fauna

Because half of the Powderhorn Wilderness is above timberline, much of the vegetation is in the form of low-growing alpine tundra grasses and forbs. Patches of willow are also common in these higher elevations. Engelmann spruce and subalpine fir are the predominant forest species, but patches of aspen also occur. The Powderhorn area contains important summer range for mule deer and elk. A variety of other mammals, including coyotes, black bears, martens, mountain lions, bobcats, marmots, and pikas, also reside here.

Geology

Much of the Powderhorn area features a layer of volcanic rock deposited between 10 million and 35 million years ago, reported to be up to 5,000 feet thick in places. Calderas that once erupted near Lake City are the probable sources of this intrusive rock.

A 4-mile-long earth flow, the Slumgullion Slide, lies just outside the southwest corner of the wilderness. Letting loose 700 years ago, the slide formed Lake San Cristobal. Movement in the slide today is as much as 20 feet per year. The Slumgullion Slide is a designated national natural landmark.

Gentle alpine plateaus typify the Powderhorn Wilderness.

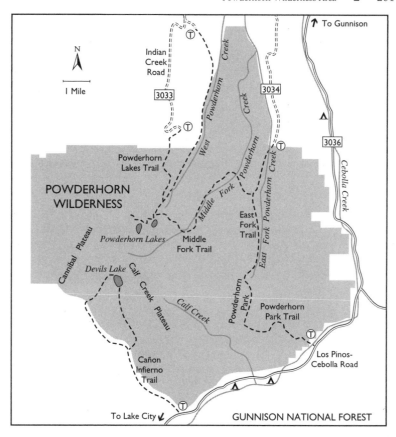

History

Cannibal Plateau was named for a dubious chapter in Colorado's history. In 1873, Alfred Packer led a prospecting party of five into the San Juans. The trip was made against the advice of the Ute Indian Chief Ouray; the men pushed on, ignoring the advance of winter. In the spring, Packer returned to report that the others had left him behind. In August of the following year, some prospectors found the cannibalized remains of his party. Packer was arrested and eventually found guilty of manslaughter.

ACTIVITIES
Hiking

Powderhorn Lakes is the premier destination within the wilderness. Situated above 11,500 feet, these two lakes offer good fishing and splendid scenery. The Powderhorn Lakes Trail from the north is the quickest route to the lakes. Beginning near the end of Indian Creek Road, this route covers 3.5 miles and climbs approximately 600 feet. Upper Powderhorn Lake is 0.5 mile beyond Lower Powderhorn Lake.

Reaching Powderhorn Lakes from the northeast is the Middle Fork Trail, which begins 2 miles up the East Fork Trail and traverses Powderhorn Swamp before picking up the Middle Fork of Powderhorn Creek. It then makes the easy climb up and over to the West Fork and Powderhorn Lakes ending a little more than 5 miles from its start. The East Fork Trail begins at the Tenmile Springs trailhead at the end of an 8-mile-long 4WD road. Following its namesake stream for 5 miles, the East Fork Trail eventually connects with the Powderhorn Park Trail near the BLM–Gunnison National Forest boundary.

Accessing the wilderness from the southeast, the Powderhorn Park Trail begins along Los Pinos–Cebolla Road and covers 4 miles before reaching Powderhorn Park. Although some grade change is involved, the terrain is generally level with views across the open expanse of alpine tundra along the trail's upper reaches. Once extending 13 miles from the trailhead to the Powderhorn Lakes, beyond Powderhorn Park the trail is now overgrown and hard to follow.

The 6-mile Cañon Infierno Trail follows Brush Creek north from Los Pinos–Cebolla Road toward Devils Lake on the Calf Creek Plateau. Since the trail begins at 10,200 feet, the ascent is not too difficult. Overgrown willows obscure the last 3 miles to Devils Lake, so be prepared to bushwhack. A compass and topographic map come in handy here.

Cross-country Skiing

Wintertime access to the Powderhorn Wilderness is confined to the west side of Los Pinos–Cebolla Road, which is regularly plowed to the Powderhorn Park trailhead 1.5 miles south of Cathedral. Los Pinos–Cebolla Road is closed to vehicles at Slumgullion Pass during the winter, but it is a level glide to the Cañon Infierno trailhead 5 miles away. Although much of the Powderhorn area is relatively flat, watch for avalanches on the steeper slopes.

42 Redcloud Peak Wilderness Study Area

Location: 2 mi SW of Lake City
Size: 37,442 acres
Status: Wilderness study area (1979)
Terrain: Alpine peaks and forested lower slopes
Elevation: 8,700' to 14,034'
Management: BLM (Gunnison Field Office)
Topographic maps: Redcloud Peak, Lake San Cristobal, Wetterhorn Peak, Uncompahgre Peak, Lake City

Rising between the Lake Fork of the Gunnison River and Henson Creek in the heart of the San Juan Mountains, the Redcloud Peak Wilderness Study Area includes a pair of "fourteeners," Redcloud and Sunshine Peaks, as well as several slightly lesser mountains. Because much of this region is above timberline, the views are fantastic and hikes are memorable. Potentially valuable mineral deposits in the area could hinder wilderness designation.

Seasons

Trails in the Redcloud are usually covered by a blanket of snow from late October or early November through June. Summer afternoons often bring lightning storms in the high country. The wildflower season takes hold in late July while mid-September ushers in the change of aspen leaves.

Flora and Fauna

Alpine tundra, with its varieties of grasses and forbs, prevails. Blue columbine and Indian paintbrush grow in the wetter meadows. Expansive areas of talus rock are present; lichens are the dominant plant species here. Marmots and pikas are common throughout the alpine reaches. Below timberline, forests consist of Engelmann spruce and subalpine fir, along with scattered aspens. Mule deer and elk reside here, as do coyotes and bobcats.

Geology

The mountains that make up this area were once part of the large Lake City Caldera, which has since collapsed and filled with volcanic debris. There are many such calderas in the San Juans. The reddish color of Redcloud and the surrounding mountains is due to mineralization—mostly iron oxides—of the rocks.

ACTIVITIES
Hiking

A few short trails penetrate drainages in the Redcloud area. Beginning on Henson Creek Road 2 miles west of Lake City and running southwest, the Alpine Gulch Trail climbs

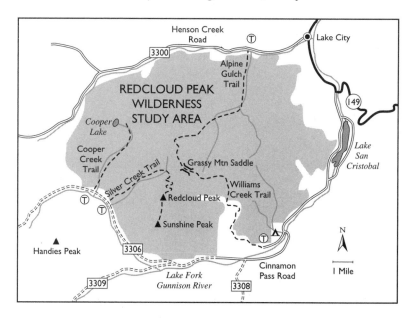

from 9,000 to 12,480 feet in 6 miles. Several old cabins left behind by nineteenth-century miners dot the route, and open parks and cliff faces are plentiful. From the Cinnamon Pass Road, the Williams Creek Trail runs northwest for 7.5 miles, gaining more than 3,000 feet. The Williams Creek and Alpine Gulch routes connect at Grassy Mountain Saddle (12,480 feet), making a 13.5-mile hike possible. Both trails are considered strenuous.

Farther west on the Cinnamon Pass Road is the beginning of the Silver Creek Trail, which covers 4.2 miles before topping Redcloud Peak (14,034 feet). It then continues another 1.5 miles to the top of Sunshine Peak (14,001 feet). The Cooper Creek Trail, which begins almost a mile beyond the Silver Creek trailhead along the Cinnamon Pass Road, is nearly 4 miles in length. Its goal, Cooper Lake, sits at 12,750 feet—approximately 2,200 feet above the trailhead. Use of the Cooper Creek Trail is comparatively light.

Cross-country Skiing
Experienced skiers occasionally attempt the Silver Creek Trail, which begins 4 miles beyond where the snowplows turn around on the Cinnamon Pass Road, but the avalanche hazard is considerable because of steep mountain faces. Extra caution should be taken. Closer to Lake City, the readily accessible Williams Creek Trail can offer good touring opportunities under the right conditions. The flip side of this route—the Alpine Gulch Trail—is reachable, but stream crossings can make it more pain than pleasure.

Mountaineering
Connected by a saddle, Sunshine and Redcloud Peaks are often climbed together. After accessing the head of a valley, the Silver Creek Trail climbs up the north face of Redcloud. A distinct trail continues from there to the summit of Sunshine. The view from both peaks is glorious in all directions.

43 Handies Peak Wilderness Study Area

Location: 18 mi SW of Lake City
Size: 16,769 acres
Status: Wilderness study area (1979)
Terrain: Alpine peaks and forested lower slopes
Elevation: 9,400' to 14,048'
Management: BLM (Gunnison Field Office)
Topographic maps: Handies Peak, Redcloud Peak

Handies Peak is situated south of the Lake Fork of the Gunnison River and southeast of Cinnamon Pass. Although one of the easiest "fourteeners" in the state to climb, it does not draw the crowds that others do, in part due to its relative isolation.

Along the trail up American Basin

Seasons

Rising quickly from the valley floor, Handies Peak and much of the surrounding terrain is above timberline. This means that finding snow-free trails is possible mostly from early July through mid-October. Wildflowers bloom in late July and August. Lightning is possible on most summer afternoons.

Flora and Fauna

Some beautiful stretches of alpine tundra exist in the Handies Peak area. Where water is plentiful, the wildflowers grow in spectacular numbers. Blue columbine, Indian paintbrush, and orange sneezeweed are most common. Pikas and marmots are abundant in this treeless landscape. Elk also summer here.

Geology

The Handies Peak area, like most of the San Juan Range, is primarily volcanic in origin. A large dome of Precambrian rock pushed upward during the Laramide Orogeny. After erosion exposed parts of this uplift, a period of volcanic activity beginning 40 million years ago spread ash, lava, and rock across much of the area. Additional erosion brought on mostly by glaciers has since shaped much of the area, rounding out valleys, carving cirques, and forming lake basins.

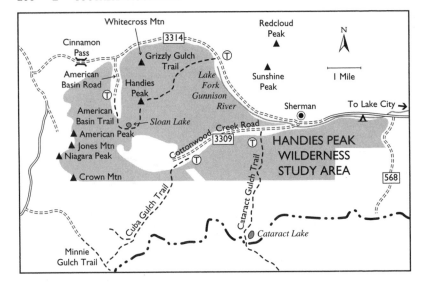

ACTIVITIES
Hiking

A number of trails follow alpine valleys into the Handies Peak Wilderness Study Area, offering climbers access to local peaks. The Cataract Gulch Trail begins on Cottonwood Creek Road west of its intersection with the Cinnamon Pass Road. It crosses 1.5 miles of the WSA and then another 2.5 miles of undesignated U.S. Forest Service land before reaching Cataract Lake and the Continental Divide, a climb from 9,630 to 12,200 feet.

The Cuba Gulch Trail begins near the end of Cottonwood Creek Road. Climbing to 12,900 feet, this trail continues 3.25 miles from the trailhead before crossing the Continental Divide and tying into the Minnie Gulch Trail in the Animas River drainage. All but 0.5 mile of the Cuba Gulch Trail lies south of the WSA boundary. It is possible to use this trail in conjunction with the Cataract Gulch Trail for an extended trip, but be sure to carry a compass and topographic maps.

The Grizzly Gulch Trail, which begins directly across Cinnamon Pass Road from the Silver Creek Trail in the Redcloud WSA, climbs 4.2 miles to the summit of Handies Peak (14,048 feet). As for the shortest (2.5 miles) and most popular route to the summit, the American Basin Trail begins at the end of 1-mile, 4WD American Basin Road. The trail passes Sloan Lake along the way.

Cross-country Skiing

Because the road to Cinnamon Pass is plowed to Sherman (where Cottonwood Creek Road forks south), skiers can reach the eastern end of the Handies Peak WSA rather easily. The start of the Cataract Gulch Trail lies 1.4 miles up Cottonwood Creek Road, while the Grizzly Gulch Trail is about 4 miles of road skiing beyond Sherman. Both trails make feasible tours for experienced skiers, but avalanche conditions should be checked before venturing into steeper terrain.

Mountaineering

Handies Peak is a walk-up from all approaches. The Grizzly Gulch Trail is one route; American Basin, which runs west of the peak, is another. Drive 4 miles beyond the Grizzly Gulch trailhead to a hairpin curve in the road. From here, 4WD American Basin Road continues another mile to the start of a trail. Following a beautiful alpine valley, this route passes Sloan Lake and ascends the south face of the mountain.

More challenging peaks include Jones Mountain (13,860 feet), Whitecross Mountain (13,542 feet), Niagara Peak (13,807 feet), Crown Mountain (13,569 feet), and American Peak (13,806 feet). With impressive couloirs running up its north face, the latter mountain offers several excellent snow-climbing routes.

Uncompahgre Wilderness Area

Location: 5 mi W of Lake City
Size: 102,525 acres
Status: Wilderness area (1980)
Terrain: Alpine summits and valleys
Elevation: 8,400' to 14,309'
Management: Uncompahgre NF, BLM (Uncompahgre Field Office)
Topographic maps: Uncompahgre Peak, Wetterhorn Peak, Lake City, Ouray, Sheep Mountain, Alpine Plateau, Dallas, Courthouse Mountain, Handies Peak

The Uncompahgre Wilderness spans a particularly high section of the northern San Juan Mountains. It includes two "fourteeners" and several slightly lower summits. Because about half of the wilderness area is above timberline, vistas in the Uncompahgre are spectacular. With 75 miles of trails to choose from, the Uncompahgre offers many places to leave the crowds behind.

Seasons

The upper reaches of the Uncompahgre Wilderness are usually snow-free from early or mid-July through September or October. Lower elevations are usually snow-free by June. During the summer months, watch out for lightning on exposed summits and ridges. Thunderstorms usually occur in the afternoon, but they occasionally gather strength by noon or even midmorning. Alpine wildflowers bloom in late July and August, and September brings the changing of aspen leaves as well as the rutting season for elk.

Flora and Fauna

Below timberline, forests consist mostly of Engelmann spruce and subalpine fir. Patches of aspen are also plentiful. Forest inhabitants include mule deer, elk, mountain lions, bobcats, coyotes, black bears, and snowshoe hares.

Above timberline—situated around 11,500 feet at this latitude—is a vast landscape of alpine tundra. A variety of grasses and sedges grow here, as do flowering perennials such as blue columbine, bistort, Indian paintbrush, and alpine sunflower.

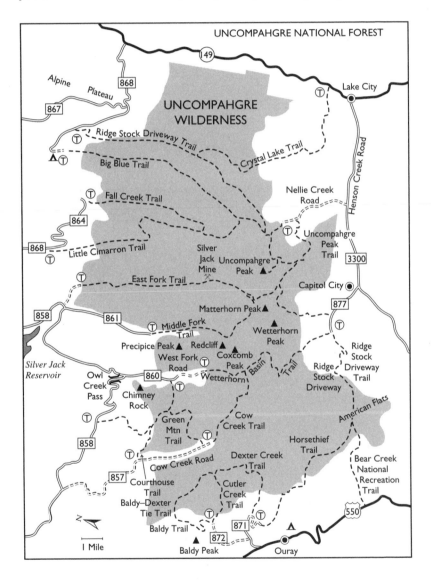

Marmots, pikes, and ptarmigan are the most frequently spotted residents of this environment, but bighorn sheep and even moose are present in some areas.

Geology

The San Juans formed as a broad dome during the Laramide Orogeny some 65 million years ago. Extensive volcanic activity during the middle Tertiary period, however, helped give the San Juans their uniquely rugged character. Uncompahgre Peak (14,309 feet) is topped with volcanic rock, as are many other summits in the Uncompahgre Wilderness. The Wetterhorn (14,015 feet) is actually a volcanic intrusion encircled by radial dikes. It was probably the conduit of a large volcano. In succeeding years, glaciers went to work etching out cirques and valleys, and sculpting the high peaks into their present-day shapes.

History

Two members of the Hayden Survey achieved the first recorded climb of Uncompahgre Peak in 1874. They discovered, however, that they had been preceded by grizzly bears. Uncompahgre is a Ute word that means "hot water," a reference to the hot springs in nearby Ouray. The Utes roamed these mountains and probably climbed many of them long before the first white men ever considered such a feat.

ACTIVITIES
Hiking

The highest peaks in the Uncompahgre Wilderness are found in its southern portion, while major streams and drainages dissect the northern side. Trails often follow this pattern of geography. Routes through the mountainous southern frontier dart between the various summits while those in the north mostly follow the drainages.

The Uncompahgre Peak Trail is probably the most popular trail. The trailhead is reached by driving west from Lake City toward Engineer Pass on Henson Creek Road, then turning north on 4WD Nellie Creek Road and driving to its end. The route climbs from 11,450 feet to 14,309 feet in 3.5 miles. While Uncompahgre is the chief attraction, this trail also provides access to other parts of the high country.

Less than 2 miles in, the Uncompahgre Peak Trail intersects the Ridge Stock Driveway Trail, which extends 21 miles from the Alpine Plateau to Matterhorn Creek just south of the wilderness boundary. Seven miles from Alpine Plateau, the Ridge Stock Driveway Trail connects with the north end of the Crystal Lake Trail (most of which runs outside the wilderness), which begins adjacent to the Lake City Cemetery. From the Ridge Stock Driveway to Crystal Lake is 7 miles, and from the lake to Lake City is another 4 miles. Because of steep terrain, the Crystal Lake Trail is considered a difficult hike.

The Big Blue Trail follows Big Blue Creek south from the Big Blue Campground (also in the vicinity of the Alpine Plateau) for 12 miles before connecting with the Ridge Stock Driveway Trail just shy of the Uncompahgre Peak Trail. Following the streambed

the entire way, the Big Blue Trail is easy save for its length. The 11.5-mile Fall Creek Trail similarly follows its namesake drainage before connecting with the upper end of the Big Blue Trail. From the trailhead the Fall Creek route covers 9 miles before picking up the end of the 8-mile-long Little Cimarron Trail. All of these trails are interconnected on their southern ends, making extended loop trips possible.

Like their eastern counterparts, the routes that follow drainages into the western half of the Uncompahgre Wilderness offer round-trip opportunities. Beginning 3 miles south of the Silver Jack Reservoir, the East Fork Trail runs 12 miles before connecting with the Ridge Stock Driveway Trail southwest of Uncompahgre Peak. Climbing to more than 12,000 feet, the route opens up to spectacular views of major summits in the area and passes the antiquated remains of the Silver Jack Mine. A mile north of Matterhorn Peak, the Middle Fork Trail comes in from the west. Following the Middle Fork of the Cimarron River south for 6 miles, this route then climbs up and over to meet the East Fork drainage. Approximately 8 miles long, the Middle Fork Trail is often combined with the East Fork Trail for an overnight hike.

The Wetterhorn Basin Trail crosses the wilderness from north to south via Wetterhorn Pass. Beginning at the end of West Fork Road (FS Road 860), the last few miles of which are 4WD, this trail climbs from 10,760 feet to the 12,560-foot pass in 2.5 miles, then drops into Wetterhorn Basin. The southern end of the trail, which is another 6 miles from the pass, is reached by driving to the end of the road up the North Fork of Henson Creek. Scenic treats along the way include Wetterhorn Basin, Wetterhorn Peak (14,015 feet), and Coxcomb Peak (13,656 feet).

The Cow Creek Trail branches off from the Wetterhorn Basin Trail and heads west to Cow Creek Road (FS Road 857), 5.4 miles away. From there, the Green Mountain Trail runs 4 miles to connect with the Courthouse Trail. After sharing a mile-long corridor with the Courthouse route, the Green Mountain Trail branches north to cover another 1.5 miles before reaching Flume Creek Road (FS Road 858). In all, the Green Mountain route covers 6.8 miles and runs between elevations of 8,400 and 10,500 feet. The Courthouse Trail covers 5.3 miles, from West Fork Road to Cow Creek Road, and reaches a high point of 11,000 feet near its eastern trailhead. All trailheads along Cow Creek Road are accessible by 4WD only. Even then, heavy spring runoff may preclude all vehicle traffic.

A separate and relatively small network of trails penetrates in the westernmost portion of the wilderness a few miles north of Ouray. Beginning at the end of Cutler Creek Road is the steep Cutler Creek Trail, which climbs 8,500 to 11,300 feet in 2.8 miles. The upper end of this route connects with the Dexter Creek Trail, which climbs up from Dexter Creek Road (FS Road 871), 5 miles distant. Heading north from the Cutler Creek–Dexter Creek Trail intersection is the 4.7-mile Baldy–Dexter Tie Trail. It hooks up with the Baldy Trail near Baldy Peak (10,603 feet), just outside of the wilderness boundary. The Baldy Trail begins 2 miles away on Cutler Creek Road (FS

Opposite: *Hiking along the Wetterhorn Basin Trail*

Road 872). From the end of Cutler Creek Road, you may follow Cutler Creek, Baldy–Dexter Tie, and Baldy trails for a 9.5-mile loop with tremendous views of the Uncompahgre Valley and the Mount Sneffels area.

Clipping across the southwest corner of the Uncompahgre Wilderness is the Horsethief Trail. Beginning at the end of Dexter Creek Road a few miles north of Ouray, this route heads southeast into the American Flats area where it connects with a continuation of the Ridge Stock Driveway 13 miles from the Dexter Creek trailhead. The Ridge Stock Driveway intersects with the Bear Creek National Recreation Trail to the west and continues east to the far northeast corner of the wilderness, as described above.

Cross-country Skiing

Wintertime access to the Uncompahgre Wilderness is quite limited. Steep terrain precludes touring out of the Ouray area. Since the Owl Creek Pass Road is not plowed beyond the vicinity of Onion Hill (at least 9 miles from the pass itself), a quick approach from this end is not possible. From Lake City, Engineer Pass Road (FS Road 877) remains open to the Capitol City area until heavy snows increase the threat of avalanches, usually in early or mid-December; after that time the plows turn around just a couple of miles from town. The road to Alpine Plateau is not normally cleared. To reach the first trailhead in this area requires a 7-mile ski along the unplowed road.

If you do plan an overnight ski trip into the Uncompahgre Wilderness, be mindful of avalanche conditions, especially on steeper slopes.

Mountaineering

Uncompahgre Peak (14,309 feet) is often climbed via the Uncompahgre Peak Trail, which winds up the summit's southeast ridge. The north face is a massive rock face too crumbly for climbing.

Matterhorn Creek is the favored approach route to Wetterhorn Peak (14,015 feet). From the head of Wetterhorn Creek, continue northwest through a basin at the foot of the summit, gain the southeast ridge, and follow it up. The climb is more technical than Uncompahgre, as it requires a lot of scrambling and crosses several exposed ledges. Bring ropes.

Matterhorn Peak (13,590 feet) rises between Uncompahgre and Wetterhorn and is considered a moderately easy climb with some scrambling. Another "thirteener" in the Uncompahgre Wilderness is Coxcomb Peak (13,656 feet) with its imposing summit. Well fortified, this is a technical climb that requires a number of belays. Approach it via the West Fork Trail. Nearby Redcliff (13,642 feet) is a walk-up from the Middle Fork. Precipice Peak (13,144 feet) and Dunsinane (12,742 feet) are two nice climbs between the West Fork and Middle Fork in the northwest end of the wilderness. Chimney Rock, which towers above Owl Creek Pass, is a striking tower of compressed volcanic rock that technical climbers occasionally tackle.

Mount Sneffels Wilderness Area

Location: 8 mi W of Ouray
Size: 16,505 acres
Status: Wilderness area (1980)
Terrain: Alpine summits and valleys
Elevation: 9,600' to 14,150'
Management: Uncompahgre NF
Topographic maps: Mount Sneffels, Telluride, Sams, Gray Head

Encompassing 14,150-foot Mount Sneffels and several surrounding peaks, this wilderness area is popular with peak baggers. It is also known for the blue columbines and other alpine wildflowers that bloom in the summer. Although long-distance hikes are nonexistent here, there are a few memorable short ones.

Seasons

Snow covers the highest terrain from late September or early October through mid-July. Rainy conditions are common during the summer, and lightning poses a frequent

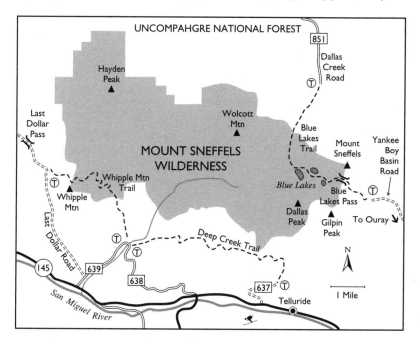

threat to hikers and climbers. Stream crossings may be a problem during high runoff periods. The flower season, for which nearby Yankee Boy Basin is known, begins in earnest in late July and lasts into August.

Flora and Fauna
Most of this wilderness area is characterized by alpine tundra, although some Engelmann spruce and subalpine fir forests are here too. Wildlife includes mule deer, elk, black bears, bobcats, pikas, and marmots. Mountain lions and golden eagles have been spotted and a small band of bighorn sheep inhabits this rugged mountain terrain. Additionally, as lynx prowl in the Telluride area, it is likely that they inhabit the Mount Sneffels Wilderness as well.

Geology
Geologists label Mount Sneffels an igneous intrusion; that is, molten rock pushed up through overlying layers of substrata. Nearby peaks were formed by lava flows from one of several calderas in the area. This part of the San Juan Mountains saw particularly heavy volcanic activity during the Tertiary period. Because vents that formed at the base of Mount Sneffels resulted in rich deposits of mineral ore, many old mines are present.

ACTIVITIES
Hiking
From the end of the 4WD Yankee Boy Basin Road in Yankee Boy Basin, the Blue Lakes Trail climbs to the top of 13,000-foot Blue Lakes Pass before dropping down the other side to the Blue Lakes themselves. From there, the route exits the wilderness to the north and ends at the 8,350-foot level on Dallas Creek Road, having covered 6.7 miles from end to end. Crowded in the summer, the Blue Lakes Trail should be avoided during peak visitation times. Impact around the lakes has been very heavy and campfires are prohibited within the entire drainage. Hikers approaching the Blue Lakes Trail via Canyon Creek and Yankee Boy Basin should keep in mind that camping is restricted to designated areas for a fee and a day-use permit (which includes trailhead parking) is required as well. Self-service stations are available.

The Whipple Mountain Trail, which traverses the southwest corner of the wilderness, is a less-traveled trail. It begins on the east side of Last Dollar Pass on Last Dollar Road outside of Telluride. Reaching an elevation above 11,000 feet, the Whipple Mountain Trail reveals fantastic views of the Sneffels Wilderness and the distant La Sal Mountains in Utah. Four miles from its start, the Whipple Mountain Trail drops to connect with the Deep Creek Trail. Although it runs outside of the wilderness boundary, the 12-mile-long Deep Creek Trail is a good route to hike in the spring and late fall when snow covers higher terrain.

Opposite: A hiker descends Mount Sneffels.

Mountaineering

Mount Sneffels (14,150 feet) is usually extremely crowded in the summer, especially on weekends. To avoid the crowds try it during the week. To climb the peak, head north from the Blue Lakes Trail through a wide gulch to a saddle above. From there ascend a narrow couloir to the left. Because of loose rocks along the way, some opt for a route southwest of this couloir.

Another interesting summit to climb is Dallas Peak (13,809 feet). Reach it by following a high ridge from Blue Lakes Pass south past Gilpin Peak. This route entails a lot of climbing and exposure in some places. On this and any other climb in the area, it is best to be off the summit by noon because of lightning.

46 Lizard Head Wilderness Area

Location: 10 mi SW of Telluride
Size: 41,189 acres
Status: Wilderness area (1980)
Terrain: Alpine summits and forested lower slopes
Elevation: 9,000' to 14,246'
Management: San Juan NF, Uncompahgre NF
Topographic maps: Mount Wilson, Dolores Peak, Gray Head, Little Cone

Straddling the heart of the San Miguel Mountains, the Lizard Head Wilderness Area contains three "fourteeners" and several 13,000-foot peaks. The area's namesake, a 400-foot spire of rock, provides a spectacular landmark for motorists along Colorado Highway 145. From all directions, the San Miguel Range strikes an impressive and alluring pose.

Seasons

Snow covers the entire wilderness area from mid-October through May, with higher trails not clearing until well into July. Several snowfields remain year-round. Wildflowers reach their peak in late July, and September brings on the colorful change of aspen leaves. Watch for dangerous lightning on summer afternoons and be prepared for sudden blasts of cold weather any time of the year.

Flora and Fauna

With timberline at 11,500 feet, much of the range features alpine tundra. Lower terrain is typified by forests of Engelmann spruce and subalpine fir, and by glades of aspen. Once home to bighorn sheep, the San Miguel Mountains lost their resident population. A game animal that does exist in large numbers here is elk. The area's thick forests and open meadows provide the ideal habitat for these magnificent beasts and the stillness of autumn is often interrupted by the eerie wail of bulls in rut. Mule deer frequent the area;

Columbine in the Lizard Head Wilderness

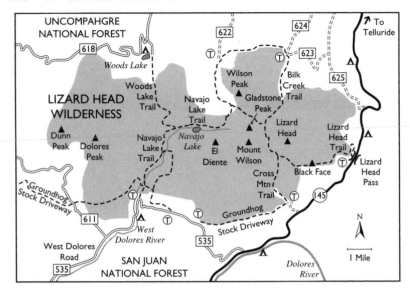

black bears and mountain lions have been sighted here as well. The high-pitched chirps of marmots and pikas commonly ring out across the high meadows.

Geology

As part of the San Juan Mountains, the San Miguels were formed during a period of volcanic activity that gave rise to many of southwestern Colorado's peaks. Beginning about 40 million years ago, during the Tertiary period, igneous intrusions pushed their way up through layers of conglomerates and shale. Three 14,000-foot peaks resulted. Lizard Head itself is composed of older volcanic ash and cinder. Glacial activity is also widely evident in these mountains. The highest peaks once jutted above glacial ice, while most valleys are U-shaped, indicating extensive glacial carving. Terminal moraines are visible south of the range.

History

Although not as extensive as in other parts of the San Juans, exploration for gold and silver did take place in the San Miguels during the late nineteenth century. A handful of antiquated mines still dot the mountainsides and scattered structures can be found. These structures and the relics associated with them are protected as cultural resources. Four miles south of the wilderness boundary, the small town of Dunton once served as a mining community. Until recently, hot springs there were open to the public.

Named by members of the Hayden Survey, the Lizard Head spire has played a prominent role in the history of the area. Early tourists flocked to see the formation after Otto Mears adopted the spire as the logo for the Rio Grande Northwestern Railroad. A 1912 report erroneously claimed that the rock had collapsed.

ACTIVITIES
Hiking

The Navajo Lake Trail, a popular entry point for the Lizard Head Wilderness, begins 1 mile north of the Burro Bridge Campground on the upper West Dolores River. After following the river northeast for 3.5 miles, the trail climbs a series of switchbacks before connecting with the end of the Woods Lake Trail. Coming in from the north, the Woods Lake Trail begins at Woods Lake, 4 miles away. From this junction, the Navajo Lakes Trail drops into Navajo Basin. Navajo Lake is a real gem, but because it serves as a base camp for folks intent on climbing nearby peaks, it receives a lot of use. Fires are banned in the Navajo Basin.

From Navajo Lake the trail continues east across talus slopes before climbing to a 13,000-foot saddle. On top the main trail drops into Silver Pick Basin to the north; a spur route descends into Bilk Basin to the east. Travel along these high ridges can be dangerous because of exposure and sliding rocks. Both trails exit the wilderness area at obscure trailheads to the north.

Bilk Basin is better reached via the Lizard Head Trail, which starts at Lizard Head Pass on Colorado Highway 145, several miles south of the Matterhorn Campground. This route climbs nearly 2,000 feet to the summit of Black Face, a 12,000-foot ridge that overlooks the highway. Six miles from its start, the Lizard Head Trail meets two other routes. The 3-mile-long Cross Mountain Trail drops south to a point on Colorado Highway 145 2 miles south of the pass. The Bilk Creek Trail heads north for 5.6 miles to a trailhead on the Wilson Sunshine Road (FS Road 623) in the Uncompahgre National Forest. An exceptionally scenic route, the Bilk Creek Trail passes through Bilk Basin, which is at the foot of Wilson Peak (14,017 feet).

Cross-country Skiing

While the heart of these mountains is too rugged for safe backcountry skiing, day tours can be enjoyed along the outer reaches of the wilderness. The Cross Mountain Trail accesses great wintertime views of Lizard Head, Cross Mountain, Mount Wilson, and Wilson Peak, and provides a gentle approach to the top of Black Face. The ski up Black Face from the east end via the Lizard Head Trail crosses some potentially hazardous avalanche chutes.

Another route follows the Groundhog Stock Driveway, which skirts the southern boundary of the wilderness area. This trail can be found a short way from Colorado Highway 145 on the Cross Mountain Trail. After you top the first major climb, you gain The Meadows with its wide open spaces and glorious views of El Diente and Mount Wilson. With a shuttle, you could end the tour at Dunton up the West Dolores Road.

Mountaineering

Three "fourteeners" tempt climbers in the Lizard Head Wilderness. The easiest to climb is Wilson Peak (14,017 feet), accessible from the ridge separating Navajo and Bilk Basins. Mount Wilson (14,246 feet) and El Diente (14,159 feet) are considered two of

Colorado's more difficult "fourteeners" because of exposure, permanent snowfields, and loose rocks. The most popular approach begins at the Rock of Ages Mine near the saddle between Navajo Lake and Silver Pick Basin. After passing below Gladstone Peak (13,913 feet), this route allows an ascent of either the northwest face of Mount Wilson or the north face of El Diente.

Lizard Head itself is a crumbling mass of rock and is considered the most difficult technical climb in Colorado. Only the most experienced climbers should attempt it.

Because peak baggers have had an adverse impact on the fragile alpine tundra of the Lizard Head Wilderness, it is recommended that they travel in groups of a half dozen or less. Additionally, poor planning and inexperience have led to climbing tragedies in the San Miguel Mountains. Climbers should watch for loose rock and exposure, be mindful of the weather, and try to be off the summits by noon.

Opposite: *Canyon scenery along the Pollock Canyon Trail*

chapter 4 **The Plateau**

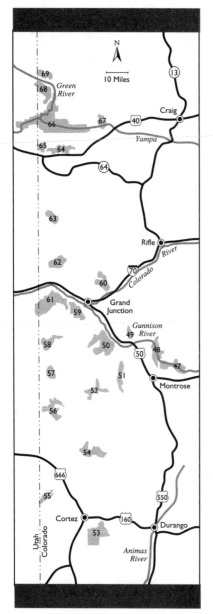

Stretching across the western quarter of the state, Colorado's Plateau region is a land of colorful mesas and canyons, sheer sandstone walls, and rugged deserts. Elevations average between 4,500 and 9,000 feet, and the climate is typically hot in the summer and cool in the winter.

While some areas represented here are designated wildernesses, many more are managed as wilderness study areas by the BLM. Because their final protection is still pending, some of these areas still allow mechanized travel. Roads and mines determine boundaries more often than the topography. Established trails within these areas are few and far between, but natural routes such as wash bottoms and canyon rims can make for pleasurable backcountry explorations. These routes often have no official name or numerical designation.

In addition to the pristine environs of Black Canyon of the Gunnison and Mesa Verde National Parks and Colorado and Dinosaur National Monuments, BLM lands described here include the Cross Canyon, McKenna Peak, Dolores River Canyon, Sewemup Mesa, Palisade, Gunnison Gorge, Dominguez Canyons, Adobe Badlands, Black Ridge Canyons, Little Book Cliffs, Demaree Canyon, Oil Spring Mountain, Bull Canyon, Willow Creek–Skull Creek, Cross Mountain, Diamond Breaks, and West Cold Spring Mountain Wilderness Study Areas. Two special management areas—Tabeguache and Roubideau—encompass sections of the Uncompahgre National Forest and adjacent BLM lands.

The Menefee Mountain, Weber Mountain, Cahone Canyon, Squaw–Papoose Canyon, Black Mountain, and Windy Gulch Wilderness Study Areas were not included here because they lack recreational opportunities and, in some cases, practical access.

Black Canyon of the Gunnison National Park

Location: 14 mi NE of Montrose
Size: 20,766 acres
Status: National park (1999)
Terrain: Steep and narrow canyons
Elevation: 5,400' to 8,563'
Management: NPS
Topographic maps: Grizzly Gulch, Red Rock Canyon

Although not as deep or as long as other canyons of North America, the Black Canyon of the Gunnison is nevertheless spectacular. With its sheer walls towering as much as 2,600 feet above the river bottom, and its north and south rims closing to within 1,100 feet, the Black Canyon of the Gunnison is unmatched in combined narrowness and depth. Fourteen of the canyon's 53 miles lie within the park. Scenic overlooks along both rims allow visitors to peer nearly straight down into the gloomy depths of this abyss. Given the fact that the river drops as much as 240 feet per mile, the canyon is nearly unrunnable; hiking is an equally difficult option for those who wish to explore the canyon's depths. Set aside as a national monument in 1933, it was upgraded to park status in 1999.

Seasons

Snowfall—up to 7 feet a year—closes the North Rim and East Portal Roads from December to March, and sometimes longer. Part of the South Rim Drive is kept open but temperatures in the winter often drop below zero at night. Summer temperatures usually do not exceed ninety degrees, and afternoon thundershowers can be expected. Late spring and fall are perhaps the nicest times to visit.

Flora and Fauna

Forests of pinyon pine and junipers are found along the rim and mesa top, as are thickets of gambel oak, serviceberry, and mountain mahogany. The canyon bottom features riparian communities of box elder trees and other water-loving plants. Of the mammals living within the national park, watch for golden-mantled ground squirrels, chipmunks, porcupines, cottontail rabbits, coyotes, and mule deer. Black bears, bobcats, mountain lions, and bighorn sheep also may be sighted here. Among the birds that inhabit the area are golden eagles and peregrine falcons.

Geology

Extending 48 miles in all, the Black Canyon of the Gunnison was formed by river erosion of the dome-shaped Gunnison Uplift. First establishing its course across softer volcanic rock, the river was forced to continue cutting through much harder underlying layers of igneous rock. The present canyon was cut within the last 2 million years and the process is still ongoing. Precambrian schist and gneiss—similar to that found within the Grand Canyon—form the dark canyon walls. Streaks of lighter rock were formed when molten rock was injected into cracks and fissures. These are quite evident in the 2,300-foot Painted Wall, Colorado's highest precipice.

History

While the Utes visited the canyon's rims, they apparently never spent much time inside Black Canyon itself. Members of the 1873–74 Hayden Expedition were the first white men to see the canyon. (Previous parties, including the Dominguez–Escalante Expedition in 1776 and Captain John W. Gunnison, who followed later, passed close by but missed the canyon completely.) In 1901 William Torrence and Abraham Lincoln Fellows became the first people to successfully travel the length of the Black Canyon. Interest in preserving its scenic beauty surfaced in the late 1920s, and in 1933 President Hoover designated the Black Canyon of the Gunnison a national monument. An act of Congress in 1999 saw the monument transformed into a park.

ACTIVITIES
Hiking

A majority of visitors to the park only see the canyon from the drive-up overlooks along the South Rim and North Rim Roads. Several short trails lead to additional view-

Looking into the depths of the Black Canyon of the Gunnison

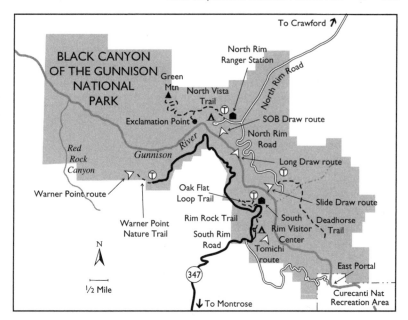

points along both rims, however. One of these is the 0.7-mile Warner Point Nature Trail, which begins at the end of the South Rim Road. The similarly short Rim Rock Trail leads from the South Rim Campground to Tomichi Point just south of the visitor center on the south rim. The 2-mile-long Oak Flat Loop Trail allows a pleasurable exploration of a benchland just below the South Rim.

On the north rim, the 1.5-mile-long North Vista Trail leads to Exclamation Point, accessing one of the most breathtaking views in the park. This route begins at the North Rim Ranger Station. A more strenuous leg of the North Vista Trail climbs an additional 2 miles to reach 8,563-foot Green Mountain, which affords wondrous views of the surrounding mountains. The 2.5-mile Deadhorse Trail begins at Kneeling Camel View southeast of the North Rim Ranger Station. Following an old road, this route provides views of the East Portal of the Gunnison River, site of the dam for a reservoir upstream.

Day hikes and overnight excursions into the canyon require a backcountry permit. These may be obtained from the South Rim Visitor Center on the south rim or at the North Rim Ranger Station. No established trails exist in the canyon, but several rugged routes are possible. Be prepared for very strenuous walking and keep in mind that the routes are not always easy to follow. Study the route as you drop into the canyon so that you can find your way back out. Bring plenty of water and a camp stove, as wood fires are not allowed.

A Park Service pamphlet on hiking the inner canyon lists six possible routes, three from the south rim and three from the north. Beginning at the South Rim Visitor Center on the south rim, the Gunnison Point route follows the Oak Flat Loop Trail for

0.35 mile before a sign indicates a turnoff for "RIVER ACCESS." This route includes a short section of safety chain part of the way down, and allows exploration of a 0.75-mile section of the river. Three primitive campsites accommodate backpackers. Dropping 1,800 feet in 1 mile, this route is very steep, but it is also the most popular descent to the canyon bottom.

Two other routes from the south rim include the Tomichi and Warner Point routes. The Tomichi route drops nearly 2,000 feet in only 1 mile from the South Rim Campground. Loose rock and steep conditions typify this route. Descending 2,660 feet in 2 miles, the Warner Point route is considered the hardest hike into the inner canyon. It begins by following the Warner Point Nature Trail, then turns left near the end of the established trail. The route accesses five primitive campsites and is considered to be best for overnight use.

From the north rim, the S.O.B. Draw route begins at a ranger station just east of the North Rim Campground. In 1.75 miles this route drops 1,800 feet to access 2 miles of the riverbank. Watch for poison ivy along the way. The 1-mile-long Long Draw route begins at the Balanced Rock View. The Slide Draw route, an extremely steep descent with a lot of loose rock, drops 1,620 feet in 1 mile; it begins at the Kneeling Camel View. Before attempting any of these hikes, discuss your plans with a park ranger and get as much information as possible.

River Running

The stretch of the Gunnison River that flows through the national park section of the Black Canyon is incredibly rugged and should only be attempted by the most experienced kayakers. The river drops 240 feet per mile in places. Sheer cliffs wall some stretches, while others disappear beneath boulders the size of houses. Ropes are needed for some portages. Allow 3 or 4 days to complete the journey and expect a lot of Class V and VI water along the way. A permit from the National Park Service is required.

48 Gunnison Gorge Wilderness Area

Location: 12 mi E of Olathe
Size: 17,700 acres
Status: Wilderness area (1999)
Terrain: River bottom and deep canyons
Elevation: 5,250' to 8,300'
Management: BLM (Uncompahgre Field Office)
Topographic maps: Red Rock Canyon, Black Ridge, Lazear

Downstream from the Black Canyon of the Gunnison National Park, the Gunnison Gorge Wilderness Area protects the wild lower reaches of the Black Canyon and the Gunnison River. Although 4WD roads reach the rim of the gorge, only primitive trails

penetrate its depths. White-water enthusiasts with the mettle to carry their gear—
or the resources to hire pack horses—can enjoy this stretch of wilderness river to
their heart's content. Although developers have long coveted the Gunnison Gorge
as a suitable site for a dam (there are already three dams upstream from the Black
Canyon of the Gunnison National Park), a number of administrative steps have ended
the battle once and for all. A law passed in 1999 carved the 17,700-acre Gunnison
Gorge Wilderness Area out of a slightly larger wilderness study area. Additionally,
this stretch of the Gunnison River is under consideration for status as a National
Wild and Scenic River.

Seasons
Summer temperatures can top ninety degrees some days, and thunderstorms occasionally march across the area. Gnats can be an inconvenience during the hottest
months. Winter brings subfreezing temperatures at night and occasional snowfalls, but
trails are not typically covered over for any length of time. Watch for ice on shaded
sections of trail, however.

Flora and Fauna
Aquatic life is plentiful along this stretch of the Gunnison. Fish species include the
endangered roundtail chub, northern pike, and three varieties of trout. River otters
have enjoyed a comeback thanks to a successful reintroduction program, and beaver
and muskrat are plentiful. Plants of this riparian community include cottonwoods,
willows, and tall grasses.

Away from the riverbanks you'll find a variety of semiarid plants, including pinyon pine, juniper, gambel oak, and sagebrush. Mule deer and bighorn sheep frequent
these areas, as well as mountain lions, coyotes, and badgers. Bald and golden eagles,
great horned owls, prairie falcons, and red-tailed hawks are among the raptors found
within the Gunnison Gorge.

Geology
The inner canyon of the Gunnison Gorge is an impressive cut through dark Precambrian granite, while the upper reaches of the gorge drop through colorful sedimentary
formations. Unlike the national park section of the Black Canyon, the Gunnison Gorge
widens considerably. This change in profile resulted from a difference in resistance
between these sedimentary and igneous formations.

ACTIVITIES
Hiking
Hikers can enjoy the pristine environs of the Gunnison Gorge via five established trails.
The BLM is currently conducting a recreation fee demonstration program in which
day-use visitors are charged $5 per person, per day. Overnight users are charged $10
per person, per night.

The Chukar Trail is reached by driving east from U.S. Highway 50 (near Olathe) on Falcon Road. After 4 miles it turns into the Peach Valley Road; in another 1.4 miles, turn right at a sign for the Chukar Trail. This road travels 7 miles more before reaching the trailhead. The last few miles may require a 4WD, depending on the weather. About 1 mile in length, the Chukar Trail drops steeply to the river below. Packhorses make regular trips along the route, making it quite dusty, but it does provide a quick access to the banks of the Gunnison River.

Three other routes similarly descend from the gorge's west rim. They include the Ute, Duncan, and Bobcat Trails. All three are accessed from the Peach Valley Road by way of 4WD spur roads. The 4.5-mile Ute Trail is the longest of the three and consequently drops along an easier grade. The Duncan and Bobcat Trails are each 1.5 miles long and descend about 800 feet. These trails are maintained, easy to follow, and have developed trailheads.

A fifth route, the North Fork–Smith Fork Trail, follows the river bottom 4 miles upstream from the BLM takeout at the junction of the Gunnison and the North Fork Rivers, north of the wilderness area. To access this trail you must first cross the North Fork River either by foot during periods of low water or by boat. It terminates at the junction of the Gunnison River and the Smith Fork. It is considered easy as it follows a mostly level grade.

Camping within the river corridor is restricted to designated sites that must be reserved. Wood fires are prohibited throughout, but stoves and charcoal fires contained in pans are acceptable.

A rafting party in the Gunnison Gorge

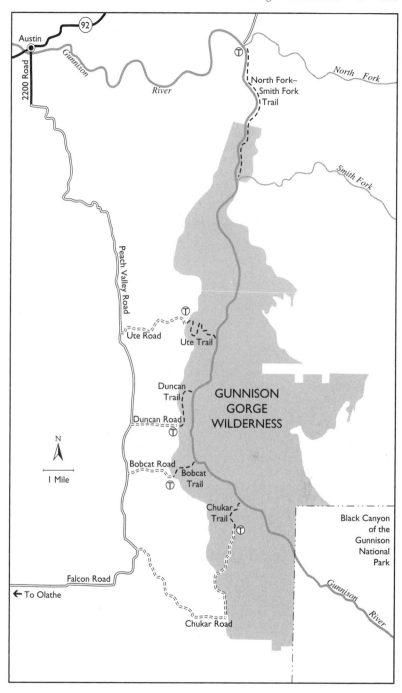

Austin

92

2200 Road

Gunnison

River

North Fork

North Fork–
Smith Fork
Trail

Smith Fork

Peach Valley Road

Ute Road

Ute Trail

Duncan
Trail

GUNNISON
GORGE
WILDERNESS

Duncan Road

N

1 Mile

Bobcat Road

Bobcat
Trail

Chukar
Trail

Black Canyon
of the
Gunnison
National
Park

Falcon Road

← To Olathe

Gunnison River

Chukar Road

River Running

Boaters who want to run the 13 miles of river that flow through the Gunnison Gorge must carry their gear a steep mile down the Chukar Trail. Several raft outfitters offer trips and hire local horsepackers to haul the gear. The gorge can be run in a day, but extra gear will allow an overnight trip. The most difficult stretch is downstream from Red Canyon in the northern section of the gorge. Expect Class III and IV waters here. Unlike the Arkansas River, which is managed for heavy use, the Gunnison Gorge is managed to protect its wilderness qualities, and permits may soon be required for private raft trips. Currently, neither rafting nor hiking parties can comprise more than twelve persons. Wood fires are prohibited and washable, re-useable toilet systems are required.

Adobe Badlands Wilderness Study Area

Location: 3 mi N of Delta
Size: 10,425 acres
Status: Wilderness study area (1978)
Terrain: Badlands formations
Elevation: 5,300' to 8,313'
Management: BLM (Uncompahgre Field Office)
Topographic maps: North Delta, Point Creek

The Adobe Badlands, as the name suggests, is a region of barren but starkly beautiful Mancos shale hills. Surreal in comparison to other wilderness lands, its smooth swells and ridges stack up against a backdrop formed by the Grand Mesa to the north. The scene is especially memorable when illuminated by the tinted rays of sunset. Unfortunately, the local population treats this area with considerable disrespect as motorcycles tear across the terrain, leaving a multitude of tracks. The BLM has concluded that scars from such activities could be erased in a few years if wilderness designation were approved, but the status of the area is in doubt simply because there is no practical way to control access to it.

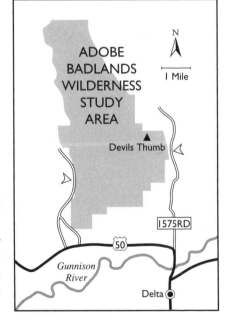

The Adobe Badlands at sunset

Seasons

Summertime temperatures can hover around the century mark, although nights do cool off. No water is available and shade is virtually nonexistent. While snow falls in the winter, it rarely accumulates thanks to the intense winter sun. Try to avoid the area after a rainstorm because the soil here can become quite sticky when wet. Spring and fall are the best times for a visit.

Flora and Fauna

Plants that manage to survive in this barren environment include saltbush, buckwheat, and desert trumpet. The threatened Uinta Basin hookless cactus is also found here, and pinyon pine and juniper grow in the area's northern portion. Among the fauna species living here are pronghorn antelope, mule deer, a few elk, coyotes, badgers, jackrabbits, rattlesnakes, and an occasional golden eagle.

Geology

Ninety-five percent of the Adobe Badlands WSA is composed of Mancos shale, a soft, claylike formation deposited by shallow seas between 65 million and 135 million years ago during the Cretaceous period. Because little plant life exists, the shale quickly eroded into well-rounded hills. The dark basalt boulders that lie scattered about originated from a volcanic cap on nearby Grand Mesa. The Devils Thumb is a noticeable monolith of the Mesa Verde Formation in the eastern end of the WSA.

ACTIVITIES
Hiking

There are no trails in the Adobe Badlands, but then, with little or no vegetation, there is also no need for them. Hiking here is a matter of going where you want for as far as you want. In dry weather, you can walk virtually anywhere with little problem. The drainages that dissect the hills can be followed, but the scenery is much better from the crests of the ridges and hilltops. To reach the Adobe Badlands, turn off U.S. Highway 50 about 1.5 miles north of Delta. Follow Road 1575RD north 3.5 miles. The WSA lies to the west.

50 Dominguez Canyon Wilderness Study Area

Location: 15 mi W of Delta
Size: 73,568 acres
Status: Wilderness study area (1978)
Terrain: Canyons and isolated mesas
Elevation: 4,500' to 7,500'
Management: BLM (Uncompahgre and Grand Junction field offices)
Topographic maps: Good Point, Escalante Forks, Dominguez, Triangle Mesa, Jacks Canyon, Keith Creek

Encompassing the drainages of Big and Little Dominguez Creeks, the Dominguez Canyon Wilderness Study Area (WSA) is a splendid parcel of canyons and mesas that lies between the Gunnison River and the Uncompahgre Plateau. Isolated by the river to the east and by rugged mesas to the west, you could spend several days hiking here without seeing another soul.

Seasons

Summers in the semiarid Dominguez Canyon area are hot, with temperatures easily approaching the 100-degree mark on many afternoons. Evenings do cool off. Gnats can be a problem during the heat of the day. Winters bring sporadic snowfalls, most of which quickly melt off. The best times to visit are in the autumn and spring when temperatures are moderate and the cottonwoods are either sprouting new leaves or turning yellow.

Flora and Fauna

A lush community of riparian plant life is found along the canyon bottoms, especially along year-round streams and creeks. Besides supporting picturesque cottonwoods of varying sizes, this ecosystem is typified by thickets of willow and tamarisk. Douglas firs find suitable habitat in the upper reaches of these canyons, and extensive forests of pinyon pine and juniper typically grow across the mesa tops. Other plants found in this classic upland desert community include sagebrush, prickly pear, bitterbrush, and a variety of grasses.

Mule deer feel at home both in the canyons and on the mesas, as do black bears, mountain lions, coyotes, and smaller mammals. Elk winter here, and desert bighorn sheep have been reintroduced to the area.

Geology

Because the canyons cut deeply into the substrata, many rock formations are exposed, some dating back 600 million years. The oldest rocks are the Precambrian schist, granite, and gneiss found along the Gunnison River. Sheer and colorful cliffs of Wingate sandstone rise in the deeper portions of the canyons. The less colorful Morrison and Dakota sandstones are exposed in much of the higher terrain. The area has a very high potential for paleontology research: dinosaur bones have been discovered in the Triangle Mesa and Cactus Park areas, including those of Ultrasaurus—the largest dinosaur ever found.

History

A number of shelters and rock art sites dating back a thousand years or more to the Fremont culture exist within the WSA. Many of these are in the sheer walls of the lower canyons. The name Dominguez refers to the Escalante–Dominguez Expedition, which passed through the area in 1776. Setting out from Santa Fe, the group's intent was to

The lower end of the Dominguez Canyon WSA

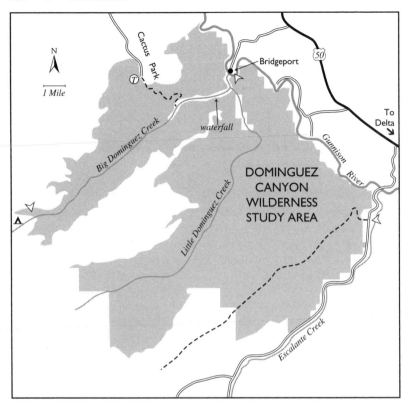

find a passage to California, but they returned home unsuccessful after several months of wandering through what are now the Four Corners states.

ACTIVITIES
Hiking

Hiking in the Dominguez Canyon WSA is often a matter of following natural corridors rather than man-made trails. Canyons extend a dozen or more miles along both Big and Little Dominguez Creeks. Big Dominguez Creek is especially easy to follow, but Little Dominguez becomes quite thick with brush near its top. Access to the lower ends of these canyons was once easy thanks to a bridge at Bridgeport, near the mouth of the Dominguez canyon system. Unfortunately, the bridge has fallen into dangerous disrepair and is currently closed to both vehicle and foot traffic. Consider a canoe crossing instead.

Compensating for the loss of the Bridgeport access, a short (about 2.5 miles) and rough trail that drops to Big Dominguez Creek originates at the BLM's Cactus Park trailhead. The canyon bottom can then be followed 6 miles upstream to the Dominguez Recreation Site, a BLM campground near the national forest border. Or you can follow it downstream for 3.5 miles to the Gunnison River. A 65-foot waterfall is one of many scenic treasures found along Big Dominguez Creek. It is located about a mile upstream from the confluence of the Big and Little Dominguez Creeks. To reach the Cactus Park trailhead, drive southwest on Colorado Highway 141 from Whitewater. The Cactus Park turnoff is signed and the trailhead is approximately 6 miles down this dirt road. When dry, it is passable to high-clearance 2WDs. Access the Dominguez campground by turning south on the Divide Road from Colorado Highway 141. Drive 5 miles to a fork in the road, turn left and drive another 5 miles.

Bordered by Escalante Creek, the southern end of the WSA is mostly open mesas and dry gulches. An old, unnamed trail begins in Escalante Canyon about 2 miles beyond the Gunnison River Bridge and eventually climbs up to a 4WD road on Camp Ridge. This trail is on BLM maps, but it hasn't been maintained so don't expect to find it in the best of conditions.

River Running

The stretch of the Gunnison River that flows adjacent to the Dominguez Canyon WSA is Class I and II, making it a nice float for canoes. Porta-potties and fire pans are required by the BLM and you need to be cognizant of private lands along the banks. The put-in is at the Escalante Bridge on County Road 1250; the takeout is at Whitewater, 27 river miles away. Plan on extra time to hike into a side canyon or two.

51 Roubideau Area

Location: 16 mi SW of Olathe
Size: 19,650 acres, plus 10,402 acres in BLM WSA
Status: Special area (1993)
Terrain: Canyons and mesa tops
Elevation: 5,300' to 9,500'
Management: Uncompahgre NF, BLM (Uncompahgre Field Office)
Topographic maps: Davis Point, Camel Back, Roubideau, Antone Springs

The Roubideau Area features a beautiful canyon that drains the eastern slope of the Uncompahgre Plateau. Much of the plateau is riddled with roads, but the bulldozers passed over this 20-mile canyon. Lush stands of spruce and fir grow along its upper reaches, while its lowest places are semidesert. Throughout, canyon walls tower to meet the sky. The Colorado Wilderness Act of 1993 prohibits mechanized travel within the Roubideau Area and directs the Forest Service to maintain its wilderness character. The lower third of the canyon falls within the BLM's Camel Back WSA.

Seasons

Temperatures in the lower canyon can rise above 100 degrees in the summer, while winter brings some snow and freezing nighttime temperatures. In these lower elevations, the snows usually melt quite quickly, making travel by foot a year-round possibility. In the upper reaches, snow often precludes hiking from November through May. Spring and fall are the best times for visiting the BLM section, while summer and early autumn are best higher up. The area is crowded during hunting season.

Flora and Fauna

Forests in Roubideau Canyon range from pinyon pine and juniper at the lower elevations to ponderosa pine, Douglas fir, Engelmann spruce, subalpine fir, and aspen up high. A riparian ecosystem of cottonwood trees, willows, and tamarisk thrives along the canyon floors. Shrubs such as bitterbrush and sagebrush are also scattered about. Wildlife found in Roubideau Canyon includes desert bighorn sheep, mule deer, elk, mountain lions, black bears, bobcats, coyotes, beavers, jackrabbits, golden eagles, peregrine falcons, wild turkeys, lizards, and rattlesnakes.

Geology

Roubideau Creek has cut hundreds of feet through layers of sandstone that were uplifted with the Uncompahgre Plateau. Included in these layers are the Dakota, Morrison, Summerville, Entrada, and Chinle formations. Stream erosion has been the primary force shaping this canyon.

Along the rim of Roubideau Canyon

ACTIVITIES
Hiking

A number of short trails cross the upper end of the Roubideau Canyon. The 5.5-mile Roubideau Trail, with its trailhead on Transfer Road 3 miles north of the Divide Road, drops west to Roubideau Creek via an old 4WD track. It then climbs up the far side of the canyon and crosses a secondary drainage, Goddard Creek, before reaching the East Bull Creek Road at the Gray Cow Camp. The Pool Creek Trail branches off southwest from the Roubideau Trail at the Roubideau Creek crossing and covers 3 miles to a trailhead just off the Divide Road.

The 7.4-mile Transfer Trail offers good access to the canyon's middle section. The eastern end of this trail is picked up near Oak Hill on the Transfer Road. From there it drops into the canyon before climbing up the other side. Skirting around Davis Point, it then picks up the end of 4WD Payne Mesa Road, which branches off the Divide Road. Elevations range between 7,500 and 8,500 feet. Roubideau Creek may be difficult to cross in the spring.

Passable to high-clearance 2WD vehicles when dry, the Roatcap Road begins at the national forest boundary, where it branches off from Transfer Road. Follow it for 4.5 miles as it jogs west, then north, and then northwest. The Traver Trail heads down into Roubideau Canyon just past the intersection. Two trails offer a choice of routes at Roubideau Creek. Continue on the 4-mile-long Traver Trail, which climbs up the

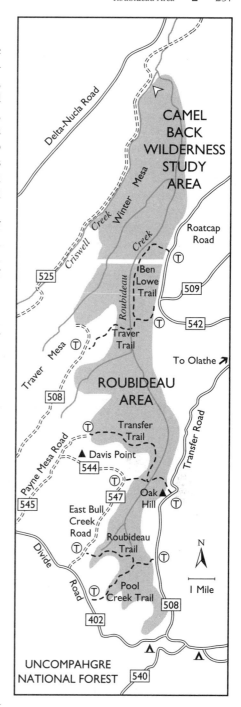

west side to meet a 4WD road on top of Traver Mesa, or turn north at Roubideau Creek and pick up the Ben Lowe Trail.

Following the creek downstream, the Ben Lowe Trail leaves the national forest in 2.5 miles. Crossing a patch of private land, the trail passes the abandoned homestead of Ben Lowe, a rancher who was killed in a shoot-out with the local sheriff around the year 1900. Just north of the Lowe cabin, the trail enters BLM land and turns east to climb up and out of the canyon. About 4 miles from the Traver Trail, the Ben Lowe Trail ends back on the Roatcap Road about 2 miles north of the Traver trailhead. From the Ben Lowe cabin, an unmaintained route continues down Roubideau Creek for about 3 miles.

Although no established trails exist in the lower end of the canyon, none are really needed. The canyon bottom is level and open, and stream crossings—of which there are many—are no problem during normal runoff. To get to the mouth of Roubideau Canyon follow the Delta–Nucla Road west from Colorado Highway 348 for 3 miles, turn left just after the second bridge, and drive 5.5 miles along a narrow road to where the canyon divides. The left-hand fork is Roubideau Canyon. Follow it for another 0.5 mile (a 4WD is suggested for this stretch) to where the track ends and the WSA begins. Roubideau Canyon and its primary tributary, Criswell Canyon, can be followed for 10 or more miles before reaching the Uncompahgre National Forest on the upper end. An old 4WD trail provides nonmotorized access to Winter Mesa. The level mesa top is fairly easy for traveling cross-country.

52 Tabeguache Area

Location: 7 mi N of Nucla
Size: 17,240 acres
Status: Special area (1993)
Terrain: Canyons and mesa tops
Elevation: 5,800' to 9,700'
Management: Uncompahgre NF, BLM (Uncompahgre Field Office)
Topographic maps: Nucla, Windy Point, Uravan, Starvation Point

The Tabeguache Area spans both Forest Service and BLM lands on the western slope of the Uncompahgre Plateau. Central to its topography is a deep canyon system carved by Tabeguache Creek. Located in an isolated part of the state, this area does not receive a lot of use, but its scenery and solitude make any visit well worth the effort. Like the nearby Roubideau Area the Tabeguache was passed up for actual wilderness designation in the 1993 Colorado Wilderness Act because of potential water rights issues.

Seasons

The climate in the Tabeguache Area can range from semiarid desert to high mountain conditions. Trails in the lower elevations stay snow-free for most of the year, but those

Tabeguache Canyon as seen from the Indian Trail

in the upper areas may be impassable from November to May. Summer afternoons can prove hot, especially in the lower elevations, and thunderstorms are a possibility all across the area. The turning leaves of aspens and cottonwoods add a lot of color to the land during September and October.

Flora and Fauna

Plant communities in the Tabeguache Area range from pinyon pine and juniper forests to sagebrush parks. There are also stands of gambel oak, Douglas fir, ponderosa, old-growth aspen, Engelmann spruce, and subalpine fir. Because the main canyon conducts cooler air down from the mountains, the distribution of these plant types does not follow elevation parameters too closely. This fact, combined with the presence of lush riparian communities along the creek beds, makes for a diverse and vibrant ecosystem.

Among the animals that roam the Tabeguache are mule deer, elk, mountain lions, coyotes, black bears, and bobcat. Native cutthroat, along with brown and rainbow trout, thrive in the creek.

Geology

Tabeguache Creek has cut through layers of sedimentary rock along the western slope of the Uncompahgre Plateau, exposing layers of Chinle, Wingate, and Kayenta sandstone and creating the Morrison, Summerville, and Entrada formations. However, it is the towering Wingate Cliffs, deposited as sand dunes during the Triassic period, that are most visible in Tabeguache Canyon.

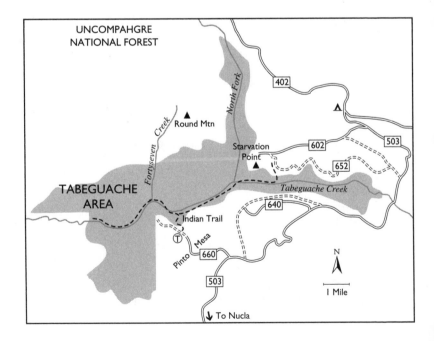

History

Today known as the Indian Trail, the route that follows Tabeguache Creek is thought to have served the Ute, Anasazi, Fremont, and perhaps even archaic cultures during prehistoric times. Several caves within Tabeguache Canyon may someday yield historical data.

ACTIVITIES
Hiking

Tabeguache Canyon is accessible from Pinto Mesa, 10 miles north of Nucla. Turn off from the road to Delta about 7 miles out of Nucla; a sign for Pinto Mesa marks the turnoff on Forest Road 660. Drive another 2 miles and then turn right onto a rough road. Follow it another mile toward the edge of the mesa. An access spur of the Indian Trail begins at an obscure trailhead here and drops quickly to the canyon bottom. The Indian Trail originally followed Tabeguache Creek upstream for a little more than 3 miles to Starvation Point, but this section has become overgrown and washed out in several places. The Forest Service now maintains the Indian Trail downstream for 1 mile to where Fortyseven Creek comes in from the north. A trail then parallels Fortyseven Creek for 2 miles to the 4WD Forest Road 600 just below Round Mountain outside the wilderness area. After following this track for a little over 1 mile, a foot trail drops back down into the North Fork drainage. It follows this creek for about 1 mile then climbs out of the canyon to meet a road on Starvation Point. The beautiful canyon scenery on this 9-mile hike includes a number of picturesque waterfalls to enjoy as well.

From Fortyseven Creek, an unmaintained BLM trail continues downstream for another 3 miles before reaching the wilderness area's western boundary. Access to this end of the trail is difficult because of private lands and the trail itself is overgrown in places.

53 Mesa Verde National Park

Location: 8 mi W of Mancos
Size: 52,085 acres
Status: National park (1906)
Terrain: Canyons and mesas
Elevation: 6,000' to 8,571'
Management: NPS
Topographic maps: Point Lookout, Moccasin Mesa, Wetherill Mesa, Cortez, Trail Canyon, Mancos

With several of the largest cliff dwellings in the Southwest, Mesa Verde National Park is the nation's premier archaeological park. The Ancestral Puebloan (formerly called the Anasazi) people built thousands of dwellings ranging in size from one to 150 rooms in the canyons that drain south from the mesa's summit; they also constructed sprawling pueblos on the mesa tops and practiced advanced farming techniques.

Most of what there is to see at Mesa Verde is stabilized and protected to minimize the impact caused by hordes of tourists. Backcountry visits are restricted to a few established trails because the park does not have enough rangers to properly patrol all of the prehistoric sites. Pot hunting by professional looters has been a problem in the Four Corners area for many years. Damage is also exacted by casual visitors who innocently pocket a single piece of pottery or who walk on prehistoric walls. Two devastating forest fires swept across Mesa Verde in the summer of 2000, greatly altering the character of the landscape for decades to come.

Seasons

Although Mesa Verde can be visited year-round, snow often precludes hiking from November through March. One cliff dwelling, Spruce Tree House, is open to visitors during these months. Summer temperatures can top ninety degrees. Spring and fall are the best times for hiking and for touring the archeological sites, although summers are most popular. Wildflowers bloom in May and the foliage becomes quite colorful in late September and October.

Cliff Palace is the nation's largest cliff dwelling.

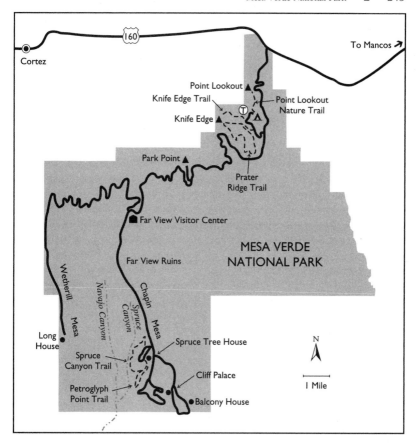

Flora and Fauna

Much of Mesa Verde supports mature stands of pinyon pine and juniper, scattered yucca, prickly pear, sagebrush, and Indian rice grass. Thickets of gambel oak grow among the higher reaches, while Douglas fir and aspen dot the shaded environs along the mesa's northern face.

Fauna in Mesa Verde includes mule deer, coyotes, mountain lions, black bears, wild turkeys, bobcats, and a variety of raptors. Wildlife is easy to spot along the roadways, especially mule deer.

Geology

As you enter Mesa Verde from the north, you will see the park's two main geological features. First is a thick deposit of Mancos shale. Deposited on a seabed some 90 million years ago, this soft formation gives fits to road builders. Above the Mancos shale are three members of the Mesa Verde Group: the Point Lookout Formation, visible in its namesake, which rises solidly above the entrance; the Menefee Formation, which often includes a seam of coal; and the Cliffhouse sandstone, which breaks away in large blocks as the softer underlying rock erodes. Mesa Verde's famous cliff dwellings were built in alcoves of Cliffhouse sandstone. The entire mesa tilts slightly southward, the result of the uplifting of the San Juan Mountains to the north. This slight angling provided the Ancestral Puebloans with just the right conditions for growing corn, beans, and squash.

History

As long as 1,400 years ago, Mesa Verde was inhabited by the Ancestral Puebloans. At first these people built subterranean homes known as pit houses; they also wove very fine baskets. Around A.D. 750 they began constructing larger communities of aboveground houses and they learned how to make pottery. By A.D. 1000 they were using primarily stone masonry rather than poles and adobe mud to build their homes. After A.D. 1100 they built the great pueblos and cliff houses that we see in the park today. It was during this period that the Ancestral Puebloans reached their peak in both population and technological achievement.

By A.D. 1300 the Ancestral Puebloans had moved out of the Four Corners area to regions to the south and southeast. Why they left is not known, but a lengthy drought, depletion of natural resources, and internal political strife are possibilities.

By the time the Dominguez–Escalante Expedition passed just north of Mesa Verde in 1776, Utes and Navajos were the only Native Americans living in the area. White settlers moved into nearby Mancos Valley in the 1880s, and two men, Richard Wetherill and Charlie Mason, came upon Cliff Palace in December 1888. Gustaf Nordenskiold conducted the first real archaeological survey of Mesa Verde in 1891. The park was established in 1906.

ACTIVITIES
Hiking

The Petroglyph Point Trail begins at Spruce Tree House and runs a little over 1 mile to a rock art panel in the cliffs above Navajo Canyon. Although the meanings of these ancient images etched in a sandstone cliff have been obscured by time, they are still interesting. The 2.1-mile Spruce Canyon Trail descends to the bottom of Spruce Canyon before looping back to the park headquarters complex. This route sees very little use.

The Point Lookout Nature Trail begins at the sprawling Morefield Campground and covers 1 mile before reaching the summit of Point Lookout, where a spectacular 360-degree panorama greets hikers. The Knife Edge Trail, which also begins at the campground, is a bit less than 1 mile long and is the easiest hike in the park. The trail reveals stunning scenery as it follows an old roadway beneath the Knife Edge, a towering escarpment of Mesa Verde sandstone. The 7.5-mile Prater Ridge Trail climbs 700 feet to the top of a rise just west of the campground. The views are outstanding, and you might spot a golden eagle in flight. A change in ecosystems is evident along this, the longest trail within Mesa Verde. Keep in mind that trails in the Morefield Campground area were greatly affected by forest fires in 2000.

54 McKenna Peak Wilderness Study Area

Location: 30 mi N of Dolores
Size: 19,398 acres
Status: Wilderness study area (1978)
Terrain: Badlands, ridges, and washes
Elevation: 6,600' to 8,600'
Management: BLM (San Juan Field Office)
Topographic maps: McKenna Peak, North Mountain, South Mountain, Glade Mountain

Situated in isolated Disappointment Valley, the McKenna Peak Wilderness Study Area (WSA) is easy to overlook. Its diverse topography and wildlife resources, however, would make it a worthy addition to Colorado's wilderness inventory. Despite this, the BLM cited pending watershed and range-improvement projects as reasons for not recommending McKenna Peak for wilderness designation.

Seasons
Because winters can be snowy and cold, and summers hot, the best times to visit McKenna Peak are late spring and fall. Wildflowers typically bloom in May and June.

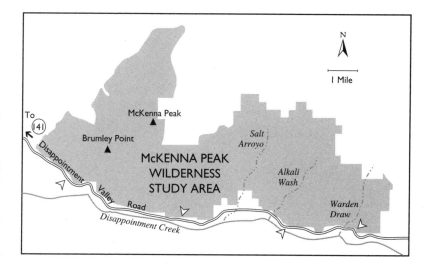

Beautiful McKenna Peak

Flora and Fauna

Pinyon pine and juniper woodlands cover much of the area, although sagebrush, saltbush, greasewood, and grasses grow in many open parks. Mountain mahogany and gambel oak grow in scattered locations. Three threatened or endangered plant species grow here: Naturita milkvetch, Uinta Basin hookless cactus, and spineless hedgehog cactus.

Mule deer reside here, as do coyotes, badgers, bobcats, red foxes, and mountain lions. Elk winter here and pronghorn antelope roam the lower elevations. A herd of wild horses has lived in the area for more than a hundred years. Every few years the BLM thins the herd down in order to maintain an ideal size of about fifty head.

Geology

The two primary geological features of the McKenna Peak WSA are the badlands formations of Mancos shale and the cliffs of the Mesa Verde Group. Deposited on a sea bottom, the grayish-colored Mancos Shale Formation is easily eroded into rounded hills. Because few plants can take root in Mancos shale soil, much of it is relatively barren. The Mesa Verde Group includes a variety of sandstones that were deposited as sediments along ancient coastal areas during the Cretaceous period. Mesa Verde sandstones often form a cap on softer Mancos shale.

ACTIVITIES
Hiking

This area has no trails, but a number of wash bottoms and the open Mancos shale badlands do allow for relatively easy access. (Avoid the Mancos shale when it is wet, as it becomes a sticky mess.) Warden Draw, Alkali Wash, and Salt Arroyo all offer entry points. Because the badlands formations stretch across the lower reaches of the area, they can be reached from the road. To reach McKenna Peak, drive east on the Disappointment Valley Road from Colorado Highway 141.

55 Cross Canyon Wilderness Study Area

Location: 50 mi W of Cortez
Size: 12,588 acres
Status: Wilderness study area (1978)
Terrain: Canyons and mesa tops
Elevation: 5,100' to 6,600'
Management: Canyons of the Ancients NM (BLM, San Juan Field Office)
Topographic maps: Ruin Canyon, Papoose Canyon

Straddling the Colorado–Utah state line, the Cross Canyon Wilderness Study Area (WSA) encompasses a canyon system that drains the Four Corners Plateau. Although scenic, it does not quite rival the spectacular beauty of other desert wilderness lands in the state. What it does offer are many prehistoric Ancestral Puebloan ruins and secretive glades of cottonwood along stream bottoms. Because two nearby WSAs— Cahone Canyon and Squaw–Papoose Canyon—include very similar terrain and recreational opportunities, the information provided here applies to them, as well. Whereas gas and oil leases helped strike all three areas from the BLM's latest list of proposed wilderness lands, they are included in the newly established Canyons of the Ancients National Monument. Set aside in 2000 by President Clinton, this 164,000-acre monument encompasses a large portion of southwestern Colorado. Because it is new and controversial (local development interests and state officials consider its establishment a land grab), it is still unclear what effect monument status will have on these WSAs.

Seasons
Stretching across the arid Four Corners region of Colorado, these canyons and mesa tops are quite hot and dry in the summer. Gnats are a nuisance in the warmest months of the year. Winter, on the other hand, can be cold but enjoyable. Snow occasionally remains on the north-facing slopes of these drainages, but it quickly melts in the canyon bottoms. Spring, for its promise of new growth, and October, for the colorful show the cottonwoods put on, are the best times of the year to visit.

Flora and Fauna
Across the higher reaches of the canyon, stands of pinyon pines and junipers are predominant. As the drainages stretch toward the southwest, the woodlands thin out, leaving scattered desert shrubs, such as sagebrush and Mormon tea. Riparian communities

A prehistoric ruin in the Cross Canyon WSA

of cottonwood, Russian olive, box elder, tamarisk, and cattails are found along the streams, some of which are perennial. Animals you might see in Cross Canyon include mule deer, coyotes, jackrabbits, and hawks.

Geology

Exposed by stream erosion are the Dakota and Morrison formations. Dating back to the Jurassic (136 million to 190 million years ago) period, the Morrison Formation was deposited in freshwater lakes and is rich in fossilized plants and animals. Capping the Morrison Formation is a harder layer of Dakota sandstone, which was formed on a sea bottom during the Cretaceous period. Responsible for the rimrock along the canyons, it is light brown and gray.

History

The Ancestral Puebloans inhabited this region for many centuries, beginning more than 1,000 years ago. In this part of the Four Corners, their architectural prowess resulted in the lonesome towers of Hovenweep National Monument, which lies a few miles south of Cross Canyon. Similar masonry structures were built in Cross and other canyons. Archaeological sites are plentiful, although they are more often piles of stone and rubble than complete structures. The remains of small pueblos can be found in

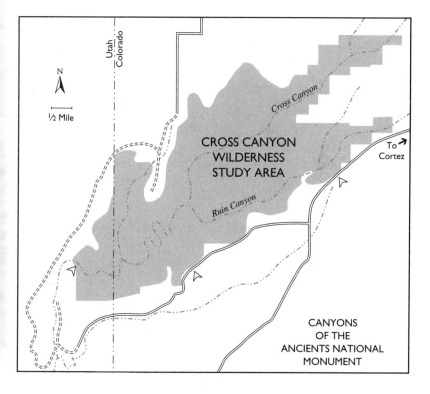

the canyon bottoms. All of these sites and their accompanying artifacts are protected by federal law; disturbing them is a felony.

ACTIVITIES
Hiking
No maintained trails exist in the area, but travel is possible thanks to the open stream bottoms and rimrock. Walking is easier in the lower elevations, where the pinyon pine and juniper growth is sparser. Although slower going than the wash bottoms, walking the rimrock offers nice vistas, occasional archaeological sites, and the enjoyment of scrambling across sandstone shelves. Gravel roads allow access to both the mouth of Cross Canyon and its rim areas, but they may be impassable when wet.

56 Dolores River Canyon Wilderness Study Area

Location: 18 mi W of Naturita
Size: 28,668 acres
Status: Wilderness study area (1978)
Terrain: Canyons, river bottoms, and mesas
Elevation: 5,100' to 6,400'
Management: BLM (San Juan Field Office)
Topographic maps: Paradox, Anderson Mesa, Bull Canyon, Davis Mesa

Gathering strength in the San Juan Mountains, the Dolores River flows west and north to a confluence with the Colorado River in Utah. Before it reaches the state line, however, it flows through some of the most spectacular canyons in Colorado. One of these, the Dolores River Canyon between Big Gypsum and Paradox Valleys, has been identified as having wilderness potential. With canyon rims soaring more than 1,000 feet above the river, a number of primitive side drainages, and several isolated mesa tops, it is easy to understand why.

Seasons
Winters bring occasional light snow and subfreezing temperatures and summers see 100-degree temperatures and infestations of gnats, so spring and fall are the best times to visit. Wildflowers bloom mostly in late April and May.

Flora and Fauna
Supporting a variety of riparian communities, the Dolores River and some of its tributaries are lined with dense thickets of willows, tamarisk, and occasional cottonwood trees. Just beyond the river and its perennial tributaries, however, a far different ecosystem takes over. In many places, and especially across the mesa tops, a mixed forest of pinyon pine and juniper predominates. In the more arid environs, this woodland is

Rafting on the Dolores River

replaced by open areas of sagebrush, squawbush, Mormon tea, and grasses.

Wildlife is plentiful in the Dolores River Canyon. Mule deer winter here in large numbers. Desert bighorn and river otters were successfully reintroduced to the area. Mountain lions, coyotes, badgers, jackrabbits, and ground squirrels are also found here. Migratory waterfowl frequent the river on their way elsewhere, and bald eagles and peregrine falcons have been spotted.

Geology

Like many river canyons in the Colorado Plateau, the Dolores River Canyon exposes a number of geologic formations. Most prevalent are the soaring cliffs of Wingate sandstone, deposited as dunes during the Triassic period. Underlying the Wingate is the Chinle Formation, a series of sandstones and shales that were deposited in large flood plains by streams and shallow lakes.

Younger than Wingate sandstone, and therefore above it on the canyon walls, is the Kayenta Formation, which was deposited in slow-moving rivers during the Triassic period. Above this is a thick layer of Navajo sandstone which, like the Wingate sandstone, was deposited as great sand dunes. Next in line is the Entrada Formation, which constitutes the rimrock in many areas. Above the Entrada is a series of less distinct formations, including the Summerville, Morrison, Burro Canyon, and Dakota sandstones, which are found in the uppermost mesa tops.

ACTIVITIES
Hiking

There are no maintained trails within the Dolores River Canyon Wilderness Study Area (WSA), but you can still do plenty of hiking, especially if you don't mind getting wet.

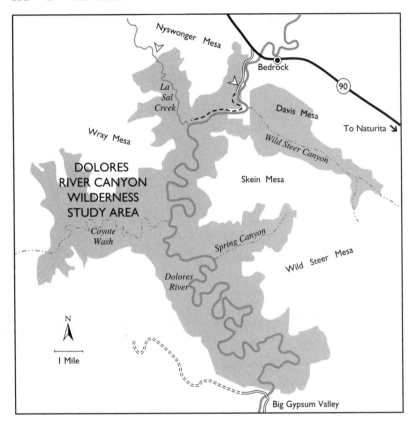

The trick is to follow the canyon bottoms along the Dolores and its many tributaries. Entrance is easiest at the mouth of the canyon near Bedrock on Colorado Highway 90. To reach the WSA boundary, drive from the store upstream along the west bank of the river for a couple of miles. When this rough 2WD road ends an old road that is closed to vehicles continues up the canyon for 3 miles or so. From here you can continue upstream provided you are prepared for river crossings. The river can be waded in low water, but an air mattress might come in handy for floating gear. Use a walking stick to check the depth of the water. River crossings and the presence of thick underbrush in places make for a difficult hike. The upper end of the main canyon is reached by driving gravel County Road 20R into the Big Gypsum Valley from Colorado Highway 141. It is 33 miles along the Dolores River from one end of the WSA to the other.

Just as the main canyon can be hiked, so too can many of its side drainages. Wild Steer Canyon branches off from the Dolores River 3 miles upstream from the Bedrock store. Although getting to it requires a river crossing, the rest of the way up Wild Steer is along a dry wash that is easy to follow. The 5-mile hike up Wild Steer will eventually put you in the vicinity of some old uranium mines on top of Davis Mesa.

La Sal Creek Canyon, a good hike along a perennial stream, can be reached by walking 3 miles beyond the Bedrock trailhead. Since La Sal Creek comes into the river from the west, no river crossing is needed to reach it. The upper end of La Sal Creek is accessible by driving 10 miles west from Bedrock on Colorado Highway 90. The road climbs Nyswonger Mesa before dropping into the La Sal Creek drainage. A dirt road continues down the canyon from the highway but is closed to vehicles partway in. It is approximately 6 miles from the highway to the river.

Other side canyons offer hiking terrain, but they are much more remote. Coyote Wash is a sizable drainage near the halfway point of the WSA. If you can get to this drainage, its many miles of canyon bottom make a nice walk. Spring Canyon, which drains off the mesas east of the river, is another possibility. For the best directions, check the topographic maps.

River Running

Thirty-three miles of the Dolores River flow through this WSA, making it one of the state's premier wilderness river corridors. Since the flow of the river is dependent on releases from the McPhee Dam upstream, boaters will want to plan their trips during peak runoff in the late spring and early summer. Float trips can last from 2 to 5 days, depending on how often you stop to hike. The put-in for the Dolores River Canyon is 2 miles upstream from the Big Gypsum Valley Bridge. This is a 35-mile float. Begin at Slickrock to extend the trip by 13 miles, but keep in mind that the put-in there is on private land and a fee is charged for overnight parking.

Rafters can enjoy a number of Class III drops, but the real treat is the slickrock scenery. Although this stretch of the Dolores has so far failed to win designation as a Wild and Scenic River (mining and development interests have too many friends in Congress), the BLM manages the river with considerable concern for its naturalness. Groups are restricted to sixteen and parties must bring fire pans, firewood, and porta-potties.

57 Sewemup Mesa Wilderness Study Area

Location: 65 mi NW of Telluride
Size: 19,140 acres
Status: Wilderness study area (1978)
Terrain: Mesa top and sheer cliffs
Elevation: 4,600' to 7,276'
Management: BLM (Grand Junction Field Office)
Topographic maps: Roc Creek, Juanita Arch

Bounded by high cliffs on virtually all sides, Sewemup Mesa is a severely isolated parcel of land that receives very little use. This is due to two factors. Access to its rolling top is difficult save for one or two breaks in the topography. And once you are on top there are no trails to follow. Regardless, if you like semiarid deserts without crowds, this is a good place to visit.

Seasons

Summers are hot, although afternoon showers do occur. Lightning can pose a threat, and gnats can be bothersome during the hottest months. Winters sometimes bring enough snow to the mesa top to impede hiking, but it often melts after a few days of sunshine. Spring and fall are the best times of the year to visit.

Flora and Fauna

The principal plant community found on Sewemup Mesa is a mix of pinyon pine and juniper, plus sagebrush, Mormon tea, bitterbrush, cactus, and yucca. Deer trails crisscross the mesa top, and coyotes can be heard yipping at night. Mountain lions frequent the area, as do peregrine falcons and bald eagles. Wildlife officials are eyeing Sewemup Mesa as a possible habitat for reintroducing desert bighorn sheep.

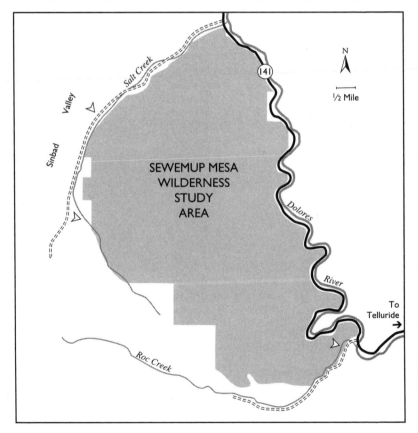

Opposite: *The backside of Sewemup Mesa*

Geology

Cliffs of Wingate sandstone are the primary geological formation in Sewemup Mesa WSA. Five hundred to 700 feet high, these rock faces are deep red in color and quite severe. The Wingate Formation was deposited between 180 million and 225 million years ago as enormous sand dunes. A wall of Entrada sandstone is exposed on the mesa's northwest corner.

The meandering Dolores River borders Sewemup Mesa on the east. Salt Creek is on the north, Roc Creek is on the south, and Sinbad Valley is to the west. Sinbad Valley is one of several salt valleys that stretch across the Paradox Basin portion of the Colorado Plateau. Once underlain by a large salt dome, the terrain collapsed after the salt migrated away from under the overlying rock. The result is broad, open valleys surrounded by high sandstone walls.

ACTIVITIES
Hiking

Barricaded by a ring of impassable cliffs, Sewemup Mesa poses a logistical riddle to those wishing to hike it. Although access points may be found hidden in the canyon walls above Roc Creek or at the southern end of Sinbad Valley, the most practical route to the mesa top begins at its southeast corner, less than a mile north of where Colorado Highway 141 crosses Roc Creek. A 4WD track climbs up this end of the mesa for about 1 mile; it can be driven or easily walked from the highway below. The track begins on private land, so access to it may be limited. From its end, follow the ridge west using high points as references. The mesa top slopes up toward its summit on the western edge. Since only game trails penetrate this terrain, hiking can be an adventure. Shallow drainages that dissect the mesa top add to the challenge, as do the thick stands of pinyon pine and juniper.

58 The Palisade Wilderness Study Area

Location: 55 mi SW of Grand Junction
Size: 26,050 acres
Status: Wilderness study area (1978)
Terrain: High ridges, mesas, and washes
Elevation: 4,600' to 9,500'
Management: BLM (Grand Junction Field Office)
Topographic maps: Gateway, Two V Basin, Fish Creek, Steamboat Mesa

A colorful fortress of sandstone, the Palisade towers over the tiny town of Gateway along the Dolores River and is reminiscent of many landforms in nearby southern Utah. In addition to its namesake, however, the Palisade Wilderness Study Area (WSA) also

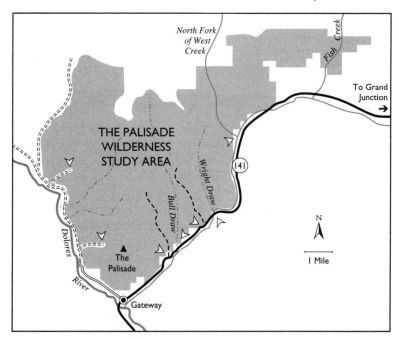

encompasses a higher mountain ridge and several Precambrian rock faces that line Unaweep Canyon. Given the awe-inspiring presence of the Palisade and the extent of the surrounding backcountry, this area would make a sensible addition to Colorado's wilderness inventory. But local sentiment and boundaries that would be difficult to administer led the BLM to recommend that no wilderness be established. Rather, it wants certain sections to be classified as an outstanding natural area, a step down from wilderness protection.

Seasons

Summer months are typically hot with occasional afternoon showers. Winter nights are cold at lower elevations, but lasting snow cover is rare. In the higher reaches, snow can last from November to May. As with other high desert areas in Colorado, the best seasons for visiting are the spring and fall.

Flora and Fauna

A forest mix of pinyon pine and juniper, along with some grasslands and sagebrush parks, is dominant across the lower lands that make up the western portion of the WSA. The pinyon-juniper ecosystem is also home to yucca, cactus, Mormon tea, and bitterbrush. Mule deer and coyotes are the most numerous large mammals here, but elk winter in this area and mountain lions are present, as well.

Stretching eastward across an arm of higher terrain, the Palisade WSA additionally encompasses ridge tops high enough to accommodate stands of gambel oak, ponderosa pine, and quaking aspen. The Palisade area provides one of two important habitats for the rare Nokomis fritillary, a butterfly under consideration for addition to the endangered species list.

Geology

The bulk of the Palisade itself consists of a several-hundred-foot-thick layer of Wingate sandstone. Atop this sheer cliff lie thinner layers of the Kayenta, Entrada, and Morrison formations. Underneath the massive Wingate cliffs are less distinct red beds of Chinle and Moenkopi. These colorful strata were deposited mostly during the Mesozoic era (between 65 million and 240 million years ago) either in flood plains and marshes or as sand dunes.

Also of interest is the geological makeup of the area's eastern half. Here, the wilderness embraces a portion of the spectacular Unaweep Canyon, an impressive slice through the Precambrian granite that makes up the core of the Uncompahgre Plateau. Unaweep Canyon today produces two small streams that could not possibly have carved such an abyss. Theories suggest that the canyon was actually carved by the Colorado River, the Gunnison River, or both, and that at some point these greater rivers changed course, leaving Unaweep virtually high and dry.

The namesake of the Palisade WSA

ACTIVITIES
Hiking
No hiking trails penetrate the Palisade WSA, but a few 4WD tracks follow some of the draws along the southern end. They are open to vehicular traffic and are mostly used by woodcutters and hunters. Beyond them, hikers can follow the washes and canyon bottoms for several miles. Bull Draw is a good drainage to walk as it reveals some spectacular geology. Other hikeable canyons in the southern end include Wright Draw and the North Fork of West Creek. In the far northeast corner of the WSA, Fish Creek features an impressive series of waterfalls.

Drainages in the western end also can be hiked. Two short 4WD tracks have been excluded from the WSA, but walking beyond them is easy thanks to open canyon bottoms.

59 Colorado National Monument

Location: 3 mi W of Grand Junction
Size: 20,534 acres
Status: National monument (1911)
Terrain: Canyons and mesas
Elevation: 4,600' to 6,890'
Management: NPS
Topographic maps: Colorado National Monument, Battleship Rock, Grand Junction, Glade Park

The slickrock escarpments of Colorado National Monument rise some 2,000 feet above the Colorado River and the Grand Valley. More reminiscent of southern Utah than Colorado, this landscape is dramatic in many respects. Canyon walls, buttes, and other landforms tower above canyon bottoms and sagebrush flats; mesa tops feature thick stands of pinyon pine and juniper. Enjoying all of it can be as easy as driving 23-mile Rim Rock Drive, or as challenging as hiking the rugged streambed of Ute Canyon. Nearly 15,000 acres of the monument's backcountry is currently classified as a wilderness study area. The Park Service manages virtually all of its backcountry as wilderness, however.

Seasons
Although winters bring subfreezing temperatures and occasional snow, hiking can be a year-round activity. Summers can be quite hot, with temperatures often approaching 100 degrees. Gnats are a problem at this time of the year and lightning can pose a hazard on exposed rims and mesa tops. The best times to visit are in the spring and fall when temperatures are moderate. Desert wildflowers bloom mostly in late April and May.

The Pipe Organ

Flora and Fauna

Much of the monument features mixed pinyon pine and juniper forest. Understory plants within these woodlands include sagebrush, rabbitbrush, and a variety of grasses. Mountain mahogany is found in many places and a few Douglas firs and ponderosa pines are scattered about. The monument's flowering plants include Indian paintbrush, aster, locoweed, sego lily, evening primrose, penstemon, and fishhook cactus. Wildlife is diverse with mule deer, bobcats, coyotes, mountain lions, ringtail cats, badgers, striped skunks, kit and gray fox, desert cottontail rabbits, wood rats, and, according to a list published by the Park Service, fifteen species of bats.

Geology

Situated at the northern end of the Uncompahgre Plateau, the Colorado National Monument was uplifted above the surrounding terrain about 70 million years ago. Within the nine exposed rock formations there is some 1.5 billion years of geologic history. The oldest rocks—Precambrian gneiss, schist, and granite—are similar to those that make up the cores of many Colorado mountain ranges. On top of this base is a layer of Chinle sandstone that dates from the Triassic period about 240 million years ago. The difference in the age of the Precambrian basement rock and the Chinle sandstone represents 750 million years of erosion. Above the Chinle Formation are prominent cliffs of the

Wingate Formation. Wingate sandstone was deposited as giant sand dunes during Triassic times. Next is a layer of Kayenta sandstone, followed by the Entrada Formation. Entrada constitutes the canyon rimrock in most areas of the monument. Above Entrada the formations become less distinct in color and physical presence and include the Morrison, Burro Canyon, and Dakota formations. Uplifting was a key factor in the formation of this landscape, but so were the forces of erosion, both water and wind.

History

Just as many other national parks and monuments had an early champion, Colorado National Monument had John Otto. Describing this place as "the heart of the world," Otto settled in these then-desolate canyons in 1907. In the years that followed, he campaigned tirelessly for national recognition and protection of the area, and constructed trails into it so that others could enjoy its beauty. His efforts paid off when the monument was established in 1911. A more recent development, the sinuous Rim Rock Drive was built during the Great Depression by several groups, including the Civilian Conservation Corps (CCC).

ACTIVITIES
Hiking

From Rim Rock Drive, four short trails—Otto's, Window Rock, Canyon Rim, and Coke Ovens (all less than a mile in length)—lead to spectacular overlooks. Although frequented by motorists looking for a quick view, these trails are still good places to learn the lay of the land and enjoy some of the best scenery around.

Other short trails include the Serpents Trail, which winds for 2.5 miles down the monument's east face. With fifty-two switchbacks, it has been called the crookedest road in the world. The 1-mile-long Alcove Nature Trail is a self-guided tour of the Kayenta sandstone benchland in the northern end of the monument. The Devils Kitchen Trail drops gradually along its 0.75-mile route to a grotto enclosed by large boulders.

Longer routes in the monument allow hikers to truly immerse themselves in a pristine slickrock desert environment. Overnight stays require a free permit and several regulations apply. Be sure to learn these before heading out.

The 6-mile Monument Canyon Trail is the most popular backcountry route. It begins at the Coke Ovens trailhead, about 7 miles from the north entrance, and drops 600 feet into Monument Canyon. Along the way it passes such picturesque features as the Kissing Couple, Independence Monument, and the Island and ends on the Broadway/Redlands Road just outside the monument.

The Liberty Cap Trail begins 10 miles from the north entrance and crosses pinyon- and juniper-covered Monument Mesa. In 5.5 miles, the route passes Liberty Cap Rock. From there it drops steeply another 1.5 miles to Wildwood Drive on the outskirts of Grand Junction.

Ute and No Thoroughfare Canyons both offer undeveloped hiking routes. The 7-mile Ute Canyon Trail descends rapidly along a trail to pick up the wash bottom. A natural arch is passed along the way, but the real pleasure of this route is the narrow

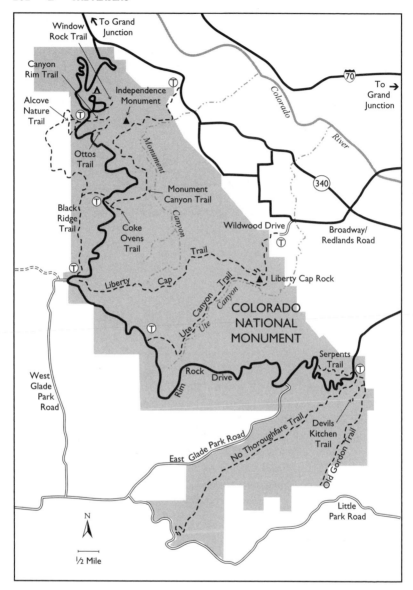

Window Rock Trail

To Grand Junction

Canyon Rim Trail

Alcove Nature Trail

Independence Monument

Ottos Trail

Monument Canyon

Black Ridge Trail

Monument Canyon Trail

Coke Ovens Trail

Wildwood Drive

Broadway/ Redlands Road

Liberty Cap Rock

Liberty Cap Trail

Canyon Trail

Ute Canyon Trail

Ute Canyon

COLORADO NATIONAL MONUMENT

West Glade Park Road

Rim Rock Drive

Serpents Trail

East Glade Park Road

No Thoroughfare Trail

Devils Kitchen Trail

Old Gordon Trail

Little Park Road

Colorado River

70

To Grand Junction

340

N

½ Mile

canyon itself, with its towering Wingate walls. The 8.5-mile No Thoroughfare Trail heads upstream from the Devils Kitchen Trail. A couple of waterfalls are found here when the stream is flowing. At the upper end, a maintained stretch of trail accesses the Little Park Road just outside of the monument.

Two other trails explore the periphery of Colorado National Monument. In the southern end of the monument, the 4-mile Old Gordon Trail was once a timber and cattle road. It can be reached by hiking a short way up Devils Kitchen Trail. The 5.5-mile Black Ridge Trail begins at the trailhead for the Alcove Nature Trail and follows its namesake in the western portion of the monument. Although mostly winding among pinyon pine and juniper stands, this trail offers outstanding views from its highest points. The canyons of the Black Ridge Canyons Wilderness stretch to the west, beyond which stand the La Sal Mountains in Utah. To the south are the San Juan Mountains, and north, across the Grand Valley, rise the Book Cliffs. The southern end of the Black Ridge Trail is across the road from the Liberty Cap trailhead. The 0.75-mile-long CCC Trail connects the head of the Monument Canyon Trail with the midway point of the Black Ridge Trail. Hike the Black Ridge Trail in conjunction with either the Monument Canyon or Liberty Cap Trail for a long-distance tour of the monument.

Cross-country Skiing

The Park Service lists both the Black Ridge and Liberty Cap Trails as possible cross-country ski routes, given enough snow.

60 Little Book Cliffs Wilderness Study Area

Location: 16 mi NE of Grand Junction
Size: 26,525 acres
Status: Wilderness study area (1978)
Terrain: Arid canyons and mesas
Elevation: 4,700' to 6,650'
Management: BLM (Grand Junction Field Office)
Topographic maps: Round Mountain, Winter Flats, Cameo

The Little Book Cliffs Wilderness Study Area (WSA) is best known as a wild horse range. Here the BLM manages a herd of between 65 and 125 wild horses, as mandated by the Wild Horse Act of 1971. But this area also offers a large expanse of desert land worth exploring. And, unlike other BLM WSAs, the Little Book Cliffs WSA features a network of backcountry trails. Pre-existing roadways and other developments have resulted in incongruities in the boundary in the Round Mountain and Monument Rocks areas. Because of existing gas and oil leases, the BLM recommended against further consideration as wilderness.

Seasons

Summers are quite hot (afternoons above 100 degrees are not uncommon) and gnats can prove a nuisance. Occasional thundershowers may pop up. Spring and fall are pleasant, but winters are not so severe as to prevent pleasurable hiking.

Flora and Fauna

Plant life consists mostly of sagebrush, rabbitbrush, and saltbush in the canyon bottoms, with pinyon pine and juniper forests at higher elevations. Indigenous wildlife includes mule deer, a few elk in the winter, mountain lions, coyotes, and badgers. Golden eagles and peregrine falcons have been spotted in the area.

The WSA falls within the 36,113-acre Little Book Cliffs Wild Horse Range. When the herd becomes too large for the land to support, the BLM rounds up the excess horses for adoption. Although wary, the horses can be spotted in most areas of the range. Typically, summers find the animals in the open canyon bottoms to the north, while winters may push them down into the lower reaches of Main and Coal Canyons. Certain areas are off-limits during the foaling season—from December 1 to July 1.

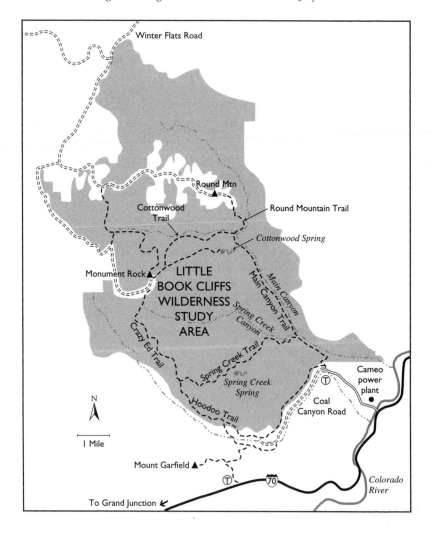

Wild horses are frequently spotted in the Little Book Cliffs WSA.

Geology

The canyons of this WSA cut into the Book Cliffs Formation, an interesting conglomerate of sedimentary rocks that runs along the north end of the Grand Valley and into Utah. This formation is visible from almost anywhere in the Grand Valley. Most prominent are the escarpments of Mancos shale, which have been eroded into fascinating badlands hills. On top of that is a cap of Mesa Verde Group sandstones. These sandstones dominate the canyon walls within the Little Book Cliffs WSA.

ACTIVITIES
Hiking

With a number of established trails, the Little Book Cliffs WSA is an ideal destination for hikers. The most convenient access is found beyond the Cameo power plant off Interstate 70. After taking the Cameo exit, cross the Colorado River and drive 1.8 miles up Coal Canyon Road to the Coal Canyon trailhead. From the parking area, the Main Canyon Trail follows a steep road to a cut in the ridge to the north where a locked gate stops vehicles. From there the route drops into Main Canyon, which it then follows for 4 miles. About 1 mile from the trailhead the Main Canyon Trail intersects the lower end of the occasionally steep and rocky Spring Creek Trail. It follows its namesake for 5 miles to an intersection with the Hoodoo and Crazy Ed Trails. The Hoodoo Trail mostly parallels a dirt road for 4 miles to return to the Coal Canyon trailhead. The

4.5-mile Crazy Ed Trail continues north to the Monument Rock area (the site of a BLM campground) and the upper end of the 3-mile long Cottonwood Trail. Because the Cottonwood Trail drops to meet the upper end of the Main Canyon Trail, a 17.5-mile loop hike encompassing the Main Canyon, Spring Creek, Crazy Ed, and Cottonwood Trails is possible.

Also continuing beyond the end of the Main Canyon Trail is the 1.5-mile Round Mountain Trail. It climbs steeply to the top of Round Mountain, a mesa top that has been cherrystemmed out of the WSA because of gas wells there.

The upper reaches of the WSA can be accessed by driving Winter Flats Road from De Beque, which is several miles to the north on Interstate 70. Passable to 2WD vehicles when dry, Winter Flats Road accesses several side roads that reach the area's northern and western boundaries. Plan on a drive of a couple of hours from De Beque to reach this end of the WSA.

61   Black Ridge Canyons Wilderness Area

Location: 10 mi W of Grand Junction
Size: 75,550 acres
Status: Wilderness area (2000)
Terrain: Canyons and mesas
Elevation: 4,650' to 6,900'
Management: BLM (Grand Junction Field Office)
Topographic maps: Battleship Rock, Mack, Sieber Canyon, Ruby Canyon, Westwater

The canyons that drain into the Colorado River from Black Ridge include some of the most picturesque terrain within Colorado's BLM holdings. Included here are several slickrock drainages, one of which contains fourteen natural stone arches—second in number only to Arches National Park. A number of established trails and trailheads facilitate access to this spectacular wild land and the Colorado River, which borders the area to the north, adds to its allure. Recognizing the value of this tract as a true wilderness, Colorado's congressional delegation successfully spearheaded the establishment of a wilderness area in 2000. The 75,550-acre Black Ridge Canyons Wilderness is included in the much larger (122,300 acres) Colorado Canyons National Conservation Area.

Seasons
The best times to hike the Black Ridge Canyons are in the spring and fall when heat and gnats are not a problem. Summer temperatures regularly climb above the century mark. Winters see occasional snowfall, but hiking is normally not impeded. Desert wildflowers bloom mostly in May and June.

Flora and Fauna

The majority of this wilderness features a forest mix of pinyon pine and juniper. This forest type is sometimes interspersed with open areas of sagebrush, saltbush, and grasses. Some canyon bottoms feature riparian communities of willow and cottonwood. Like most desert areas of the Colorado Plateau, much of the barren ground here is covered with cryptogamic soil. Formed by lichens and mosses, this crust helps stabilize soil and is quite fragile. Hikers should avoid walking across such areas as even footprints can have a lasting effect.

Wildlife residing here includes mule deer, coyotes, mountain lions, and badgers. A band of desert bighorn sheep inhabit the area, the result of a transplant project. Endangered birds of prey found here include bald eagles and peregrine falcons.

Geology

The geology of the Black Ridge Canyons really makes this area spectacular. Seven major canyon systems dissect the northern reaches of the wilderness, and a stunning variety of sedimentary rock is vividly displayed. Beginning with the Morrison Formation, these abysses drop through the Summerville, Entrada, Kayenta, Wingate, and Chinle formations. The arches within Rattlesnake Canyon are carved into the Entrada sandstone, which rims the canyon, while the spectacular pinnacles within Mee and Knowles Canyons are made of Wingate sandstone. Precambrian rock is also exposed in the Black Rocks at the mouth of Moore Canyon.

One of many arches in Rattlesnake Canyon

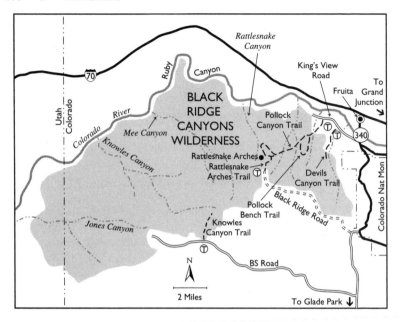

ACTIVITIES
Hiking

The Pollock Canyon Trail is a good place to start an exploration of the Black Ridge Canyons Wilderness. Drive south from Fruita on State Highway 340 1.2 miles to the King's View Road. Turn right and drive 3.3 miles to the well-developed trailhead. This rugged, 7-mile trail crosses Pollock and Flume Creek Canyons before climbing to reach the Rattlesnake Arches along the upper rim area of Rattlesnake Canyon. Rough in places, this route is marked with rock cairns as it climbs in and out of drainages. Within the first mile of the Pollock Canyon Trail, the start of the Pollock Bench Trail takes off to the left. It loops across its namesake before connecting back up with the Pollock Canyon Trail a bit farther on. A hike along the Pollock Bench Trail involves a round-trip of about 4 miles.

The Devils Canyon Trail begins along the same road as the Pollock Canyon Trail. From a trailhead about 1 mile closer to State Highway 340, it explores its beautiful and occasionally rugged namesake. A round-trip hike of 5 miles can be enjoyed here.

A shorter and therefore more popular route to the Rattlesnake Arches follows the 1.5-mile Rattlesnake Arches Trail. To get to the trailhead, drive 11 miles from the north entrance of the Colorado National Monument to the turnoff for the Glade Park store. Drive another 0.2 mile and then turn right onto Black Ridge Road. The BLM calls this a 4WD route, but the first 8 miles are passable to high-clearance 2WD vehicles in dry weather. Follow the Black Ridge Road for 11 miles to the trailhead; the way is marked at each fork in the road by small brown public-access signs. From here it is about 1 mile to the first arch. To get to other arches, climb down through this arch and follow the bench below. Considerable care should be taken because of precipices in the area.

About 0.5 mile from the trailhead, the Pollock Canyon Trail branches off to the north.

Knowles Canyon is another drainage with trail access from above. The Knowles Canyon trailhead is reached by driving the BS Road from Glade Park. From the trailhead, hike 3.5 miles into the bottom of Knowles Canyon, which can then be hiked to the Colorado River. Other canyons also can be accessed from their upper ends, although the way is not so clear. To get into Mee Canyon, hikers must follow a very specific route to get below a ring of sandstone walls. Jones Canyon is the same. For descriptions of these routes, check with the BLM office in Grand Junction. These and other canyons that dissect this wilderness are accessible to boaters on the Colorado River.

River Running

Nearby Ruby Canyon provides some of the most spectacular wilderness boating in the state. Because the 25-mile stretch of the Colorado River from the Loma boat launch to the Westwater Ranger Station in Utah is mostly Class I water, it is ideal for canoeists, but kayakers and rafters can also enjoy the scenery and hiking opportunities. Ruby Canyon can be run in one long day or in two leisurely days. This part of the lower Colorado River is being considered as a National Wild and Scenic River.

62 Demaree Canyon Wilderness Study Area

Location: 28 mi NW of Grand Junction
Size: 21,050 acres
Status: Wilderness study area (1978)
Terrain: Deep canyons and narrow mesa tops
Elevation: 5,000' to 7,500'
Management: BLM (Grand Junction Field Office)
Topographic maps: Howard Canyon, Carbonera

The Demaree Canyon Wilderness Study Area (WSA) encompasses a series of rugged canyons that penetrate the southern face of the Book Cliffs near the Utah border. Perhaps due to its isolation and the fact that other desert wildlands in western Colorado are considered more scenic, the Demaree Canyon WSA receives comparatively few visitors.

Seasons

Because summer temperatures are typically hot, sometimes topping 100 degrees, and winters may bring occasional snows and muddy, impassable roads, the best seasons to visit are spring and fall. Watch for colorful desert blooms in mid- to late spring.

Flora and Fauna

Canyon bottoms mostly feature low-profile sagebrush, saltbush, and grasses, while the sloping terrain above includes stands of pinyon pines and junipers. Gambel oak and mountain mahogany also grow in places. Although wildlife is sparse, mule deer may be sighted here. Coyotes and mountain lions also roam the region.

Geology

The Demaree Canyon WSA encompasses a portion of the Book Cliffs, a grand escarpment rising more than 2,000 feet above the desert lands to the south. Exposed in the strata of the Book Cliffs, both along its face and in the canyons carved within, are the Mesa Verde Group and Mancos shale. Whereas the sandstones of the Mesa Verde Group lack the colorful hues and definitive profile of the Entrada and Wingate formations, eroded Mancos shale typically presents a classic badlands look that can be quite scenic.

ACTIVITIES
Hiking

Although the Demaree Canyon WSA has no established trails, it is dissected by four major canyons, all of which make for suitable hiking. The largest of these drainages, Demaree Canyon, is accessed by driving approximately 13.5 miles north from Interstate 70 (exit at Loma) on State Highway 139. Turn left on a dirt road that heads west. This occasionally rough track passes a stock pond and then crosses East Salt Creek (a trickle for most of the year). In another mile or so, the route reaches the mouth of Demaree Canyon, the bottom of which may be followed for 5 miles or more.

The mouth of Howard Canyon is about 2 miles north of the mouth of Demaree Canyon, while Camp Gulch opens a little more than a mile west of Demaree. Access to either of these drainages is gained by walking cross-country along the base of the Book Cliffs.

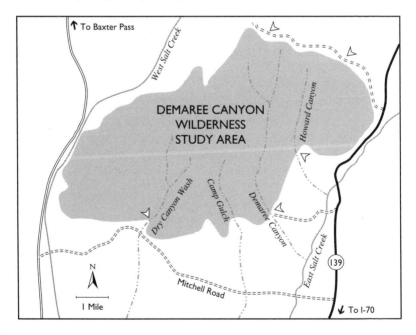

Sagebrush flats in the Demaree Canyon WSA

Dry Canyon Wash, which drains the south-central portion of the WSA, is accessible via Mitchell Road, which branches east from an improved gravel road running west of the WSA between Mack and Baxter Pass. As with Demaree Canyon, Dry Canyon Wash and its various tributaries offers several miles of canyon bottom hiking.

Additionally, a rugged 4WD route parallels the northern boundary of the WSA, thereby accessing the higher reaches of the Book Cliffs. This road begins a few miles north of the access road to Demaree Canyon.

63 Oil Spring Mountain Wilderness Study Area

Location: 20 mi S of Rangely
Size: 17,740 acres
Status: Wilderness study area (1978)
Terrain: Forested mountain and bottomland
Elevation: 6,000' to 8,550'
Management: BLM (White River Field Office)
Topographic maps: Big Foundation Creek, East Evacuation Creek, Texas Creek, Texas Mountain

Rising above a sea of oil and gas wells, Oil Spring Mountain is an oasis of sorts. The mountain's flat top is covered with virgin stands of fir, while its lower reaches feature sculpted rock formations and beautiful grass and sagebrush parks. This wilderness study area (WSA) is one of the last remaining wild areas in the southern portion of the Rangely oil field. Because of the pending development of leases within its boundaries, however, the BLM dropped Oil Spring Mountain from its list of recommended wilderness areas.

271

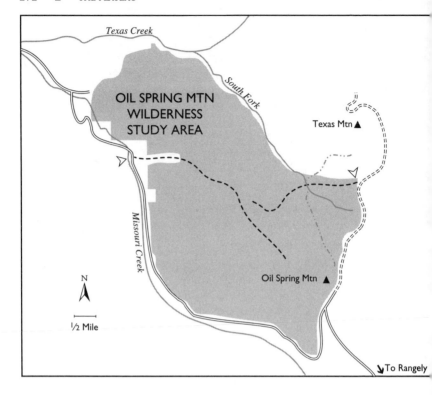

Seasons

Across the highest reaches of Oil Spring Mountain, snow usually precludes hiking from November through May. Summer afternoons are occasionally hot at these elevations and thunderstorms sometimes move across the area during July and August. In the lower sections, gnats can be a problem and temperatures are hot on some afternoons. The best times to visit are late spring and fall.

Flora and Fauna

Forests of Douglas fir grow across the mountain's higher elevations, while pinyon pine and juniper are most common in the lower western end. Stands of gambel oak and mountain mahogany are scattered throughout. Lower elevations also feature open areas of grasses or sagebrush. The Oil Spring Mountain WSA is considered important summer range for mule deer and elk. Black bears, mountain lions, and coyotes reside here, and a herd of wild horses roams across the area's western and northern ends.

Geology

Oil Spring Mountain consists mostly of the Green River Formation, a shale that was deposited as mud in the ancient Lake Uintah about 40 million years ago. The Green River Formation is said to be the greatest undeveloped source of petroleum in the world.

Most of the interest in developing its oil shale reserves has been directed toward the huge Roan Plateau north of Rifle.

ACTIVITIES
Hiking
Two bootleg trails enter the Oil Spring Mountain WSA. One comes in from the northeast corner near Texas Mountain and one via a drainage bottom along the western border. Because both routes are unofficial, neither has a name, and because they are not maintained, they may be hard to follow in places. Nevertheless, both access the open forests on top of the mountain and together they offer 6 to 8 miles of hiking.

64 Willow Creek–Skull Creek Wilderness Study Area

Location: 20 mi N of Rangely
Size: 27,553 acres
Status: Wilderness study area (1978)
Terrain: Canyons and mesas
Elevation: 5,800' to 8,200'
Management: BLM (White River Field Office)
Topographic maps: Plug Hat Rock, Lazy Y Point, Skull Creek

The Willow Creek–Skull Creek Wilderness Study Area stretches across a band of rugged canyons that run east of the Harpers Corner Scenic Drive and north of U.S. Highway 40. Colorful geology and a heavily dissected topography are the key attractions here. The old road that separates Willow Creek and Skull Creek, originally identified as two separate WSAs, has been closed and is slowly being rehabilitated.

Seasons
Hiking can be a year-round experience here, although summers typically bring high temperatures and gnats, while winters include below-freezing temperatures and occasional snow. Spring and fall provide the best overall conditions for visiting this upland desert. Desert wildflowers bloom in late spring. Since precipitation is scant at best, be prepared for arid conditions.

Flora and Fauna
Most of this area includes mature stands of pinyon pine and juniper. A study conducted by the University of Arizona revealed that many of these trees have reached their maximum age of 600 years. In the wake of large wildfires that have swept across the area, many forests are now blackened skeletons, beneath which a variety of grasses grow. Associated plants of the pinyon pine–juniper ecosystem include sagebrush and saltbush. Riparian communities of willows, tamarisk, cottonwoods, and box elder trees

In the Willow Creek drainage

are found along streambeds. Among the wildlife species that live here are mule deer, elk, coyotes, mountain lions, and golden eagles.

Geology

The Willow Creek–Skull Creek WSA features a fascinating conglomerate of geologic formations and structures. Running along much of the area's southern border is the Dakota Hogback, an upturned layer of Dakota sandstone that eroded into a sharp and narrow ridge. This landform is common throughout the state. Beyond the Hogback are the green and purple shales of the Morrison Formation and deep-red Triassic sandstones. As in nearby Bull Canyon, imposing cliffs of Entrada sandstone head many drainages.

History

A number of prehistoric sites have been discovered here, including some Paleo-Indian artifacts dating back 10,000 years. Fremont rock art, a stone shelter, and a few granaries also have been found among the canyon walls.

ACTIVITIES
Hiking

Hiking in this area is mostly a matter of following drainage bottoms and canyons in from the south. Normally a simple process, this means of access is complicated by the fact that private land blocks the lower ends of many canyons.

Willow Creek, a major drainage in the western half, can be hiked by driving nearly

1 mile east of where the stream crosses U.S. Highway 40. Walk through a small gap in the hill just north of the highway and cross over the Dakota Hogback. Here Willow Creek is a broad drainage bottom of sagebrush and grass, but 2 miles upstream the canyon walls close ranks to make the scenery more interesting. Willow Creek is passable for 1 or 2 more miles. Bull Draw makes an interesting side trip from Willow Creek. There is also an old 4WD track that climbs along a drainage just west of upper Willow Creek and ends on Buckwater Ridge about 3 miles to the north. To find the road on top, turn right off Harpers Corner Road 2 miles beyond the Plug Hat Rock Picnic Area and then continue another 2 miles along a high-clearance 2WD road to the road closure. From here it is a 1.5-mile walk to where the route drops off the ridge.

In the eastern portion of the WSA (the Skull Creek section), private lands make access to draws and canyons difficult, but Box Canyon provides an exception. It can be reached by driving 1 mile west on County Road 165 from where Red Wash crosses U.S. Highway 40. A faded track heads north from County Road 165 for 0.5 mile to a section of state land. No trail enters Box Canyon, but the wash bottom is passable.

Red Wash and Little Red Wash are blocked on the lower ends by private land, but they can be entered from the top. To reach them, drive 6.2 miles north on County Road 95 from Skull Creek (a cluster of buildings on County Road 104), then drive west on a dirt road (a high-clearance 2WD vehicle will suffice in dry weather) for 2 miles. Two gates about 1 mile apart mark either side of an inholding of private land that can be crossed. Beyond the second gate, the road eventually drops into Red Wash. Because it is closed to vehicles not far beyond the second gate, the road makes a nice 5-mile hike across the mesa top. This is the road that originally divided the Willow Creek and Skull Creek WSAs.

A less distinct pack trail drops into Little Red Wash. To find it, head down a faded road that turns south just before the second gate; the trail branches to the left off this track. Because a recent forest fire obscured the route, it is best to obtain more complete directions from the BLM office in Meeker.

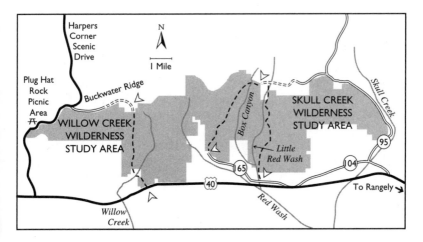

65 Bull Canyon Wilderness Study Area

Location: 20 mi N of Rangely
Size: 13,187 acres
Status: Wilderness study area (1978)
Terrain: Canyons and mesas
Elevation: 5,600' to 7,400'
Management: BLM (White River Field Office)
Topographic maps: Plug Hat Rock, Snake John Reef

Although small, the Bull Canyon Wilderness Study Area (WSA) offers a wonderful se-lection of rugged gulches and canyons along the Colorado–Utah border. In fact, 520 acres of the WSA are in Utah. Thousands of visitors peer into Bull Canyon from scenic overlooks along the Harpers Corner Scenic Drive—a popular paved route into Dino-saur National Monument. But very few ever bother to set foot there.

Seasons
Although winters may bring cold temperatures and some snow to Bull Canyon, hik-ing here is mostly a year-round activity. Summer temperatures can rise above 100 de-grees and gnats are a nuisance during hot spells. The best seasons for visiting Bull Canyon, then, are spring and fall. Spring is also when most desert flowers bloom. Be-cause this is arid country, be sure to bring plenty of drinking water.

Entrada sandstone cliffs ring the head of Bull Canyon.

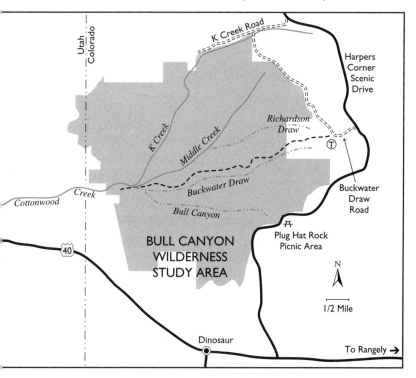

Flora and Fauna

The primary ecosystem here is a forest mix of pinyon pine and juniper. Scattered Douglas firs grow in the canyons and lush riparian communities of box elders, cottonwoods, and willows characterize many stream bottoms. Open areas of sagebrush and grasses are also present, especially in the higher eastern end of the wilderness. Mule deer, some elk, mountain lions, and coyotes inhabit the area. Golden eagle nesting sites have been spotted here as well.

Geology

Bull Canyon's most impressive feature is the sheer cliffs of the Entrada Formation that form the upper rims of the canyons. Entrada sandstone was deposited 150 million years ago as gigantic sand dunes. Below these prominent cliffs is a smaller layer known as the Carmel Formation, which consists of silt and mud that was deposited as fine sediments.

History

In September 1776, the Dominguez–Escalante Expedition made camp near the mouth of Bull Canyon. They reportedly drew water from a spring and hunted buffalo while staying here.

ACTIVITIES
Hiking

To get a good feel for the Bull Canyon Wilderness, stop at the Plug Hat Rock Picnic Area on the Harpers Corner Scenic Drive. Situated at the edge of the WSA, this facility overlooks most of Bull Canyon and its associated drainages. From this developed site it is possible to walk north along the mesa's edge for a mile or more—if for no other reason than to enjoy that "land's end" feeling of being at the canyon's rim. Several picturesque pinyon pine and juniper snags grow here.

For a more substantial hike into the Bull Canyon WSA, follow Buckwater Draw via an old 4WD track that is closed to vehicles. To find this route, drive 3 miles north of the Plug Hat Rock Picnic Area, turn left on a dirt road, and park just inside the fence. This route drops through sagebrush parks before entering pinyon pine and juniper forest below. Beyond the gate it is a 7-mile hike to the WSA's western boundary. Buckwater Draw, like other drainages in the wilderness, narrows to a spectacular slickrock canyon.

Other canyons also can be accessed from their upper ends, but they do not include trails of any kind. The trick is to follow stream bottoms. Three possible hikes follow K Creek, Richardson Draw, and Middle Creek. K Creek is reached via K Creek Road, which branches off Harpers Corner Scenic Drive 4 miles beyond Buckwater Draw Road. A spur off K Creek Road crosses the upper ends of Richardson Draw and Middle Creek. Unfortunately, access to the mouths of all of these canyons is blocked by private land. Recognizing the recreation potential of the area, however, the BLM is working to remedy the situation.

66   Dinosaur National Monument

Location: 45 mi N of Rangely
Size: 210,844 acres
Status: National monument (1915)
Terrain: River canyons and mesas
Elevation: 4,740' to 9,006'
Management: NPS
Topographic maps: Canyon of Lodore South, Canyon of Lodore North, Jack Springs, Jones Hole, Stuntz Reservoir, Hells Canyon, Tanks Peak, Zenobia Peak, Haystack Rock, Greystone, Indian Water Canyon

The premier attraction at Dinosaur National Monument is the Dinosaur Quarry in the monument's western quarter. Here paleontologists have dug up the bones of such ancient giants as Apatosaurus, Stegosaurus, and the sharp-toothed Allosaurus. Visitors see a vast array of exposed bones in the large building, but actual digging occurs outside of the quarry in remote locations.

In addition to its collection of oversized reptilian bones, however, Dinosaur National Monument offers an enormous spread of backcountry that rivals most other national parks of the Colorado Plateau in both size and geographical variety. Within Dinosaur two major rivers of the West—the Green and the Yampa—join forces. The configuration of the monument reflects this as one arm extends north from the confluence along the Green River, another extends east with the Yampa, and a third takes up the Green as it flows west into Utah. Because of these two rivers, Dinosaur National Monument offers some of the best wilderness boating in the nation. Its backcountry is extensive enough to satisfy the desires of most hikers, as well. About a third of the monument—54,446 acres—is in Utah.

Seasons
Summers can be hot in Dinosaur as temperatures occasionally rise above the century mark. Gnats are a common nuisance during the hottest months, and lightning can pose a hazard on exposed ridges and mesa tops. Winters often bring subzero temperatures and snow. Spring and autumn are the best times of the year for a visit, with wildflowers blooming from late April through early June. Because this is an arid land with very little precipitation, backcountry travelers should bring plenty of water; a gallon per person per day should suffice.

Flora and Fauna
A variety of upland desert plant communities are represented in Dinosaur National Monument. Open parks of sagebrush, saltbush, and greasewood are found across the

Prehistoric petroglyphs in Dinosaur National Monument

lower drainage bottoms. Pinyon pine and juniper forests grow along hillsides and on mesa tops, with occasional stands of aspen and Douglas fir in the higher reaches.

Riparian ecosystems are frequent along river and stream banks. Members of these water-loving communities include box elders, cottonwoods, willows, and tamarisk. Wildflowers that bloom here include the arrowleaf balsamroot, sego lily, evening primrose, yellow beeplant, desert plume, lupine, globemallow, and sunflower.

Wildlife species inhabiting Dinosaur National Monument are equally diverse. Mule deer and elk are present throughout. Coyotes and mountain lions haunt out-of-the-way places. Peregrine falcon numbers are on the rise. And several endangered fish species swim the waters of the Green and Yampa Rivers, including the razorback sucker, humpback chub, roundtail chub, bonytail chub, and Colorado pikeminnow.

Geology

Dating back 150 million years to the Jurassic period, the treasure chest of bones found at Dinosaur Quarry was deposited when floodwaters washed several dinosaur carcasses down to a sandbar. These sands eventually formed part of the Morrison Formation, a layer of rock that has produced similar relics of the past in other locations.

While the Morrison Formation commands much of the attention in Dinosaur National Monument, it is but one small chapter in what experts consider to be one of the most complete geologic records anywhere. The oldest rock found within Dinosaur is the Uinta Mountain Group, which dates back 1.09 billion years. These are Colorado's oldest rocks. Unlike other Precambrian formations, they are sedimentary rather than igneous in nature.

The Uinta Mountain Group sandstone is most prominent along the Canyon of Lodore in the north end of the monument. On top of the Uinta Group is a thick layer of limestones and shales. These were deposited in the bottom of ancient seas during the Cambrian, Mississippian, and Pennsylvanian periods. Next in line is the salmon-colored Weber sandstone, which formed as sand dunes during middle Pennsylvanian times. It is responsible for many of the monument's best-known landmarks, including Steamboat Rock at Echo Park and Split Mountain in Utah.

While the formations of Dinosaur cover an incredible span of years, the fascinating landscape was shaped by a great amount of faulting and folding. This displacement is most evident at Harpers Corner, a promontory that overlooks both the Yampa and Green Rivers. River and stream erosion also added much to Dinosaur's geologic countenance.

History

Dinosaur National Monument has been home to a number of Native American cultures, the oldest of which dates back some 10,000 years. Known to archaeologists as Paleo-Indians, these nomadic people hunted such extinct megafauna as mammoths, giant bison, and camels. Following the Paleo-Indians were the Desert Archaic groups, which subsisted by gathering wild food and hunting small game. Dating back to A.D. 200, the Fremont Culture is responsible for many of the intricate panels of rock art in Dinosaur. They made their living mostly by hunting and gathering, but they also farmed.

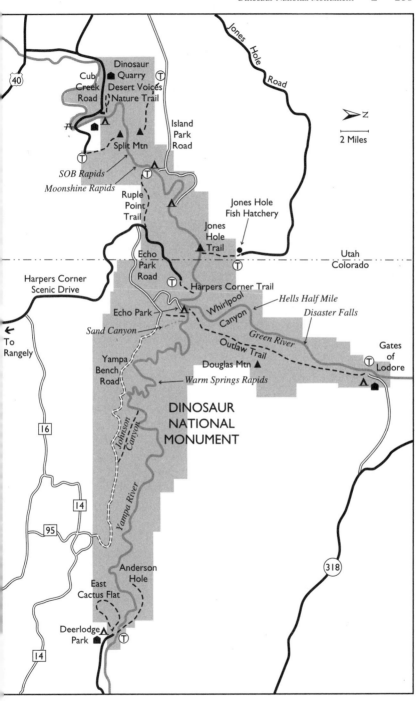

Droughts around A.D. 1150 may have helped push the Fremont out. The Utes, who lived a hunting-and-gathering subsistence, eventually replaced them.

The first Europeans to visit the Dinosaur area were members of the Dominguez–Escalante Expedition in 1776. The trapper William Ashley floated the Green River on a crudely constructed bull boat in 1824, and Mormons were settling most parts of Utah by the 1850s. John Wesley Powell made his epic voyages down the Green River in 1869 and 1871.

In the summer of 1909, Earl Douglass, a paleontologist, arrived to search for dinosaur bones. After months of looking he happened upon the exposed tailbones of a brontosaurus. His find led to the excavation of literally hundreds of tons of dinosaur bones from the quarry. An 80-acre national monument was established in 1915. President Franklin Roosevelt added 210,000 acres to the monument in 1938. Despite this expanded protection, controversy over a proposed dam at Echo Park erupted in the 1950s. Under mounting opposition orchestrated by conservationists, the project was squelched in 1955. The federal government instead authorized the construction of dams in Glen Canyon, Flaming Gorge, and other locations in the West.

ACTIVITIES
Hiking
Hiking trails access most parts of the monument, but backpackers must first obtain a free backcountry permit at the monument headquarters, the Dinosaur Quarry, or at any of the ranger stations. Because this is a pristine desert, extra care should be taken so as not to damage the fragile environment. Measures include not walking across cryptogamic soil, using a stove instead of a wood fire for cooking, and not bathing or washing dishes in springs, streams, and pools.

A good introductory hike in Dinosaur is the 1-mile-long Harpers Corner Trail at the end of Harpers Corner Scenic Drive. With a guide pamphlet in hand, hikers can learn a lot about the geology and ecology of the monument's eastern half. Although the scenery is outstanding all along the trail, the views reach their peak at the very end. To the east are Echo Park and the sandstone labyrinths of the Yampa River; to the north and west, within the depths of Whirlpool Canyon, runs the Green.

The Ruple Point Trail also starts along Harpers Corner Scenic Drive. Four miles long, this less-developed trail begins at the Island Park Overlook 28 miles north of monument headquarters near the town of Dinosaur. Generally level, this walk gives a spectacular view of the monument's western half, including Split Mountain Canyon.

Thirteen-mile Echo Park Road branches off Harpers Corner Scenic Drive. Passable to most 2WD vehicles in dry weather (rain can make it impassable even to 4WDs), this drive results in an up-close view of Steamboat Rock and the confluence of the Green and Yampa Rivers. A new campground allows for an overnight stay—provided that it is not full—and a ranger is on hand during the summer months. A possible hike from Echo Park follows the Yampa upstream to Sand Canyon (high water can make the mouth of Sand Canyon impassable). Follow the canyon to where 4WD Yampa Bench Road crosses it, and then follow that back to Echo Park Road. It is possible to avoid walking along the road by crossing the open bench land north of the road. No actual trail exists along this route, but the walking is still easy. The entire hike is 8 miles.

Another hike that doesn't necessarily follow a clear path is the Outlaw Trail. Twenty miles long, this route runs from Echo Park to the Gates of Lodore in the northern end of the monument. To begin at Echo Park you will need to find a ride across the Yampa. From here the route crosses Douglas Mountain, traversing a variety of rough terrain in the process. Rated as difficult in places, it is best to mark the route on a topo map with the help of a knowledgeable ranger.

Branching off the Echo Park Road, the high-clearance 2WD Yampa Bench Road accesses Johnson Canyon, which can be hiked 5 miles to the Yampa River. From here it is possible to continue downriver 1 mile to Bull Canyon for the return trip.

Two hikes access the wilds of the monument's eastern end. One trail follows Disappointment Draw southwest from the Deerlodge Park area (a campground and ranger station are located here) for 3 miles. It accesses East Cactus Flat above the Yampa, across which hikers will find mostly open terrain. The other hike, a cross-country route, accesses Anderson Hole and Corral Springs Draw on the north side of the Yampa. You will need to catch a raft ride across the river at Deerlodge Park. Expect moderate to difficult hiking conditions along the way and, again, check with a knowledgeable ranger for the exact route. A hike of up to 30 miles is feasible along this route.

At the Gates of Lodore—the dramatic abyss that the Green has carved in the park's northern area—a short nature trail follows the river for almost 1 mile. The northern end of the rugged Outlaw Trail can be picked up here.

Several interesting hiking routes are accessible on the Utah side of the monument. The 2-mile Desert Voices Nature Trail loops through a variety of geologic formations. It begins 4 miles beyond the Dinosaur Quarry at the Split Mountain Campground. Beginning near Elder Spring on Cub Creek Road, a 3-mile hiking route tops Split Mountain east of the river. A 7-mile route to Split Mountain from the west begins near Bear Wallow on the Island Park Road. Both routes reveal spectacular views of Split Mountain Canyon, but, because they are unsigned and unmarked, they require good maps.

From the Jones Hole Fish Hatchery at the end of Jones Hole Road, the Jones Hole Trail follows Jones Creek for 4 miles to the Green River. An easy walk along a clear-running creek, this trail features lush riparian growth, prehistoric pictographs, and a waterfall. Because of the hike's popularity, however, camping is allowed only at the Ely Creek backcountry campsites.

River Running

Perhaps the most inviting environs that Dinosaur has to offer are its river canyons. Float trips lasting from one to several days are possible. The white water can be exciting, and the scenery seldom fails to amaze the thousands of people who float the rivers of Dinosaur annually. Such numbers make it necessary for the Park Service to control access by means of a permit system. To apply for a permit, contact the monument headquarters at 970-374-2468.

The most popular float trip is the one-day run down the Green River through

Split Mountain Canyon. From the put-in at Rainbow Park, it is 9 river miles to the Split Mountain takeout ramp. Four rapids—Moonshine, SOB, Schoolboy, and Inglesby—thrill boaters with white-water challenges.

Upriver from Island Park, the Green flows through Whirlpool Canyon with its Class II water. The put-in for this stretch is at Echo Park. A 3- or 4-day, 45-mile trip is possible with a put-in at the Gates of Lodore. Through 3,300-foot deep Canyon of Lodore—the monument's deepest gorge—the Green tumbles through such drops as Disaster Falls, Triplet Falls, and Hells Half Mile. Class III waters are the toughest you will find here.

Unlike the Green River, whose flow is controlled by the Flaming Gorge Dam, the Yampa is one of the last free-flowing rivers in the Colorado River Basin. This allows nature to play a much greater hand in any float trip down its waters. With only one put-in at Deerlodge Park, trips on the Yampa can run all the way to Echo Park, a distance of 45 miles, or to Split Mountain, 72 miles. Expect Class III–IV waters at Warm Springs Rapids, a drop that did not exist prior to June 1965, when a flash flood sent boulders tumbling down Warm Springs Draw. Boating season on the Yampa typically lasts only to July, as low water makes passage difficult.

67 Cross Mountain Wilderness Study Area

Location: 55 mi W of Craig
Size: 14,081 acres
Status: Wilderness study area (1978)
Terrain: Mountains and canyon
Elevation: 5,700' to 7,750'
Management: BLM (Little Snake Field Office)
Topographic maps: Twelvemile Mesa, Lone Mountain, Peck Mesa, Cross Mountain Canyon

Although small by comparison to other mountains in Colorado, Cross Mountain possesses many noteworthy qualities. The 1,200-foot-deep abyss that the Yampa River has carved in the southern end of the mountain affords a vivid lesson in the geology of the West. The area provides suitable habitat for a number of endangered fish, bird, and plant species. And, because it is situated in an isolated portion of the state, it offers visitors outstanding opportunities for finding solitude.

Seasons

Cross Mountain is usually free of snow from May to late October. Summers bring hot afternoons, especially in the lower elevations. Lightning can be a hazard on exposed ridges and hilltops. Winters often see subzero temperatures and lasting blankets of snow. Early summer and fall are the best times to visit.

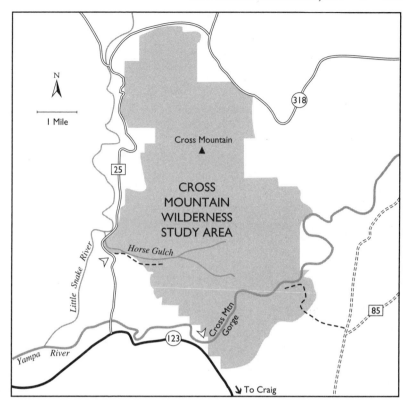

Flora and Fauna

Most of the Cross Mountain WSA is typified either by forests of pinyon pine and juniper or by open areas of sagebrush and grasses. Two rare plants—Ownbey's thistle and a penstemon—both grow within the confines of Cross Mountain Gorge.

A sizable population of mule deer winters here, as do some elk. Bighorn sheep were transplanted here in 1977, but inadequate sources of water have limited the herd's growth. Seven golden eagle nests have been spotted in the WSA and peregrine falcons frequent the area. The Colorado squawfish and humpback chub, both of which are federally recognized endangered species, migrate through the canyon.

Geology

From a distance, the 9-mile-long profile of Cross Mountain appears less than spectacular. Up close, however, the geological complexity of this uplift becomes evident. Much of the mountain consists of limestones deposited in seas during the Mississippian period, but the Yampa has revealed the mountain's Precambrian heart. Because Cross Mountain is an eastern extension of the Uinta Mountains, the rock displayed in the gorge is of the Uinta Mountain Group. The river, geologists tell us, was superimposed onto Cross Mountain as surrounding layers of younger rock were

The mouth of Cross Gorge

stripped away. Other geologic formations found within the WSA include Mancos shale, Chinle sandstone, and Weber sandstone.

ACTIVITIES
Hiking
No maintained trails exist in the Cross Mountain area, but unmaintained routes and plenty of open terrain allow some backcountry explorations. A closed road begins on County Road 25 along the western end of the WSA and climbs for perhaps 1 mile just south of Horse Gulch. From its end a trail of sorts—more of a game trail than anything—continues to the gorge's north rim, a walk of about 5 miles from the county road.

Find your way to the southern rim of the gorge by cutting up from the southeastern end of the mountain. Similarly, the flat summit of Cross Mountain in the northern part of the WSA is approachable by following game trails and open spaces up from the eastern slope. The top is open and easy to walk. Be sure to begin this hike on BLM land and not from one of the private tracts in the area.

River Running
Boulder-choked and extremely wild, the 3.5-mile stretch of the Yampa that flows through Cross Mountain Gorge is nearly unrunnable by rafts. Because kayakers will find Class V and VI waters within the vertical walls of the gorge, this float is strictly for experts. Most kayakers wait for low water before attempting it. State-maintained put-ins are located on the east side of the canyon above and below Maybell. A spur road off County Road 85 puts you at the upper end of the canyon. Takeout is along the road into Deerlodge Park in the eastern end of Dinosaur National Monument. With drops like Mammoth Falls and the Snake Pit, you need to do plenty of scouting before successfully tackling this river corridor.

Diamond Breaks Wilderness Study Area

Location: 90 mi W of Craig
Size: 35,380 acres
Status: Wilderness study area (1978)
Terrain: Mountainous with canyons
Elevation: 5,400' to 8,673'
Management: BLM (Little Snake Field Office)
Topographic maps: Canyon of Lodore North, Lodore School, Hoy Mountain, Swallow Canyon

The Diamond Breaks Wilderness Study Area (WSA) encompasses rugged Diamond Mountain, an extension of Uinta Mountains. It is bordered to the north by the Browns Park National Wildlife Refuge, which includes several lazy bends of the Green River.

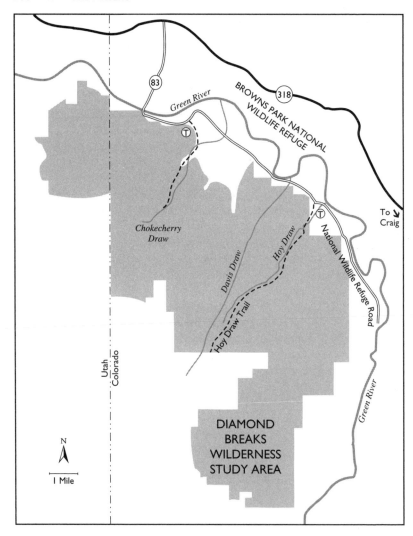

It adjoins the northern arm of Dinosaur National Monument and backs up to an isolated region of mountains along the Colorado–Utah border. In short, few wild areas in the state offer the kind of "back-of-beyond" feeling as the Diamond Breaks. Three thousand nine hundred acres of the WSA lie west of the Utah–Colorado line.

Seasons
Hiking is feasible from April or May through October. Summer afternoons can exceed 100 degrees in the lower elevations, but nights generally cool off. Wildflowers bloom in late spring and early summer. Listen for elk bugling during the rutting season in September.

Flora and Fauna

Across the lower elevations, pinyon pine and juniper forests are interspersed with sagebrush and grassland parks. Aspens, gambel oak, mountain mahogany, limber pine, and Douglas fir become more common in the upper reaches of the wilderness. Riparian communities are also represented in some draws.

Wildlife in the area includes mule deer, elk, coyotes, black bears, and mountain lions. It is likely that golden eagles nest here, as well.

Geology

The Uinta Mountain group is the primary geologic feature of the Diamond Breaks. Although dating back to the Precambrian era, this formation does not include the granite, schist, and gneiss found in most Colorado mountain ranges. Rather, it consists of sedimentary rock well hardened by more than a billion years of existence. Faults and stream erosion have given the Diamond Breaks their rugged character.

History

Nearby Browns Park enjoyed a colorful though somewhat notorious past. Because it provided ready access to three different states, outlaws such as Tom Horn, Annie Bassett, and Butch Cassidy and the Sundance Kid hid out here. Save for a few roads and a store, Browns Park is nearly as remote today as it was a century ago.

ACTIVITIES
Hiking

To reach the Diamond Breaks WSA, turn off Colorado Highway 318 and head south on County Road 83. In 2 miles you will reach a single-lane swinging bridge. Because this bridge is very narrow and the load limit is 6,000 pounds, RVs and travel trailers should not cross it. Turn left just beyond the bridge and drive east on a U.S. Fish and Wildlife Service road that extends along the periphery of the Browns Park National Wildlife Refuge.

To reach the first of the two established trails within the WSA, drive 1.7 miles to a 4WD road that branches off to the right. This road is closed to vehicles at the WSA boundary, which is within a mile of the turnoff. From there an old 4WD track extends about 4 miles up Chokecherry Draw to a beautiful grassland park. Here some old fence posts, the foundation of a house, and an abandoned fruit tree or two are all that remains of a homestead dating back to the early part of the twentieth century. From the top of a rock outcrop at the upper end of the park you can get a splendid view of Chokecherry Draw and Browns Park below. No trail extends beyond this point.

The Hoy Draw Trail is reached by driving a little more than 7 miles east from the swinging bridge along the National Wildlife Refuge road. This trail was a wagon route at one time, but today it is only adequate for hiking. It follows Hoy Draw for a few miles, then crosses over to the upper end of Davis Draw. In all, this route covers about 5 miles before topping out at the far boundary of the WSA. In that distance it climbs approximately 2,000 vertical feet. Access to the upper end of the Hoy Draw Trail (and the southwestern boundary of the WSA for that matter) is blocked by private land.

69 West Cold Spring Wilderness Study Area

Location: 80 mi W of Craig
Size: 17,682 acres
Status: Wilderness study area (1978)
Terrain: Mountainous with canyons
Elevation: 5,800' to 8,200'
Management: BLM (Little Snake Field Office)
Topographic maps: Beaver Basin, Willow Creek Butte

Overlooking Browns Park, the West Cold Spring Wilderness Study Area (WSA) includes the steep southwest slope of West Cold Spring Mountain. A deep canyon dissects the western end of the mountain, and lesser streams drain from the eastern end. Not long ago, a large forest fire left a highly visible scar across part of the mountain. In part because of proposed rangeland improvements, the BLM dropped the West Cold Spring WSA from its list of proposed wilderness areas. But given the area's great beauty and the opportunities it provides for finding solitude, it would make a fine addition to Colorado's wilderness lands. Three thousand two hundred acres of the WSA fall into Utah.

Seasons
Hiking here is possible from late April or May through October. The winter months usually bring subzero temperatures and a lasting snow cover. Most wildflowers bloom in May or June. Summer afternoons can be hot, and lightning is sometimes a hazard on prominent ridges.

Flora and Fauna
Woodland areas of pinyon pine and juniper, interspersed with sagebrush parks and grasslands, characterize much of the area. Up high, aspen, limber pine, and mountain mahogany grow in scattered locations. Two drainages feature riparian communities of box elders, cottonwoods, willows, and occasional poison ivy.

    Mule deer and elk live here in promising numbers. A herd of Rocky Mountain bighorn sheep roam the rugged western area, the result of a transplant project in 1983. Pronghorn antelope reside in the Utah section, and, true to its name, Beaver Creek is the site of several beaver dams. The Colorado Division of Wildlife recognizes Beaver Creek as a High Priority Fishery Resource. Once home to the rare Colorado River cutthroat, the stream now contains Yellowstone cutthroat, brown, and brook trout.

Geology
An extension of the Uinta Mountains, West Cold Spring Mountain consists mostly of Red Creek quartzite. Some 2.3 billion years old, this is Colorado's oldest exposed rock.

Across the flats below the mountain is the Browns Park Formation, a Tertiary sandstone that is often crossbedded.

History

Besides serving as a hideout for outlaws, Browns Park witnessed another colorful era in the history of the old West. From 1824, the year William Ashley floated down this stretch of the Green River, to 1840, Browns Park witnessed some of the largest Mountain Man Rendezvous ever held. Annual reenactments are held near the mouth of Beaver Creek Canyon.

ACTIVITIES
Hiking

Beaver Creek Canyon offers the best opportunity for hiking within the West Cold Spring area. From the canyon's mouth near the Utah–Colorado border, a cattle trail runs 3.5 miles up canyon to the far boundary of the WSA. Although not maintained for hiking, this route is easy to follow as it provides passage around the tangled creek bottom. Beaver Creek Canyon is indeed quite beautiful, but watch out for large patches of poison ivy and rattlesnakes along the way. To get to the start of Beaver Creek Canyon, drive 0.8 mile west of the Browns Park National Wildlife Refuge headquarters and turn north on a rough road which is 4WD in places. From here it is 3 miles to the mouth of the

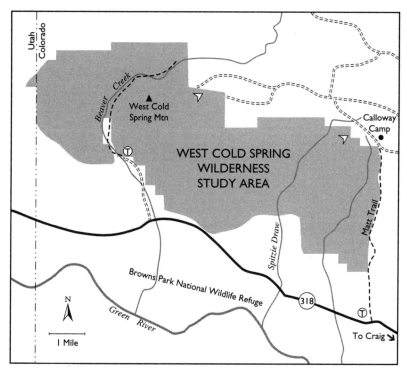

canyon. Since the last 0.75 mile of this road is on private property, obtain a detailed map of the area to avoid trespassing.

The Matt Trail runs along the WSA's eastern boundary. An old 4WD track, this route runs 4.5 miles up the face of the mountain before reaching the top. It is dry along this trail, so bring plenty of water. To find the trail's start, drive 4.6 miles west of the Browns Park store and watch for tracks leading north across the flats. A sign prohibiting motor vehicles marks the start.

The highest reaches of West Cold Spring Mountain can be walked for much of the way (at least 5 miles) along shelf rock and through open areas. Dirt roads access this area from the north. A good place to start is at the undeveloped Calloway Camp near where the Matt Trail ends. The views are dramatic from this high terrain.

APPENDIX: RECOMMENDED RESOURCES

National Forests

    Arapaho/Roosevelt National Forests

www.fs.fed.us/r2/arnf/

Boulder Ranger District
2140 Yarmouth Avenue
Boulder, CO 80301
303-444-6600

Canyon Lakes Ranger District
1311 South College
Ft. Collins, CO 80524
970-498-2770

Clear Creek Ranger District
101 Chicago Creek
P.O. Box 3307
Idaho Springs, CO 80452
303-567-3000

Sulfur Ranger District
9 Ten Mile Drive
P.O. Box 10
Granby, CO 80446
970-887-4100

Grand Mesa, Uncompahgre, and
    Gunnison National Forests

www.fs.fed.us/r2/gmug/

Gunnison Ranger District
216 North Colorado
Gunnison, CO 81230
970-641-0471

Norwood Ranger District
1760 Grand Avenue
P.O. Box 388
Norwood, CO 81401
970-327-4261

Ouray Ranger District
2505 South Townsend
Montrose, CO 81401
970-240-5400

Paonia Ranger District
North Rio Grande Avenue
P.O. Box 1030
Paonia, CO 81428
970-527-4131

Pike and San Isabel National Forests
www.fs.fed.us/r2/psicc/

Leadville Ranger District
2015 North Poplar
Leadville, CO 80461
719-486-0749

Salida Ranger District
325 West Rainbow Boulevard
Salida, CO 81201
719-539-3591

San Carlos Ranger District
3170 East Main
Cañon City, CO 81212
719-269-8500

South Park Ranger District
320 Highway 285
P.O. Box 219
Fairplay, CO 80440
719-836-2031

South Platte Ranger District
19316 Goddard Ranch Court
Morrison, CO 80465
303-697-0414

Routt National Forest
www.fs.fed.us/r2/mbr/

Hahns Peak/Bears Ears Ranger District
925 Weiss Drive
Steamboat Springs, CO 80487
970-879-1870

Parks Ranger District
612 5th Street
Box 158
Walden, CO 80480-0158
303-723-8204

Yampa Ranger District
300 Roselawn Avenue
P.O. Box 7
Yampa, CO 80483
970-638-4516

**San Juan and Rio Grande National
    Forests**
www.fs.fed.us/r2/srnf/

Columbine Ranger District
110 West 11th Street
Durango, CO 81301
970-385-1283

Divide Ranger District
13308 West Highway 160
Del Norte, CO 81132
719-657-3321

Mancos-Dolores Ranger District
100 North Sixth
P.O. Box 210
Dolores, CO 81323
970-882-7296

Pagosa Ranger District
180 Second Street
P.O. Box 310
Pagosa Springs, CO 81147
970-264-2268

Saguache Ranger District
46525 Highway 114
Box 67
Saguache, CO 81149
719-655-2547

White River National Forest
www.fs.fed.us/r2/whiteriver/

Aspen Ranger District
806 West Hallam
Aspen, CO 81611
970-925-3445

Blanco Ranger District
317 East Market Street
Meeker, CO 81641
970-878-4039

Dillon Ranger District
680 Blue River Parkway
P.O. Box 620
Silverthorne, CO 80498
970-468-5400

Eagle Ranger District
125 West 5th Street
P.O. Box 720
Eagle, CO 81631
970-328-6388

Holy Cross Ranger District
24747 U.S. Highway 24
P.O. Box 190
Minturn, CO 81645
970-827-5715

National Parks, Monuments, and Recreation Areas

Black Canyon of the Gunnison
   National Park
102 East Elk Creek
Gunnison, CO 81230
970-641-2337
www.nps.gov/blca/

Colorado National Monument
Fruita, CO 81521-0001
970-858-3617
www.nps.gov/colm/

Dinosaur National Monument
4545 East Highway 40
Dinosaur, CO 81610
970-374-3000
www.nps.gov/dino/

Great Sand Dunes National Monument
   and Preserve
11500 Highway 150
Mosca, CO 81146-9798
719-378-2312
www.nps.gov/grsa/

Mesa Verde National Park
P.O. Box 8
Mesa Verde, CO 81330-0008
970-529-4465
www.nps.gov/meve/

Rocky Mountain National Park
1000 Highway 36
Estes Park, CO 80517-8397
970-586-1206
www.nps.gov/romo/

Bureau of Land Management
www.co.blm.gov/

Glenwood Springs Field Office
50629 Highway 6 & 24
P.O. Box 1009
Glenwood Springs, CO 81601
970-947-2800

Grand Junction Field Office
2815 H Road
Grand Junction, CO 81506
970-244-3000

Gunnison Field Office
216 North Colorado
Gunnison, CO 81203
970-641-0471

Kremmling Field Office
1116 Park Avenue
P.O. Box 68
Kremmling, CO 80459
970-724-3437

Little Snake Field Office
455 Emerson Street
Craig, CO 81625
970-826-5000

Royal Gorge Field Office
3170 East Main Street
Cañon City, CO 81212
719-269-8500

San Juan Field Office
15 Burnett Court
Durango, CO 81301
970-247-0471

San Luis Field Office
46525 Highway 114
Box 67
Saguache, CO 81149
719-655-2547

Uncompahgre Field Office
2505 South Townsend
Montrose, CO 81401
970-240-5300

White River Field Office
73544 Highway 64
Meeker, CO 81641
970-878-3601

INDEX

ABOUT THE AUTHOR

Scott S. Warren is an outdoor enthusiast who has lived in the Southwest for the last thirty years. He is also a photographer, holding a bachelor of fine arts degree in photography from Utah State University. His images have appeared in *Audubon, Outside, Sierra, Travel & Leisure, Time, Smithsonian,* and various National Geographic publications. He is also the author of *Exploring Arizona's Wild Areas, 100 Classic Hikes in Arizona,* and *100 Classic Hikes in Colorado* from The Mountaineers Books.

THE MOUNTAINEERS, founded in 1906, is a nonprofit outdoor activity and conservation club, whose mission is "to explore, study, preserve, and enjoy the natural beauty of the outdoors. . . . " Based in Seattle, Washington, the club is now the third-largest such organization in the United States, with 15,000 members and five branches throughout Washington State.

The Mountaineers sponsors both classes and year-round outdoor activities in the Pacific Northwest, which include hiking, mountain climbing, ski-touring, snowshoeing, bicycling, camping, kayaking and canoeing, nature study, sailing, and adventure travel. The club's conservation division supports environmental causes through educational activities, sponsoring legislation, and presenting informational programs. All club activities are led by skilled, experienced volunteers, who are dedicated to promoting safe and responsible enjoyment and preservation of the outdoors.

If you would like to participate in these organized outdoor activities or the club's programs, consider a membership in The Mountaineers. For information and an application, write or call The Mountaineers, Club Headquarters, 300 Third Avenue West, Seattle, WA 98119; 206-284-6310.

The Mountaineers Books, an active, nonprofit publishing program of the club, produces guidebooks, instructional texts, historical works, natural history guides, and works on environmental conservation. All books produced by The Mountaineers fulfill the club's mission.

Send or call for our catalog of more than 450 outdoor titles:

 The Mountaineers Books
1001 SW Klickitat Way, Suite 201
Seattle, WA 98134
800-553-4453
mbooks@mountaineersbooks.org
www.mountaineersbooks.org

 The Mountaineers Books is proud to be a corporate sponsor of Leave No Trace, whose mission is to promote and inspire responsible outdoor recreation through education, research, and partnerships. The Leave No Trace program is focused specifically on human-powered (nonmotorized) recreation.

Leave No Trace strives to educate visitors about the nature of their recreational impacts, as well as offer techniques to prevent and minimize such impacts. Leave No Trace is best understood as an educational and ethical program, not as a set of rules and regulations.

For more information, visit *www.lnt.org*, or call 800-332-4100.